Praise for
THE INTERNET POLICE

"No one can finish this book thinking the Internet remains a disorderly wasteland. The West is being tamed, if slowly.... [Anderson's] storytelling is brisk and lucid, often pithy but never glib."
—Robert Kolker, *New York Times Book Review*

"A comprehensive history of governments' attempts to corral the online universe into more controllable form.... [A]n effective primer for anyone looking to catch up on what's been happening in the shady realms of online anarchy and surveillance.... The book does an excellent job of delineating the positive and negative qualities of each 'side.' "
—Nick Kolakowski, *Washington Independent Review of Books*

"Nate Anderson shows where the Internet's flourishing underworld meets international law enforcement. From stories of good guys, bad guys, and people that can't be pigeonholed, Nate gives the background to tomorrow's headlines."
—Cliff Stoll, author of
The Cuckoo's Egg and *High-Tech Heretic*

"As soon as the Internet turned mainstream, a new breed of criminal appeared. The police, who were trained on Agatha Christie novels, took about a decade to catch up. This entertaining and informative book tells their story."
—Bruce Schneier, author of
Liars and Outliers: Enabling the Trust Society Needs to Thrive

"A nuanced study of crime on the Internet and how government and law enforcement agencies have been tackling it. . . . A thought-provoking primer on the state of cybercrime." —*Kirkus Reviews*

"[His] takes on landmark digital cases are valuable, colorfully drawn, primers. . . . Anderson meticulously tracks the evolution of Internet policing." —*Publishers Weekly*

THE INTERNET POLICE

HOW CRIME WENT ONLINE— AND THE COPS FOLLOWED

Nate Anderson

W. W. Norton & Company

New York   London

Portions of Chapter 3, "'I Feel That He Is Watching Me': Privacy on the Computer" were
first published in *Ars Technica*.

For information about permission to reproduce selections from this book,
write to Permissions, W. W. Norton & Company, Inc.,
500 Fifth Avenue, New York, NY 10110

For information about special discounts for bulk purchases, please contact
W. W. Norton Special Sales at specialsales@wwnorton.com or 800-233-4830

Manufacturing by Courier, Westford, MA
Book design by Daniel Lagin
Production manager: Anna Oler

Library of Congress Cataloging-in-Publication Data

Anderson, Nate, editor
The internet police : how crime went online, and the cops followed / Nate Anderson.
— First Edition.
pages cm
Includes bibliographical references and index.
ISBN 978-0-393-06298-4 (hardcover)
1. Computer crimes. 2. Computer crimes—Investigation. 3. Internet—Security measures.
4. International crimes. I. Title.
HV6773.A53 2013
364.16'8—dc23
                     2013013978

ISBN 978-0-393-34945-0 pbk.

W. W. Norton & Company, Inc.
500 Fifth Avenue, New York, N.Y. 10110
www.wwnorton.com

W. W. Norton & Company Ltd.
Castle House, 75/76 Wells Street, London W1T 3QT

1 2 3 4 5 6 7 8 9 0

for leah

CONTENTS

THE INTERNET POLICE

1
CHAOS, STRENGTH
OF THE INTERNET

Ryan Lackey's bedroom had already driven men to madness. As the head of HavenCo, an ultrasecure Internet data center housed in a rusting North Sea naval fort seven miles off the English coast, Lackey spent months at a time during 2000 and 2001 sleeping inside one of the fort's two concrete legs. But when you want to escape the eyes of Government—and change the world while you're at it—you expect to put up with some discomfort. Lackey got plenty, later comparing life on the site to "squatting in an abandoned warehouse."

Even when new, this had not been a comfortable place. The hulking structure known as HM Fort Roughs Tower had been one in a series of forts built at a wharf in Gravesend during World War II, then hauled to its current location in the waters of the English Channel east of Harwich, where it was sunk to provide an antiaircraft platform. The fort's installation came close to catastrophe; film of the event shows the monstrous structure nearly capsizing with a full crew on board before the massive legs settle on the sea floor.

For the rest of the war, 100 enlisted men bunked at the fort for shifts of six weeks on, ten days off, spending much of their time inside the lightless, circular legs. Each leg contained seven levels, each level a concrete room 24 feet in diameter and lit with a single light bulb. A 120-foot steel deck, rising 60 feet above the frigid seawater, lay across the two squat legs and provided space for latrines, radar, and gun emplacements.

"While the officers' sleeping quarters were in the upper part of the cylinders, where there was adequate light and oil heating," noted a *Der Spiegel* article on these forts, "it was intolerable for the crews, who spent their nights below the surface of the water." The claustrophobia, isolation, and fear—crews routinely shot at Luftwaffe bombers and V-1 flying bombs from guns mounted on the deck—commonly led to psychological distress; crews called the condition "fort madness."

In 2005, artist Stephen Turner spent six weeks alone in a nearby North Sea fort called Shivering Sands in order to conduct an "artistic exploration of isolation." Turner found in the rusting workshop there "a ball of beautifully preserved and colourful cottons," created as part of the compulsory recreation program ordered by the fort's wartime commander, Major J. Sharman. Sharman had ordered his men to build "fully rigged galleons, kids' toys, and so on" as a way of keeping the mind's demons too busy for free play.

Fifty years in the briny air had not improved the comfort of the forts. "Rusty precipitation falls on the tent every night with a slow but regular patter," wrote Turner of his experience at Shivering Sands. "All my equipment would be covered in a film of new deposits if I did not regularly dust it down. Every day I ritually sweep around the tent, an act akin to maintaining a clearing in a wood."

Roughs Tower was farther up the coast from Shivering Sands. On approach, the two pillars and the rusting platform of Lackey's redoubt looked more like Neptune's abandoned banquet table than the spot from which the next great Internet revolution would be launched. The tower had not deteriorated as badly as the abandoned Shivering Sands, but conditions could still be brutal. Shower facilities were minimal, since the muddy North Sea water created problems for the desalinator (not that a visitor would want to take many showers; as Lackey put it later, "our shower wasn't properly grounded and thus led to shocks"). Lackey also admitted that North Sea winters were "worse than I expected." Weather grew so rough that even helicopter access to the fort was impossible for a week at a time, while getting up to the deck from the more common rigid inflatable boat required a winch-powered ride over the roiling ocean while sitting on a wooden plank.

Not everyone involved with HavenCo wanted to live this way. Original CEO Sean Hastings and his wife both left the company soon after HavenCo began operations. ("They didn't like living on a tiny platform in the middle of the sea," was how Lackey put it in a conference presentation.) Even the cook found a better opportunity, according to Lackey, "She went off to the north of England to become a stripper."

But the miserable conditions gave HavenCo something unique: a true libertarian paradise. The company had grand plans to run fiber-optic cables from Roughs Tower to English and Dutch Internet exchange points, to stuff one leg of the fort with computer servers and diesel generators, and to host just about any sort of Internet activity that might be frowned on in less liberty-loving jurisdictions. Hence HavenCo's motto: "The free world just milliseconds away."

The entire project was about pushing free speech to its radical limits. Apart from child pornography and spam, most activities were fair game. No rules governed "copyright, patents, libel, restrictions on political speech, non-disclosure agreements, cryptography, restrictions on maintaining customer records . . . music-sharing services, or other issues," according to HavenCo's website at the time.

This sort of talk wasn't likely to please countries like the United States, where online gambling was forbidden. For their part, European states tended to frown on speech with Nazi overtones. China wouldn't like "free Tibet" sites, while Saudi Arabia wouldn't tolerate even adult pornography. And the extraordinarily powerful global music and movie lobbies weren't about to sit idly by while a North Sea naval fort turned into Pirate Central. But what were any of them going to do—summon HavenCo to court?

"If somebody comes to us with a subpoena—one, they're going to have a pretty long boat ride and two, we're going to probably laugh at them," Lackey told a gathering of hackers at the 2001 DEF CON convention in Las Vegas. "We're either going to laugh at them or shoot at them—probably laugh at them." The crowd loved it. Lackey went on to lay out his vision of an alternative to existing nation-states—which in his estimation were already overregulated and were heading in the direction of less, not more, personal liberty.

"There's really no middle ground," he continued. "You're either going to have uniform laws across all the countries . . . [or] it's going to be a few of the big countries like the US and the UK that don't really respect personal liberty as much as they might ideally do. . . . The alternative that we have is to create ways that you can use technical means or use structuring or anything else to sort of take some of the bite out of some of these regulations. Really, nothing we're doing is enabling a truly new thing that you couldn't do if you were willing to break the law. It's just that we're making it legal."

Could sticking some servers inside the leg of a sea fort really make such behavior "legal"? Perhaps Lackey had picked up a bit of "fort madness" already—but he had a reason for thinking HavenCo might work.

Roughs Tower wasn't just a rusting North Sea fort. It also claimed to be the world's tiniest country, called "Sealand." The gun platform's strange journey to quasi-statehood began when libertarian-leaning UK citizen Roy Bates decided that he would take one of the rusting gun platforms long abandoned by the British armed forces and turn it into a pirate radio operation, blasting pop and rock music back into the United Kingdom in an era when licensed broadcasters did not do so.

Bates was a true character, who had gone off to fight in the Spanish Civil War at age fifteen and later saw action in places like Italy, Iraq, and Syria. His family said that Bates was taken prisoner—among many other adventures—during the war and put on a plane that then crash-landed on Rhodes. Bates tried to escape but was "captured stealing a fishing boat by the Fascista and later rescued from execution by firing squad by a passing German officer."

Of course he was—it was just the sort of life Bates led. (He once told an interviewer, "I might die young or I might die old, but I will never die of boredom.") In the two decades after the war, Bates tried his hand at many businesses: meat importer, swimming fins manufacturer, commercial fisherman, butcher shop operator, real estate–agency owner. In 1965, hooked on the pirate radio trend, Bates decided to seize Knock John, a Roughs Tower clone that stood closer in to shore, to house his radio transmitter. Knock John was already occupied by other pirate radio operators, so Bates and a small crew physically ejected the men and set up their own Radio Essex station there. But Knock John was within the United Kingdom's three-mile territorial waters, and Bates was soon hauled into a UK court on charges of illegal broadcasting.

Undeterred, Bates and his then fourteen-year-old son Michael packed up their gear and moved a few miles farther out. On Christmas Day 1966, they took a boat to Roughs Tower. It too was already occupied by radio pirates running a station called Radio Caroline, but Bates dealt with the problem just as he had on Knock John. He seized the platform by force and left his own men in charge, but bad weather meant they could not be resupplied with food; they eventually had to be rescued by a government lifeboat sent from the mainland.

Roughs Tower was soon reoccupied by Radio Caroline, but Bates remained determined to secure the fort. In April 1967, he partnered with Radio Caroline and agreed to share the platform. When a Radio

Caroline crew member suffered severe rope burns and was taken ashore, however, Bates found himself in sole possession of the place. He refused to let Radio Caroline staffers reboard.

"Radio Caroline didn't go down without a fight," writes New York Law School professor James Grimmelmann, who in 2012 completed the definitive archival history of Sealand. "It sent a boarding party by boat on April 27; [Radio Essex employee] David Barron and Michael Bates repulsed them with an air rifle and flaming bottles of paraffin. Defiant, Roy Bates painted his name on the side of the platform in large white letters. Caroline tried again, more dramatically, on June 27. Bates and company again fought off the attackers with petrol bombs. When they withdrew, one man was left dangling from a ladder for two hours until a lifeboat from nearby Walton-on-Naze rescued him."

Soon after the clashes with Radio Caroline, Bates announced that Roughs Tower was its own country, the Principality of Sealand, and that he was its prince. (Bates gave his wife Joan the title "princess" as a birthday present in 1967.) Sealand's history over the next decades only got more bizarre. Bates took potshots at passing ships, the UK cabinet drew up plans to seize the tower, Bates was abducted and sent by boat to the Netherlands, he used a helicopter assault to retake the fort, and the German government sent a diplomat to check on one of Bates's "prisoners." The stories quickly deteriorate into legend and rumor, but between the romantic episodes that punctuate Sealand's history, the Bates family had a constant ambition: having Sealand recognized as a real country.

It hasn't happened. No state formally recognizes Sealand, nor does the United Nations. Sealand can make a few credible claims to being a de facto state, however, including the visit from the German diplomat and decades of benign neglect from a UK government often embarrassed about Sealand goings-on but unwilling to force the issue.

Running one's own country can be an expensive proposition. Bates has stated publicly that he has invested over one million pounds in the place for refurbishment, security guards, boats, food, and diesel (others claim this is gross exaggeration). What is clear is that Sealand hasn't produced much money in recompense. Plans for grand projects like a floating hotel have come to nothing, though Sealand did launch a short-lived online casino in 2007. (The local newspaper called it "the latest in a string of bizarre stories to emerge from the former war-time fort.") Sealand has had better luck selling its own stamps, passports, and even titles of nobility.

In 2000, HavenCo looked like a credible, long-term opportunity to put Sealand's remote location to good use—and to do so in a way that appealed to the Bates family's libertarian leanings—while making a bit of money. HavenCo would use the reach of the Internet to "arbitrage" between various legal schemes. Customers who wanted total Internet freedom could use HavenCo servers to run their online gaming sites or pro-Tibet blogs with impunity, but they could reside and play in places where people actually wanted to live. Thanks to the Internet's amazing ability to publish globally, it had become a simple matter to stick servers in one country with a favorable set of laws, but use them to reach the wealthy residents of countries whose governments were less excited about whatever was on offer.

For HavenCo to succeed, its founders needed somewhere with fewer restrictions, but they didn't want mere anarchy. The ideal location would have just enough order to avoid arbitrary lawmaking and to enforce private contracts. It also needed protection from unhappy governments who might simply show up in force and shut down the scheme. What HavenCo wanted, in other words, was a minimalist sovereign state.

Such states can be hard to find. Lackey and partner Sean Hastings met at a 1998 financial cryptography conference on Anguilla, an island nation just east of Puerto Rico, and decided to start such an operation. Hastings lived at the time in Anguilla, which had access to decent Internet connections and was quite close to the US mainland, but he didn't believe it was right for HavenCo due to perceived corruption and also to laws against gambling and pornography (likely to be some of a data haven's best clients).

States with minimal regulation also tend not to have easy Internet connections to wealthy Western countries, or they lack a robust and predictable judicial system, or both. Sealand looked like a solution. As a nominal state, it could make HavenCo's activities legal, and it had about as few laws as it was possible to have. Other nations would do nothing to assault the Sealand platform given its proximity to the United Kingdom, which had extended its territorial waters out to twelve miles—five miles past Sealand—in the 1980s. As Lackey put it in his 2001 DEF CON talk, he wasn't worried about foreign forces, since "the British will deal with it. We don't need to do anything." (This was neither the first nor the last time that Sealand had thumbed its nose at UK law while relying on the country as a supply base, defense force, emergency rescue hub, place to live, and home to Bates businesses.)

The only challenge for HavenCo was preventing the Bates family from arbitrarily changing Sealand's laws. HavenCo believed that the money it promised to pay the family would ensure that agreements were honored. Lackey made much of this legal security when talking up HavenCo in 2000 and 2001. It's "very dangerous to be in a country that can change its laws on a whim," he said in reference to that über-arbitrary nation-state, Australia. "And because Sealand gets all of its revenue pretty much from HavenCo, it's unlikely to do anything."

Lackey believed he had found paradise in Sealand: third-world regulation, first-world Internet connectivity, and a veneer of fixed law for the whole operation. The agreements were all there, written on pieces of paper. Unchangeable. HavenCo was going to make millions by selling access to total freedom—something that looked a lot like total chaos.

This was the Internet, after all; chaos was built into its bones. HavenCo's founders weren't alone in believing that governments could not—and should not—stop their offer of anonymity and an anything-goes jurisdiction to anyone who could cough up at least $1,500 a month.

/////

"Governments of the Industrial World, you weary giants of flesh and steel, I come from Cyberspace, the new home of Mind," declared John Perry Barlow in his infamous 1996 manifesto, *A Declaration of the Independence of Cyberspace.* "On behalf of the future, I ask you of the past to leave us alone. You are not welcome among us. You have no sovereignty where we gather."

Barlow was a Wyoming rancher, a sometime-lyricist for the Grateful Dead, and a passionate defender of early online communities like the Whole Earth 'Lectronic Link (WELL). He helped to launch the Electronic Frontier Foundation (EFF), a pioneering digital rights group still prominent and effective today. His declaration was an over-the-top howl of dissent against US government actions regarding the Internet—but the delightful bombast staked out quite a serious position, one appealing to the well-off, technically savvy early netizens: the Internet would solve its own problems, thank you very much.

With the benefit of fifteen years' perspective—hardly a fair advantage, to be sure, when critiquing a visionary statement—Barlow's frantic repudiation of existing institutions looks breathtakingly radical and improbably utopian. Penile enlargement e-mails, offers from Nigerian princes, phishing attempts from "your bank," million-strong computer botnets, cyberwarfare, stolen credit cards traded openly in hacker forums, online "sextortion" using stolen nude photos, corporate espionage, the underground online market for child sex abuse imagery, anonymous defamation in online forums—all these would be addressed how, exactly, without government?

Barlow anticipated the question; even in 1996, bad behavior online was rampant. He insisted that voluntary self-governance would diagnose and treat most ills. "You claim there are problems among us that you need to solve," he wrote in the declaration. "You use this claim as an excuse to invade our precincts. Many of these problems don't exist. Where there are real conflicts, where there are wrongs, we will identify them and address them by our means."

This online self-government would arise from "ethics, enlightened self-interest, and the commonweal," and Internet "laws" would be based only on the Golden Rule—it was the only rule recognized by "all our constituent cultures." Any good declaration is a place for slogans, not specific solutions, but Barlow hinted that some of the perceived "problems" on the Internet were really just free speech issues—and they couldn't be addressed without doing serious damage to the 'Net.

"All the sentiments and expressions of humanity, from the debasing to the angelic, are parts of a seamless whole, the global conversation of bits," Barlow wrote. It simply wasn't possible to "separate the air that chokes from the air upon which wings beat."

Cyberspace, the "new home of Mind," refused all attempts at building Internet air scrubbers. Indeed, the new home of Mind denied that such scrubbers were even a theoretical possibility. You simply couldn't design one without suffocating the emerging public Internet, so rich with both promise and pollution. Such, at least, was the claim.

Animating the entire declaration was the concept of jurisdiction. Barlow claimed that existing institutions had, quite literally, no say in what happened in cyberspace, envisioned as a place of its own, completely firewalled from the actual locations where Internet users lived. The rushing static of a modem handshake had opened the door into a new world; stepping through it onto the 'Net put you in a separate legal space.

The entire document was a bit overripe with these cyberlibertarian pronouncements, and it wouldn't take much imagination to see this Golden Rule, new-home-of-Mind business as hippie-dippie claptrap.

Hadn't Barlow seen the sorts of things that people got up to the moment someone handed them a keyboard, anonymity, and an Internet forum?

Indeed he had. Barlow was a shrewd thinker and an engaging writer, and he was well plugged in to the global conversation then ramping up over the future of the Internet. (The declaration was written in Davos, Switzerland, best known as the host resort for the World Economic Forum's annual swankfest of global luminaries.) But Barlow embraced the chaos of the Internet, believing it did so much more good than harm—and he wasn't alone in that view. Even key members of the US federal judiciary shared it, with one going so far as to explicitly embrace chaos as "the strength of the Internet."

/////

1996 was a remarkable year for the flourishing Internet, which saw the World Wide Web surge in popularity after the recent arrival of graphical Web browsers. Amazon.com had been online for a year. Pornography was common. Forums sprung up on every conceivable topic—and even a few inconceivable ones. Getting a website, then publishing your thoughts for the entire world to see, was suddenly cheap and (relatively) easy. Intoxicated by the 'Net, people shouted and spammed, prayed and cursed, bought and sold. They made friends and flamed enemies. It was glorious, maddening chaos.

Into that chaos stepped an unlikely defender: seasoned federal judge Stewart Dalzell, who handed down the most famous Internet-related ruling of the 1990s when his three-judge panel in Philadelphia considered a legal challenge to the Communications Decency Act (CDA). The CDA was a congressional attempt to clamp down on the Internet free-for-all with the specific goal of shielding the offline eyes of children from online pornography. (Its passage had spurred Barlow to write his declaration.) To the CDA's backers, this hardly seemed a controversial idea; various laws enforced a similar scheme at newsstands and bookstores. Where Barlow saw a separate realm of Mind in the online world, Congress saw one more venue in which the same offline principles should apply. If the CDA worked, online porn would resemble a copy of *Penthouse*—kept up high behind the blinder rack so that only adults could buy a copy.

The Web posed thorny problems, however. How could one tell if any particular Internet visitor to a pornographic website was a child? In the real world, it was simple enough to pick out most children by sight, and government-issued photo IDs could be used to verify age. But a cloak of anonymity governed the Web by default. It could be pierced, but only by serious effort (and a subpoena). IDs couldn't be checked; visitors couldn't be eyeballed.

The CDA's backers suggested various proxies for age—key among them a credit card screen. Plenty of online porn sites already sucked up credit card information in order to bill visitors, and cardholders were generally over eighteen, so a solution presented itself: require sites wanting to traffic in the erotic urges of the human race to block access to anyone without a credit card, then penalize any site that did not set up such a screening system. The kids were protected; the adults could view their "adult" content. Problem solved.

Except that it wasn't, because the CDA was written so broadly that it would have affected all sorts of "indecent" but not "obscene" material, including plenty of nonpornographic material. Would sex education or health nonprofits really have to set up a credit card screen to avoid criminal activity? How would this work for sites that weren't "selling" anything? And how could the government pass constitutional muster with a law requiring that access to this sort of material online required citizens to possess a credit card?

In 1996, several months after Barlow's declaration, a three-judge panel struck down the CDA (later confirmed by a 7–2 Supreme Court decision). But only one judge's opinion attracted all the attention—and with good reason. Judge Dalzell was ready to out-Barlow Barlow with his own ode to Internet chaos. He had a host of arguments on his side, including the obvious practical point that the Internet was international. With the contents of millions of servers located outside the United States available to US browsers, content regulation of the Internet looked in 1996 like a truly quixotic act, a tilting at digital windmills.

"Pornography from, say, Amsterdam will be no less appealing to a child on the Internet than pornography from New York City," Dalzell wrote, "and residents of Amsterdam have little incentive to comply with the CDA."

While not agreeing with Barlow that the Internet was beyond the jurisdiction of existing governments, Dalzell did offer support to the jurisdictional model that would later be appropriated by HavenCo: it was simple to move servers to a favorable legal location, after which other governments could do little to stop the content streaming forth. So what was the point of one nation passing an Internet law?

Even if the US government could exert perfect pressure on every noncompliant website operator in the world, Dalzell argued against stifling the Internet's incredible conversation. "Congress may not regulate indecency on the Internet at all," he asserted. "Any content-based regulation of the Internet, no matter how benign the purpose, could burn the global village to roast the pig."

Here was an echo of Barlow—even making the *attempt* at regulating Internet content was out of bounds. In his concluding paragraphs, Dalzell issued a poetic encomium to chaos worth quoting at length:

> True it is that many find some of the speech on the Internet to
> be offensive, and amid the din of cyberspace many hear discordant
> voices that they regard as indecent. The absence of governmental

regulation of Internet content has unquestionably produced a kind of chaos, but as one of plaintiffs' experts put it with such resonance at the hearing:

"What achieved success was the very chaos that the Internet is. The strength of the Internet is that chaos."

Just as the strength of the Internet is chaos, so the strength of our liberty depends upon the chaos and cacophony of the unfettered speech the First Amendment protects.

Reaction to the decision was immediate and worldwide. When an interviewer from an oral history project later asked about his proudest moment as a judge, Dalzell immediately singled out the CDA decision. "I just couldn't believe it," he said. "I was very gratified and touched that it was so well received. World-wide. It's funny to see your stuff in a foreign language; somebody sent me . . . oh, I forget, was it *Der Spiegel*, or one of the German magazines, and there was my picture and—I took a few years of German in school, I can assure you I was never as eloquent as that fellow in *Der Spiegel*. But they just translated what I wrote into German and—that was pretty extraordinary."

Everyone agreed that the opinion was extraordinary; critics just thought it extraordinarily bad. In 1996, Cathleen Cleaver was director of legal studies at the conservative advocacy group Family Research Council and she immediately went after Dalzell's "roast the pig" assertion with a deboning knife. "Really? What about fraud—may we not protect consumers in cyberspace?" she asked. "May we not ban child pornography or enforce copyright violations on-line? Would these content-based regulations burn the village, too?"

While this line of attack did sound promising, it neglected a key point in the case: the CDA regulated pornographic and sexual speech that was in itself legal for adults. Dalzell was concerned with limits upon legal speech that might quiet the Internet's grand conversation. Fraud, child pornography, and copyright violations were all illegal, and thus unprotected, activities.

But it was Dalzell's more general embrace of "chaos" as a governing principle of the Internet that truly drew Cleaver's ire. "If the First Amendment's promise to this new technology is indeed chaos and anarchy, then perhaps Judge Dalzell is right," she concluded. "But before we too quickly agree with this visionary from the federal bench, we ought to ask ourselves how we have survived and thrived as a democracy for two centuries upon the bedrock of ordered liberty, the enemy of chaos and anarchy."

Support for "ordered liberty" would have a long shelf life among groups hoping to impose more controls on the Internet. Fourteen years after Dalzell's ruling, the music trade group Recording Industry Association of America (RIAA) was still banging on the same drum as it asked Internet providers to take steps to curtail online copyright infringement.

"We all share the goal of a robust Internet that is highly accessible, secure, and safe for individuals and commerce," wrote the group in a statement. "An Internet predicated on order, rather than chaos, facilitates achievement of this goal." Under this view, the Internet was something to be brought under control. Where it could not, it became the enemy.

This line of thinking presupposed one crucial fact: that the forces of order actually could control the Internet. Even in the mid-1990s, that claim was disputed. "US Customs officials have generally given up," wrote law professors David Post and David Johnson in a well-known 1996 *Stanford Law Review* article that summed up this attitude. "They assert jurisdiction only over the physical goods that cross the geographic borders they guard and claim no right to force declarations of the value of materials transmitted by modem."

Post and Johnson saw the Internet as a take-it-or-leave-it proposition; if you wanted your country hooked up to the 'Net, you had to accept all of the 'Net. "Individual electrons can easily, and without any realistic prospect of detection, 'enter' any sovereign's territory," they wrote. "The volume of electronic communications crossing territorial boundaries is just too great in relation to the resources available to government authorities to permit meaningful control."

The Internet had three features that made it especially difficult to control in any centralized way. The first was technical. The Internet's architecture put much of the network's intelligence at the edge, in people's computers. The core of the network funneled bits back and forth, but it didn't care what they were. Crafting a new kind of Internet application—instant messaging, video chat, online games, even building something as crucial as the World Wide Web—required no permission from network operators, only new code on people's computers. Having few gatekeepers produced an explosion of creativity and commerce, but it also meant the Internet was not well suited to centralized surveillance and law enforcement.

Second was geography. Since anyone on the 'Net could reach anyone else, attempts at controlling Internet content would require dealing with many countries and wildly different legal environments. National law couldn't reach people in all these other countries. Sure, rich democracies might have their extradition treaties, but Internet servers and the people behind them could move to Kiev and continue their activities. Nigerians could spend the day in an Internet café and dash off fake e-mails from a "prince" in desperate need of some help to move money out of the country. And twentysomethings could stack racks of servers inside a rusting sea fort with the explicit goal of tweaking national governments and expect to have no problems getting away with it. What was any particular government going to do? Did national law have any meaning on the "borderless" Internet?

Third was anonymity. The Internet was built without any means of validating identity, which resulted in plenty of productive anonymous speech, plenty of illegal and obnoxious activity, and that ubiquitous *New Yorker* cartoon about how, when you're online, no one knows you're a dog. Simply learning an Internet user's real identity was a chore; if the user was from another country, it might well be impossible. The identity issue wasn't just academic theorizing. As the CDA battle showed, the inability to identify Internet users reliably could lead to the overturning of major pieces of legislation.

Mix all three factors and many saw a potent poison, one fatal to traditional ideas about government control. In 1997 law professor James Boyle summed up the views of these "Internet exceptionalists," writing, "Viewed through this lens, the 'Net is the ultimate natural environment for information and trying to regulate the 'Net is like trying to prohibit evolution." Whatever governments might want the Internet to be, the exceptionalists argued, they were going to get the Internet as it actually was.

/////

HavenCo was happy to provide all the chaos that money could buy. From its Sealand base, the company hosted the Tibetan government-in-exile, a move certain to irritate China's leaders. It refused to identify any other customer by name, but Lackey did eventually reveal that his main customers were casinos and their affiliates, often trying to access the lucrative US market where online gambling was forbidden.

"We were worried we'd get some terrorist group that would want to set up a server with us, but really all of our customers right now are customers that we're pretty proud to have hosted with us," he said at his 2001 DEF CON presentation.

Not that HavenCo was likely to know about any terrorist activity; it accepted digital payments using anonymous services, and it provided "tamper-resistant computing hardware, designed to protect customer transactions from all possible attackers, including HavenCo and its staff" along with "advanced cryptographic protocols" and "cryptographically-secured servers."

In answer to a question about terrorist or criminal groups using the service, Lackey added, "If hypothetically someone were to host something with us that we didn't know what it was, we wouldn't know what it was so we wouldn't have any reason to complain.... So if you buy a server, use it, have a bunch of encrypted traffic to it, we're not going to really notice. It's not a big deal." HavenCo's unofficial motto might well have been "We don't want to know."

The company began with a bang in the middle of 2000 after raising some capital. Lackey arrived on Sealand with little more than a laptop and a cell phone—Sealand residents could access UK mobile phone towers from the top of the deck when conditions were right—but the sheer cheek of HavenCo's operations combined with the improbable location were enough to grab a *Wired* magazine cover story in July 2000. HavenCo launched alongside the story and soon said it was breaking even on monthly expenses and had between ten and a hundred clients; as in many matters relating to the company, details were vague.

As for the future—well, Lackey had big plans. The *Wired* story chronicled them in all of their improbable glory:

> The huge support cylinders will contain millions of dollars' worth of networking gear: computers, servers, transaction processors, data-storage devices—all cooled with banks of roaring air conditioners and powered by triple-redundant generators . . . HavenCo's onboard staff will come and go on helicopters and speedboats. Four security people will be on hand at all times to maintain order; six computer geeks will run the network operations center . . . Simply entering one of the machine rooms will require putting on scuba gear, because the rooms will be filled with an

unbreathable pure nitrogen atmosphere instead of the normal oxy-
gen mix—a measure designed to keep out sneaks, inhibit rust, and
reduce the risk of fire.

And that was just the beginning. Give HavenCo time to reap the
profits from its data haven and the company would build out Sealand,
perhaps adding a hotel and casino. "Five years from now," Lackey told
the magazine, "we are either going to be completely broke or we're going
to be fantastically wealthy."

HavenCo, like Dalzell and Barlow years earlier, believed in the
freedom-enhancing potential of a chaotic Internet. The company
neatly summed up the law professors' arguments about the Internet's
jurisdiction-busting, censorship-evading, privacy-enhancing abilities.
In 2000, one would have been hard pressed to find a better example of
every point made by the Internet exceptionalists.

But the HavenCo story took a curious twist. The poster child for
Internet chaos, it turned out, actually liked law and order quite a bit. After
living on Sealand from mid-2000 through December 2002, Lackey left
the gun platform and eventually left HavenCo. The company went into
stasis; no one seemed sure if it was in fact still operational. Then Lackey
showed up at the 2003 DEF CON hacking conference in Las Vegas—two
years after his first, hugely optimistic presentation there—and delivered a blistering indictment of both Sealand and his own management
abilities.

"A good deal of this is actually my fault," he said while walking
through a slide deck titled "What really happened." He admitted that
"media attention got in the way of judgment."

HavenCo never had the speedy Internet connections it bragged
about. Instead it relied on a painfully slow 128 Kbps satellite link with
terrible delay (bouncing signals up to a satellite and back to earth, then
passing them through a ground station and onto the terrestrial Internet

was—and still is—a relatively slow process). Two or three thousand potential customers besieged HavenCo after the *Wired* cover story, but the Internet situation was so bad, and the company so disorganized, that customer sign-ups had to be delayed. Most never returned.

Lackey had taken to telling the press about the massive racks of servers hidden in the "secure" nitrogen-filled leg of Sealand, but in reality HavenCo had just five racks holding around twenty inexpensive servers, which it kept up top in a space referred to as the "demo room." The secret room stacked with gear simply didn't exist; the nitrogen atmosphere was a fantasy, too.

The press loved the entire Sealand/HavenCo story, but Lackey admitted to "so much press inquiry that nobody did any other work." With only ten customers, HavenCo tried to slash costs and stopped paying employee salaries; it barely managed to break even in 2001. But the original agreement with Sealand promised a large cash payment to the Bates family, a payment not included in the profitability calculations.

Michael Bates became the "prince" of Sealand when his aging father Roy retired (Roy finally died on October 9, 2012, after a long battle with Alzheimer's). Michael eventually took over as HavenCo's CEO, despite a lack of technical knowledge and a day job running a two-boat UK fishing company called Fruits of the Sea. Relations between Sealand and HavenCo soured. Lackey worried about Sealand statements to the press saying that HavenCo wouldn't support any "offensive" conduct and might cooperate with authorities from other countries in investigations. Sealand, still concerned with being recognized as a nation, seems to have realized that hosting an anything-goes business with customers who flouted other countries' laws would not be helpful in securing this recognition. After the September 11, 2001, terrorist attacks in the United States, Lackey realized that any hint of turning a blind eye to terrorism could cause problems. And his plan to launch a totally anonymous gold-backed, electronic currency was nixed by Sealand.

Worse, in Lackey's view, the "fixed" laws of Sealand that he had counted on had suddenly became mutable. "Informal and inconsistent restrictions were placed on HavenCo's operations, but largely ignored, in the truest form of banana republic," Lackey later wrote in his 2003 DEF CON slide deck. He began launching new, unofficial projects like a popular anonymizing mail server without even telling Bates.

At this low point, in need of cash and customers, potential salvation appeared in the form of Malaysian movie-site operator Alex Tan. Tan's companies rented films over the Internet without permission from the studios; when chased out of Taiwan, Tan's Film88.com site registered its domain name in Iran—a country unlikely to acknowledge the concerns of US copyright holders. But Iran doesn't have great connectivity to the rest of the world, certainly not enough to distribute films, so the Film88.com servers providing the movies were actually located in the Netherlands. After US movie studios asked the site's Dutch Internet provider to shut off access, Film88 went down. Tan then came to HavenCo, looking for a secure location to stash his servers. In May 2002 Tan set up a meeting with Lackey and Bates.

Tan had a new idea that he hoped might be legal even in places like the United States. He wanted to rip films off DVDs and then stream them over the Internet—but each DVD rip would go to only a single customer at a time. In essence, this was the digitization of the existing movie rental business, doing away with the need to rent and return a physical disc to a store or kiosk. (The idea was good enough that a company called Zediva actually tried it from within the United States in 2011. Zediva was sued out of business almost immediately.)

Lackey had no problem with Tan's idea. As HavenCo's terms of use made clear, everything but child porn, hacking, and spam was welcome. Sealand decided, however, that it wasn't about to host a major business so likely to irk powerful countries. At this point, Lackey quit, claiming that HavenCo had been effectively "nationalized" by Sealand.

I asked Michael Bates for his side of the Film88.com story. "Ryan got the hump because we were offered a deal with a film pirating company that was being chased out of Taiwan by Uncle Sam and the film industry," he told me. "Apart from the fact the company in question had no money to finance it, it went against our principles to 'steal copyright'—even libertarians have to have some regulation!"

As for Lackey's quip about Sealand acting like a "banana republic," Bates was having none of it. "So the answer is actually we didn't behave like a third world country; we acted responsibly on the international stage," he said. "We just didn't do what Ryan wanted!"

Sealand, still concerned about its reputation, had embraced international norms like copyright after all. This should have been clear as far back as 2001, when Roy Bates told an NPR reporter, "[W]e wouldn't do anything which was anti-British or unethical or whatever, you know." HavenCo, believing Sealand to have almost no laws, appears to have been unaware of this attitude until after it set up shop on the fort. Lackey's data paradise had become distinctly hellish—and there was little he could do about it. Whether or not it was truly a country, Sealand had no courts, no police, and no parliament—and it was presided over by a self-styled prince whose family had a long history of resorting to force to seize and hold Roughs Tower. When a dispute arose over law or contracts, HavenCo had nowhere to turn.

Grimmelmann sums up the situation. "Thus, HavenCo was not an exercise in pure lawlessness," he wrote. "Indeed, the viability of its offer—and indeed, its very existence—depended on law, specifically the international law of states. HavenCo's product differentiator was Sealand law ... [But] Sealand 'law' was never much more than a formality or a tacit agreement, and when things on Sealand deteriorated, HavenCo found itself boxed into a corner, precisely because it had rejected national and international authority over what happened on Sealand. In the end, HavenCo failed not from too much law, but too little."

As Lackey himself admitted after the Sealand experience, "Political and contract stability is critical. . . . Promises that shares will be issued in the future, debts will be repaid, etc. are meaningless without documentation, and often are meaningless with documentation."

Lackey walked away from the project bitter and in debt. At the end of his 2003 DEF CON talk, he held up his Sealand passport. "This cost me $220,000 and three years of my life," he announced.

/////

As far back as 1997, James Boyle had warned that the cyberlibertarians "should not be so quick to write off the state." The Internet needed baseline order for its chaos to be productive rather than destructive, and governments soon showed themselves willing to provide it. Theorists might insist on the self-contained, self-regulatory nature of the Internet, but government forces weren't going to hold back after Internet-delivered ills proliferated in the boom years of the late 1990s and early 2000s. As the Internet exploded in popularity and huge new populations of less tech-savvy people came online, the authorities worried that they would quickly be overwhelmed. The drumbeat was for order in the face of too much chaos.

"Our [cybercrime] case load is increasing dramatically," FBI director Louis Freeh told Congress in 2000. "Even though we have markedly improved our capabilities to fight cyber intrusions, the problem is growing even faster . . . The problem of Internet crime has grown at such a rapid pace that the laws have not kept up with the technology."

Hamid Ghodse, president of the International Narcotics Control Board, warned in 2001 that "enhanced vigilance at the local level and international cooperation in the investigation and prosecution of cyber crime are essential to preventing the Internet from turning into a worldwide web of drug trafficking and crime."

By the early 2000s, governments had lost any patience they once had for letting Internet engineers solve the problems of child porn, copyright infringement, and hacking with some self-regulatory Golden Rule magic. Laws proliferated. "Internet governance" became a buzzword. The United Nations even got a piece of the action with its Internet Governance Forum. By 2003, the libertarian-leaning Cato Institute worried that "the Internet's good old days as a global cyber-zone of freedom—where governments generally take a 'hands off' approach—may be numbered."

In 2008, law professor Milton Mueller gave an address at the Technology University of Delft in which he praised that older dream of a chaotic Internet—and said that it was his dream too. But he acknowledged that reality had made Barlow and Dalzell's approaches to the 'Net unrealistic. "Let this dream now come into full contact with reality," he said. "The Internet is a mess. It is an organism infected by viruses and worms; a planet invaded and colonized by alien botnets. For every innovator, there is an imposter. The more it brings us together into social networking sites, the more we discover how bizarre and even horrifying social relations can be. All of our contemporary and historical social problems are manifest there: war, hate, discrimination, cruelty, perversion and domination. And yet we cannot escape it because it is invading our pockets through our mobile telephones."

Governments got increasingly serious about online crime. By May 2011, a gathering of the wealthy G8 countries could confidently assert in a postmeeting declaration that "governments have a role to play, informed by a full range of stakeholders, in helping to develop norms of behaviour and common approaches in the use of cyberspace." Separately, the United States and United Kingdom announced that they would work towards "building consensus on responsible behavior" online through the "same kinds of 'rules of the road' that help maintain peace, security, and respect for individual rights" in the offline world.

The vaunted "information superhighway" of the 1990s could soon have a speed limit.

How was this even possible? Authorities had eventually learned, after some trial and error, that the Internet's three great "exceptions" could be overcome. Unlike the older telephone network, the Internet had been built for intelligence not at the center but at the edges, where people wrote crazy programs and put this new tool to all manner of crafty uses—but even a decentralized network has pressure points. The new breed of Internet police forces found the most promising and learned to lean on them.

And anonymity—well, true online anonymity turned out to be the province of the deeply skilled; even noted black-hat hackers found it difficult or impossible to maintain over time. While practical anonymity might be the rule in daily life online, the police and then private actors soon found that with a court order, much of this anonymity could be pierced.

As for the geography/jurisdiction question, it wasn't quite the problem the exceptionalists believed. If an Internet user (or a server) was within your country, you could seize him or her (or it). If in a friendly foreign country, you could have local police make the grab. If in a hostile country, you could lure the user to your soil—or to a country with an extradition agreement—and make an arrest. You could seize the domain name—or block all access to the site from within your country for users who wouldn't be baited.

The "borderless" Internet has in many ways become a bordered place, with local law governing Internet use in a way thought almost impossible or impractical a decade ago. Though of concern to the early cyberlibertarians, this rebordering of the 'Net didn't concern another group of legal scholars known as the Internet "unexceptionalists." In the unexceptionalist view, the Internet provides nothing truly novel when it comes to legal enforcement. Regulation-evading jurisdictions of convenience? The offline world had them, too—think tax havens or pirate radio. Worldwide publishing? Globalization and the telegraph had created similar issues more than a century earlier. Nothing new to see here.

In 1998, Harvard Law professor Jack Goldsmith laid down a direct challenge to the exceptionalist camp with his paper "Against Cyberanarchy." "Cyberspace transactions are no different from 'real-space' transnational transactions," he wrote. "They involve people in real space in one jurisdiction communicating with people in real space in other jurisdictions in a way that often does good but sometimes causes harm . . . As the wave of real world regulation and enforcement indicates, there is no reason to believe that territorial governments will permit cyberspace participants to opt out of real world regulatory regimes."

In a 2006 book, *Who Controls the Internet? Illusions of a Borderless World*, Goldsmith joined forces with fellow law professor Tim Wu. The two came from different worlds—Goldsmith served as a legal advisor to the George W. Bush administration, while Wu went to work as a senior advisor for Barack Obama's Federal Trade Commission—but they agreed that cyber-utopianism suffered from delusions. "What we have seen, time and time again, is that physical coercion by government—the hallmark of a traditional legal system—remains far more important than anyone expected," they concluded. "This may sound crude and ugly and even depressing. Yet at a fundamental level, it's the most important thing missing from most predictions of where globalization will lead, and the most significant gap in predictions about the future shape of the Internet."

Those early pronouncements that existing institutions of control like US Customs had "given up" had the ring of truth to them—for a few years. A new generation of officials and a new generation of digital tools took years to install, but it's impossible now to look around and say that any policing agency has abandoned the Internet's chaos to its own devices.

Consider the range of agencies that now investigate crimes involving the Internet, zooming out from the local to the national level. Carol Stream, Illinois, isn't a national center of power; indeed, it isn't known to most people outside the Chicago area, yet local police there routinely arrest citizens for sharing child pornography over the Internet. The DuPage county government, which encompasses Carol Stream, runs its own SPEED (Sexual Predator Electronic Exploitation Division) unit to hunt for predators online. The state of Illinois operates an Internet Crimes Against Children task force, a High Tech Crimes Bureau, and the Illinois Computer Crime Institute to train police in Internet and computer-related investigations.

At the national level, the FBI runs the Innocent Images National Initiative to catch "cyber sexual predators" and has a significant "cyber squad" presence in FBI offices all across the country. The Secret Service investigates credit card theft online, sending agents as far away as Dubai and Estonia to investigate cases. The Department of Justice (DoJ) has a Child Exploitation and Obscenity Section focusing in large part on Internet activity. Numerous assistant US attorneys across the country now specialize in Internet caseloads. US postal inspectors regularly investigate child pornography and sex abuse on the Internet. The Federal Trade Commission recently hired its first chief technologist to help its own Internet-based work against fraud.

HavenCo's hope to sit offshore and pump bits that were legal in Sealand into other countries where they weren't, and to do so without difficulty, quickly became roadkill on the Information Superhighway. If Internet activity had disagreeable local effects, governments simply weren't going to allow it uncontested. Increasingly, they gained the tools to fight back against the chaos—sometimes too well.

/////

Why was Immigration and Customs Enforcement (ICE) director John Morton speaking at a Washington, DC "State of the Net" conference in January 2011? He had the same question. "What does ICE have to do with the Internet?" he asked. "I am here because my business—investigating crime—has brought me to the Net. Crimes that in the past occurred almost exclusively on the street or through the mails—counterfeiting, child pornography, copyright infringement—now take place in cyber space. I am here because the Internet has changed ICE's world as well as yours."

Morton had already showed himself to be a thoroughgoing unexceptionalist. His agency hadn't "given up" on the Internet, having just spent the last year on a major initiative to seize hundreds of domain names that the government alleged were linked to illegal file sharing, to counterfeiting, or to child pornography.

"We will follow criminal activity wherever it occurs, including the Internet," Morton continued. "In short, we are going to stay at it. I am unapologetic on that last point, just as we are when a crime occurs at our physical border, in your home, or at the proverbial corner of Fourth and Main. Crime is crime."

Companies like HavenCo, visionaries like Barlow, judges like Dalzell—they all pushed variations on an early vision of the 'Net in which governments had little say in the content available within their borders. Whatever theoretical advantages this view possessed, governments weren't going to accept the resulting chaos long enough to see if it was ultimately freedom-enhancing. When they saw problems online, they were predictably going to act, react, and sometimes overreact.

As his speech wrapped up, Morton tried to make one point clear: "ICE is not the police of the Internet." In the narrowest sense, Morton was right; ICE is not the Internet police. Indeed, no major country has a single, separate Internet police force. But in every way that matters,

Morton was wrong. As the Internet filled with people, people filled the Internet with everything that was worst and best about humanity. Those angel wings of which Barlow spoke often beat upon an online atmosphere black with the residue belching forth from factories catering to every dark human desire.

In response, all police became the Internet police. Here's what they've been up to.

2

OPERATION NEST EGG: ALL POLICE ARE INTERNET POLICE

On the morning of September 10, 2008, US Postal Inspector Lori Heath had a team assembled in Baltimore to raid the ramshackle Independence Street home of a suspected Internet child pornography kingpin. They got an early start; with help from the local cops, Heath put the house under surveillance at 6:00 a.m. By 8:30 a.m., the twelve-person team of postal inspectors, digital forensics specialists, and police officers was in position, but they couldn't act—Heath was stalled down at the District Court, still scrambling to get her search warrant signed. Without it, the raid was on hold.

Their target was Roger Lee Loughry Sr., a fiftysomething mechanic with a high school education, a handlebar mustache, and a love for motorcycles. Heath, in constant communication with her team back on Independence Street, wanted her warrant before Loughry got spooked by the surveillance. While she waited, Loughry stepped out into the morning air, unkempt hair hanging to his shoulders. To ensure he didn't leave the property, the surveillance team broke from their vehicles and detained him next to his home, but they could proceed no further.

At 9:00 a.m., Magistrate Judge Beth Gesner signed off on the search warrant. Heath called her team the moment she obtained the warrant, and they took Loughry back inside his home. Heath arrived shortly, crossed the dirt driveway, and let herself into the yard through the chain-link gate in the front fence. The vinyl-sided home was dilapidated. Heath's inspectors went two steps down into the basement, but the stairs were so rickety that she worried someone might fall through them.

On the main floor, the team tried to enter a room where two dogs, agitated at the agents' presence, barked repeatedly. The agents called Baltimore Animal Control, though Loughry told them the dogs simply belonged to a lodger who was renting rooms and were not being mistreated.

The warrant team sat Loughry on a living room couch just to the right of the front door, then spent an hour and forty minutes combing the house. Much of that time was spent on the second floor where Loughry had his bedroom and a home office.

The team had broad license to grab material. The warrant authorized them to take cameras, films, address books, mailing lists, mortgage documents, utility bills, diaries, notebooks, disks, computers, login names and passwords, P2P (peer-to-peer) software, and records "in any format or medium" that dealt with child pornography or child erotica. Loughry had a trove of such stuff, including a webcam, a burned CD hand-labeled "Vids+," and three internal hard drives that had been removed from computers and set atop a stack of DVDs.

The agents sought information that would tie Loughry to an Internet message board called "The Cache," which existed to share links to child pornography photos and videos. The government had already penetrated the board's security and knew the online "handles" of its members. The leader went by "DAS" while one of the coadministrators preferred "Mayorroger"; Loughry was suspected to be the latter.

Agents searching Loughry's home couldn't yet see what was on the hard drives they collected, but they did find a piece of paper with a cryptic address fragment in the lower right corner: "6 West Barney." Turning it over, they saw another address: "Mr. D. A. Savigar, [house number redacted], Leyland, Preston, Lancashire, United Kingdom, PR251AH." It was the address for one Delwyn A. Savigar—"DAS"—who was at that moment being arrested by the Lancashire Constabulary. (Savigar would later plead guilty to possessing 100,000 child pornography images, to running The Cache, and to sexual assaults on two thirteen-year-olds and one sixteen-year-old in the north of England.)

Confident now that she had her man, Heath went downstairs to speak with Loughry. He signed a waiver acknowledging his willingness to talk without a lawyer present and he freely admitted to using the Mayorroger screen name for all sorts of online accounts; he had chosen it in the wake of a failed 1999 bid for mayor of Baltimore. He then volunteered that he was an admin for The Cache—before Heath had even mentioned the site. Loughry said the position was just "honorary"—what most interested him about the site was a simple arcade game called "Army Corps." And what harm was there in that?

After Heath pointed out that The Cache had actually dropped support for the game some time ago and then asked him about child pornography on the site, Loughry told her that he "figured" such material was being traded on the board. But he claimed that he had worked to thwart the child pornographers. "The only functions I performed there was I banned people for posting child pornography," he wrote in a signed statement at the end of this interview. "I did click the links to see their posts and then banned them. . . . My understanding of 'The Cache' was they had adult porn and games. I have since left the site." He told Heath that viewing child porn was a "sickness."

As a government lawyer would later put it, "We expect his essential defense in substance to be, I was only an administrator of an adult porn game board, 'The Cache.' I didn't know. I didn't intend to do any of the things that the other people are doing." The government didn't buy it. Would a jury?

//////

The long road to Loughry's run-down Baltimore home stretched back to Australia, where in 2006 a Queensland investigator came across a video of child sex abuse. Investigators routinely scrutinize such videos after seizure, looking for any scrap of evidence—a school logo, a poster—that might help identify either child or abuser. The Australian video depicted a man and a young girl who spoke with a Flemish accent. Queensland police therefore passed the video to counterparts half a world away in Belgium, where officials launched Operation Koala.

Incredibly, the Europeans found the man shown in the video—a father who was raping his two daughters. The man led police to the forty-two-year-old Italian photographer who had taped the abuse. He had set up a studio in the Ukraine, where he produced child pornography and ran a website from which he sold more than 150 homemade creations. (The site masqueraded as a legitimate child modeling site; a secret, password-protected section contained the child porn.)

The photographer was soon arrested by Italian police, and a real breakthrough came when investigators seized his archive of 50,000 e-mails from potential customers in twenty-eight countries. The cops suddenly had more leads than they could handle. Europol, the regional version of the international police coordination organization Interpol, put together detailed planning sessions at The Hague. Police from across Europe got involved, eventually using the e-mail addresses to identify 2,500 individuals; they then launched coordinated raids in nineteen countries and arrested hundreds of suspects.

While Europe planned its crackdown, Europol sent the e-mail list to US officials, who found that the United States had the dubious distinction of originating 11,000 of the messages. The FBI could turn only

700 of these into "workable investigative leads," but pursuing that many individuals was itself a huge job that required massive federal resources.

The US investigation that resulted was named Operation Joint Hammer. When US Attorney General Michael Mukasey revealed Joint Hammer at a press conference in December 2008, sixty US residents had just been arrested, including a New Jersey man who pled guilty to "producing sexual images of his 9-year-old daughter" and an Arizona fifth-grade teacher eventually accused of "sexual contact with female students at his school."

That might not sound like a large haul after the application of so many resources, but the Europol e-mails had set in motion a complex series of investigations that ran for years—indeed, as of 2013, they remain ongoing. Joint Hammer provided a new entryway into the shadowy child pornography subculture, where users built relationships of trust with one another, took pains to use security measures, and operated on small boards that did not advertise their existence. In such cases, simply knowing that a particular child porn board existed was half the battle; such sites might operate in secrecy for years. And because so many users had accounts on multiple boards, cracking one often led to the next, which led to the one after that.

With Joint Hammer, the pattern held. In 2007, a US postal inspector named Jeffrey Arney had followed up on some of the Europol e-mails when he interviewed an Alabama suspect who was a member of several boards. The man eventually turned over his online identity to the inspector, offering up his e-mail accounts, his usernames, and his passwords, including credentials to a site known only as The Cache. Suddenly, the feds had a new board name—and a way inside.

Visitors to The Cache accessed thecachebbs.com and saw nothing special—just a simple log-in screen asking for a username and password. Signing up for a new account required approval from an administrator, and such access wasn't given out easily. But with access to the informant's account—his username on The Cache was "Retard"—authorities bypassed the login barrier.

At first glance, the view was unremarkable. Like most online forums, The Cache hosted numerous text-based discussion sections including sections on politics and sports. It also explicitly banned child pornography; indeed, this was rule number one. The Cache demanded that users "not request, offer, and/or post child pornography" and said that "violation of this rule will result in an immediate ban, and your law enforcement agency will be notified of the infraction." An entire subsection of the rules spelled out what constituted "CP" in tremendous detail—"no dildos or sex toys even if it is not used. This can include a girl suggestively sucking a cucumber or other phallic symbol. You get the idea?"

The child porn ban didn't mean The Cache was a wholesome place. Instead, the rules were apparently driven by a particular definition of "child pornography" as hard-core sex acts. The site banned those but trafficked in all sorts of other images and videos, mostly of young children posed to display their genitals for the camera. (Federal law makes such "lascivious exhibition" material illegal, despite the distinction drawn by The Cache.)

Users were cautioned to "always surf safe. Have your Internet settings at the highest settings. Take caution when surfing the links." Members would be "pruned" from the board if they didn't participate regularly, which included posting material—but not posting anything too tawdry directly to The Cache. Members instead compressed videos and pictures, slapped innocent-sounding names on them, applied passwords, then uploaded them to anonymous file-hosting sites across the Internet. They would then post a link on The Cache to this material while also providing the file password in bold letters.

But the links they provided couldn't be clicked; they were purposely defective. As one site rule explained, "Even though these [images and videos are compressed as] zips and RAR'd files remember, they still cannot be direct link." Users were told to prefix links with "hxxp://" instead of the normal Web prefix "http://." This made links impossible to click on accidentally and also provided The Cache with some protection. Any link clicked on directly from a website generates a "referrer" ID that the linked website can read and record; if Cache members began clicking on links directly from the board, third-party sites or police might one day have an easy-to-assemble list of things that Cache members were downloading. Instead, members had to copy the link, paste it into a Web browser, and correct it by hand—thereby removing The Cache's referral.

As Postal Inspector Arney looked around the site, he found such things as a "nude" gallery, which was further subdivided into an "18+" nude gallery, a "13-to-18" nude gallery, and an "under-13" nude gallery. Following the links and using the passwords revealed the material being traded. With 1,000 members at its height, The Cache was a big deal. Because of the scale of the site, the government soon spun off The Cache probe into its own operation—Operation Nest Egg.

Arney had his evidence of wrongdoing, but he couldn't identify the people behind the site. They were merely names on a screen— Mayorroger, Devil, Legend, Spit4branes. To access real identities, he needed the actual computer serving up The Cache. In February 2008, seven months after gaining access to their informant's Cache account, US postal inspectors obtained a warrant to seize the actual machine serving up thecachebbs.com from North Carolina hosting company Caro.net.

Caro pulled the machine offline and turned the hard drive inside over to postal inspectors, who passed it on to the DoJ's Child Exploitation and Obscenity Section (CEOS) back in Washington, DC. James Fottrell served as head of the High Technology Investigative Unit at CEOS, and he used the main database found on the hard drive to rebuild The Cache locally in his office, creating a private version of the site that looked just as it would have to the site's users. When infiltrating the board, Arney had been merely a regular user with a regular user's limitations; now Fottrell had complete run of the site.

A few weeks later, Fottrell took his copy of The Cache out to the Immigration and Customs Enforcement (ICE) Cybercrimes Center in Fairfax, Virginia, to get more space. He set up shop in a training room with twenty-four computers. For a week, federal, state, and local agents sat at those computers and probed this locally re-created Cache, following its links, downloading evidence, and preserving it for prosecution. The team eventually assembled investigative lead packets on every member of the site, packets that included usernames, profile information, and the Internet Protocol (IP) addresses of every machine used to access the site.

These IP addresses, four-part numbers such as 192.168.0.1, could often identify individual Internet accounts, but only with the help of service providers like AT&T or Comcast. The government sent a set of subpoenas to Internet providers across the country, asking them which subscribers had been assigned particular IP addresses at the dates and times in question. When the responses came back, the government suddenly had real names, though agents knew that an IP address alone could not tell you who had actually been using the computer at the time. Still, it provided a good place to start.

The investigative lead packets went to field agents around the country who lived close to the suspects. Mayorroger's IP address matched a Comcast account belonging to one Roger Loughry of Baltimore, so his investigative lead packet went to an agent in the Baltimore/Washington area. Which is how Loughry's name ended up on the desk of Postal Inspector Lori Heath.

/////

In 1999, Roger Loughry wanted to run for mayor of Baltimore—despite being out of work and on probation for driving while intoxicated. "I didn't see any problem with running for mayor," Loughry told a *Baltimore Sun* reporter at the time. "With Marion Barry getting busted and still getting elected [as mayor of Washington, DC], why not me?" His bid didn't go far; Baltimore's official results for the 1999 mayoral election show no record of his name on the ballot.

Born in March 1953, Loughry was in rough shape as the new millennium rolled in. Almost deaf in his left ear, he had brushed with the law over a pair of gun charges, marijuana possession, and a situation in which he was accused of threatening the manager of a pizza shop. He had married and fathered a pair of children, serving as their primary caregiver in the 1980s and early 1990s, a period of time during which he also admitted to using marijuana on a daily basis. Then his wife took ill; he tended her for three years, until she died. She was followed to the grave by Loughry's mother Margarete, whose name remained on the deed of the Independence Street home where Loughry lived at the time of his arrest. He grew estranged from his family and had no "healthy support system since the death of your mother and your wife," as a federal judge would later put it.

At some point, Loughry discovered MySpace. His profile, now frozen in time, describes him as a TRAMP—"terrific, responsible, adventurous, mystical, and profound." (Digital forensics would later establish that "tramp" was one of his online passwords.) He most wanted to meet "real people in a real world," he wrote. "We all need to stand together and kill the monster that is known as 'Government.'" Pictures posted to the account show Loughry, often bare-chested, his reddish hair spilling down onto his chest. In one, he stands smiling and shirtless beside a sixties-style door studded with diamond-shaped windows. He clutches fourteen birthday balloons. Plaster and paint flake away from the background walls and ceilings.

Loughry joined The Cache in 2005, soon after its creation by Delwyn Savigar. His profile's signature line was "Bow down to the masses" and he used a Confederate flag as his profile image. His Mayorroger account was made a coadministrator, one step below Savigar's all-powerful root administrator. Loughry could create and change accounts, move and delete forum posts, even delete most of the board if he chose.

Far from ratting out the child pornographers, Loughry appeared to appreciate their work. A member provided access to images called the "school passion" series that the member had ripped from another site "quite a while back when I was on dial-up." Mayorroger responded, "Totally awesome, guys. Great work. Many, many thanks for these cuties."

On March 9, 2007, Mayorroger contributed to a general Cache discussion thread about the "general definition of our topic interest." "You could say I was sexually molested as a child, but I wouldn't," he wrote. "I learned the true beauty of the young female form long before I should have. I learned to do things that a lot of men can't do no matter how old they are, and that is truly—and that it is truly please that luscious creature. I'm gonna tell it like this. I was five and she was six, no joke. After that I was six and they were seven, eight, nine, 14, 15, 16; again, no joke."

He said that, as he grew older, mature female bodies never became appealing. "I used to look at LGs [little girls] and think how sweet it was back then," he continued. "Then I happened onto RLbbs [Russian Lolita BBS], and it was all over for me. I was seeing the very things I had been imagining for so long. For me, it was like a trip back to my youth. I wouldn't lay a hand on any LG, but to look and remember, ah, yes."

By October 2007, the breezy tone turned chilly; Loughry was running scared. He sometimes hung out on another board where he met a man known as "Cranckrack." Loughry and Cranckrack formed enough of a friendship that they sometimes spoke on the phone; both eventually joined The Cache, and once they actually met in person at a Baltimore "gentlemen's tavern" called Haven Place. Shortly after this meeting, Cranckrack called Loughry and told him that postal inspectors had just seized his computer.

The raid on Cranckrack spooked Loughry, as it did other Cache admins; they knew that a raid on a Cache user might result in government infiltrators. Michael James Baratta, a Sacramento, California, resident who operated as "DublHelix" on The Cache, would later cop a plea deal and testify that Cranckrack's account on The Cache was shut down immediately after news of the raid broke.

"If he were in custody, they . . . probably would have confiscated his computer and possibly be—what is the word?—impersonating him online, perhaps," Baratta said at Loughry's eventual trial. "We just wanted to make sure that there was no way that anybody else except the person that we knew as Cranckrack would be able to use that account."

Loughry's response was to send an instant message to DublHelix on October 3, saying, "Delete me from the board." But when DublHelix went to the other admins with news of Loughry's "paranoia" about arrest, site leader DAS got involved. "Paranoia about what?" he wrote back. "Don't delete him, just downgrade his account to master. If he then wishes to come back, his account will be active."

On January 11, 2008, seeing that nothing had happened in the last three months, Loughry's confidence returned and he logged into The Cache once more. "Yes, it was paranoia," he wrote when he returned. "Besides, way too much live pussy running around my house to need pics. LMFAO [laughing my fucking ass off]." He resumed his coadmin duties.

Loughry's confidence was supremely misplaced; the feds were actually tightening the noose around The Cache, but no one on the site appeared to notice. When postal inspectors seized The Cache's main server from Caro.net in February 2008, the site stopped functioning—but admins didn't spend much time investigating what had happened. People who run this sort of operation don't want to bring themselves to the attention of their own Internet providers by filing trouble tickets when their servers have problems and so, while the episode should have waved a huge red flag repeatedly in their faces, the admins instead retreated to a backup server kept in place for just such moments of downtime.

This backup server wasn't a traditional backup containing an exact mirror of the original site, but a secondary communications channel that members could use to regroup. The Cache eventually rebuilt its main site with a different Internet hosting provider, leaving Caro.net for Atomic Colo in Minnesota. (In September 2008, when the feds were finally ready to make arrests, they seized the new Cache server—but this time also found and grabbed the backup server from Future Hosting in Dallas to ensure this wouldn't happen again.)

Membership declined to around 530 as the noose tightened and suspected infiltrators were purged, but the core members showed signs of addiction. William Weyrick, a forty-seven-year-old Cache member from Aurora, Indiana, operated under the name "Sammybear"—a combination of names from his two dogs. After his own arrest, he plea-bargained a lower sentence for testifying about the site. When asked during Loughry's trial if pictures on The Cache were "not right to have," Weyrick answered, "Yes, sir. There—I, I don't know. I guess I was just addicted. I had problems, but I, I, I know it is wrong."

Like many members of The Cache, Loughry just couldn't stay away even when the danger was obvious. In late 2008, investigators raided homes across the country, including Loughry's, where Heath and her team put their target under arrest and began a meticulous search of Loughry's digital devices.

/////

Investigators executing a search warrant have long been instructed to find all active computer equipment, shut it down, and bag it for study back at a forensic lab. Called "data preservation," the approach takes as its mantra: "Don't touch anything—you might contaminate it."

Evidence remained unspoiled, but the delay in looking through it caused problems. When police surprise a suspect on a search, running computers in the house might contain key information. Perhaps the suspect has just logged into a secret Internet board with his credentials; perhaps he has decrypted the hard-drive partition where the worst material is stored. Turn off the computer, haul it away—and you've lost your advantage.

The Cache investigators trialed a more recent technique known as "on-scene computer triage." Under this model, search-warrant teams arrived with their own digital forensics specialists and began sifting the data while the suspect sat on a living room couch. The technique "treats forensics data on someone's computer like a martini," Assistant US Attorney Steve DeBrota, who oversaw the entire set of Cache prosecutions, told me. "If you let it get warm, it's not worth drinking."

On-scene computer triage had been developed in part at Purdue University, an hour north of DeBrota's base in Indianapolis. It wasn't widely known in 2008, but DeBrota pushed his teams in Indiana to use it with terrific success: confession rates went up. Investigators raided one Indiana man involved with The Cache and brought in Hamilton County's child exploitation task force to help. The suspect had taken precautions, encrypting his hard drive, but when he saw the techs at work in his home he grew convinced that they were only minutes away from breaking in. During on-site questioning, he voluntarily surrendered the passwords.

As data use increases, so does the time needed to do an exhaustive search of that data in forensics labs. In one case, investigators came across a suspect with twelve terabytes of data spread across seventy-two hard drives in his apartment. Sifting it all could take months, which wasn't a problem if investigators wanted to convict one guy but became a huge liability when they wanted to take down a still-thriving network.

The government could build more labs, of course, but on-scene triage suggested a new approach: skim the data quickly on-site looking for other suspects, user passwords, and obvious items of value. Then—act on it. Immediately. Said DeBrota, "Very dangerous offenders have very dangerous friends," who may be hard to locate if the trail goes cold.

The rest of the data can always be examined at leisure. In Loughry's case, that job fell to computer forensics specialist Matthew Kiley, who had been at the Department of Justice's CEOS unit for only a few months when Operation Nest Egg material began to arrive from across the country. In November 2008, Kiley copied the two 160 GB hard drives found inside Loughry's computer onto separate drives that he could examine without fear of tampering with the original evidence; in December, he moved on to the smaller drives found atop Loughry's stacks of DVDs. With the help of professional forensics software, Kiley rifled through Loughry's files, the websites he had visited, and his instant messaging logs looking for evidence of child pornography—and it wasn't hard to find.

Loughry had used the Internet Explorer Web browser to visit sites like the Russian Lolita BBS and the Lair of Young Art Lovers (LOYAL). As a simple security measure, he had configured the browser to retain the list of websites he had visited for only a single day instead of the default twenty days, but this caused almost no problems for detailed forensic analysis. Little was well hidden; links to The Cache had even been bookmarked and 181 child porn pictures still sat in the Windows recycle bin.

Loughry had also used LimeWire, a peer-to-peer file-swapping application that has since been shuttered by a federal judge in a copyright infringement lawsuit. When his computer was seized, LimeWire logs showed attempts to download files with deeply incriminating names. A Windows Live Messenger log showed a conversation between Loughry and someone claiming to be a sixteen-year-old girl; Kiley's final report noted that "the content of the chat includes sexual overtones."

Kiley also found a host of child sex abuse videos in the Loughry evidence. A CD burned back in 2005 was labeled "LS_Movies," an apparent reference to the huge Lolita Studios series of pictures produced by organized operators in Eastern Europe and sold around the world. A DVD burned on September 7, 2008—only three days before Postal Inspector Heath raided Loughry's home—contained "approximately 200 pictures and 40 videos of suspected child pornography."

Loughry had collected this material for many years. An old, disconnected hard drive showed that he had visited the Lolitafix website 321 times between October 2002 and January 2003, and the Russian Lolita BBS 889 times over the following three months.

Numerous Cache defendants turned out to be "contact" offenders, too—people who went far beyond just looking at pictures. "It was immensely satisfying to catch people who had gotten away with child molesting for at least ten years on multiple victims," DeBrota told me. "If you prosecute sex crimes cases, at the end of the day what sustains you is knowing that you made an individual difference. I've met some of the victims that were victims of the material in The Cache case—I've met them. They don't like that their material is out there. It causes them continuing chronic pain."

In the end, of the twenty-six top usernames on The Cache, twenty-two were successfully mapped to real people. Relying in large part on digital forensic evidence, prosecutors got every other person arrested in Operation Nest Egg to plead guilty, including leader Delwyn Savigar in England. ("We had what they said to each other, there wasn't much they could do," DeBrota said.) Not Loughry, though—he alone elected to fight the sixteen counts against him on the grounds that he had actually been working from the inside to bring down the child abusers. The government was incredulous, calling The Cache "the largest child pornography conspiracy ever prosecuted by anyone anywhere" and claiming that Loughry was one of the five most culpable people. But Loughry would not bend, even if it might have meant a plea deal with a lower sentence, so his case trudged toward a trial.

After the arrests, the second innovation of the Cache investigation became clear: the government sought to hold the site's leadership accountable for a group conspiracy rather than charging them separately. The tactical decision meant that the suspects could be consolidated into a single criminal case handled by DeBrota in an Indiana federal court. It simplified the discovery process and involved fewer prosecutors, who found it easier to get a handle on the complicated linkages between suspects in the case.

For fifteen years, DeBrota had argued for this approach to handling such cases; he told me that he felt "vindicated" by what happened with The Cache. "There's always somebody you miss, but if you aggressively pursue groups as groups you can get a class of offenders that's hard to find any other way," he said. "They're very good at hiding in plain sight."

But charging The Cache defendants with conspiracy had a drawback—it limited the government to talking in court only about activities directly related to The Cache. Although far worse material was taken from suspects' homes, the men weren't charged with its possession—yet the government's temptation to show this material to the jury anyway was powerful. And in Loughry's case, the government indulged, with dramatic results.

/////

Loughry had little money to mount a legal defense, and he accepted court-appointed attorney Joseph Cleary of Indianapolis. After meeting with Loughry for two hours on January 16, 2009, Cleary learned that a Baltimore doctor suspected Loughry of bipolar disorder or schizophrenia but that Loughry had been arrested before meeting with a psychiatrist who might have confirmed the diagnosis. Loughry spent the meeting with Cleary explaining—again—that he had only been on The Cache because he wanted to "clean up the problem" of child porn. He was being persecuted, he told Cleary, for "attempting to do the right thing."

Cleary had his doubts that his client was in a position to go to trial.

"Loughry's fixation extends to his efforts to clean up the city of Baltimore (figuratively and literally)," he told the judge overseeing the case. "Loughry claims to have run for mayor of Baltimore and [said] that he sought expertise in running the particular computer bulletin board at issue in this case in order for him to use a computer bulletin board to run for President of the United States. Counsel cannot get past Loughry's fixation with being persecuted.... Counsel is unwilling to proceed without some medical assurance that Loughry is capable of making such a decision in this case."

The Federal Bureau of Prisons examined Loughry; a doctor concluded that he suffered from severe maladaptive personality features that included a grandiose sense of self-importance and a lack of remorse—but they concluded that he was still competent to stand trial. Cleary eventually agreed. "I did not re-raise the issue in this case because I was satisfied that Mr. Loughry was competent," he told me after the case ended.

On April 12, 2010, the trial began at the US District Court for the Southern District of Indiana in downtown Indianapolis. Loughry said almost nothing during the four days of testimony. Federal agents, including Heath and Fottrell, reconstructed the story of The Cache for the jury and walked through the contents of Loughry's computer. Other members of The Cache testified as part of plea deals, each dispelling the idea that anyone might have used the site only to play games or to discuss politics.

Back in 2007, Marc "Kingbee" Reeder of Pennsylvania had posted a link on The Cache saying, "Once again I have decided to bestow my graciousness upon ye and post some more sets from Lolita Castle. I hope you enjoy!" At Loughry's trial, Reeder admitting to possessing 200 GB of child pornography and to being a regular on The Cache. When asked what The Cache was, he was clear: "It was a place where we traded links to images of underage girls, nude underage girls."

Loughry declined to take the stand in his defense. He called no witnesses. Cleary's closing argument concluded that Loughry "should be found not guilty"—a tough sell for a lawyer who also has to admit that his client "had child pornography in his house, but he is not charged with what is in his house, ladies and gentlemen, he is not. He is charged with these things on 'The Cache.'"

I asked Cleary later what it was like to give this speech. "My job is to zealously advocate for my client and try to convince the jury that the government has failed somewhere in its burden of proof and thus my client should be acquitted," he told me. "That was certainly difficult in this case, given the evidence arrayed against Mr. Loughry."

The jury left the courtroom at 2:41 p.m. and returned at 4:11 p.m. In an hour and a half they had found Loughry guilty of advertising and distributing child pornography. Loughry was taken back to prison to await his eventual fate; as a coadmin who had refused to plead out, the sentence was unlikely to be lenient.

In the four months before the judge ruled on his punishment, Loughry may have seen the jail terms piling up against the other Cache defendants: 120 months, 180 months, 240 months, even 378 months in one case, depending on how senior each man had been in the site hierarchy. Helping the government nail Loughry paid off for some. William "Sammybear" Weyrick, who showed up at Loughry's trial to admit that he knew The Cache trafficked in child porn, received only sixty months in prison after most of the charges against him were dropped.

While awaiting their sentencing in various jails scattered about the region, The Cache defendants had time to find God. One wrote in a letter to the court that "I realize now that my actions were not those of a God-fearing man; and I am deeply ashamed of what I have done. My actions, which I deeply regret, I realize now were cries for help; and because of what my cousin had done to me when I was a child, I was already in a prison of my own making, yet I did not realize at the time how imprisoned I truly was."

Others led lives so lonely that they couldn't find anyone to help them prepare for a long stretch in prison. Jason "Pikachu 71" Milano had lived in his Clinton Township, Michigan, mobile home for twenty-two years before his Cache-related arrest. Unable to find friends or family members who could put his possessions in storage, sell his trailer, and take care of his two Dodge Neons, Milano was reduced to begging the judge for a temporary release from jail to dispose of his assets.

As for Loughry, he found only violence in the Kentucky prison where he was held. On August 18, 2010, he appeared before Judge William T. Lawrence for sentencing. For the first time in the case, Loughry's voice comes through clearly. "I've had my face rearranged in Kentucky, literally," he told the judge when given a chance to speak. "I'm really bad almost—well, the vision is really blurry in the right eye because it's be being held in by a piece of titanium mesh now from this beating."

His possessions had gone missing while he was recovering from the assault; Loughry blamed prison officials. "The deputy here or guard, whatever you want to call him, stole all my property that day," he said. "When I come back from the hospital my property's gone. . . . My stuff was in a locked cell. The only person who could get in that cell is a deputy. If it come up gone, who could've took it?"

Loughry saw his life as one subject to a "system" of overlapping authorities, each with minimal competence and in little contact with one another. "This system really does suck," he said. "It's not just on the outside, in Baltimore, it's all over." He claimed to have spent years filming gang violence on his street—but said that police refused to respond to his calls or to watch his VHS recordings. He claimed to have filmed his postman tossing Loughry's mail in the rough direction of the porch; half the time it fell short and would be covered in rain or snow. The Postmaster General would, he said, do nothing. He claimed that his garbage collector tossed trash in front of his house—yet it was Loughry who got a citation for littering. His ninety-seven-year-old neighbor threw "dirty diapers among other trash" into his yard and onto his roof, but "she don't care. I've got it on videotape since '97."

After his arrest, the City of Baltimore fined him $3,000 "because I was not there this past winter to shovel the seven feet of snow off the sidewalk," he said. Those fines went unpaid; Loughry heard that the city eventually seized his mother's home, but he didn't know. (His probation officer said the issue was actually one of back taxes.)

The "system" couldn't even get his previous criminal record correct. "Everything pertaining to this case has been lies actually," he said. "There was like things that happened in places that it never happened in. It looked like somebody just took my record, threw it up in the air and just scrambled it."

The judge took note of all these complaints, concluded that none posed a material challenge to the case, and prepared to pronounce the sentence. Loughry received permission for a final oration. He spoke about the "positive things that I've tried to do." His statement, the longest single one he made during his case, reveals Loughry's view of himself as a fundamentally decent person:

> At my wife's prodding, I took a bunch of old computer parts I had laying around the house, built computers for some of the kids in the neighborhood that couldn't afford it and parents couldn't afford 'em. Granted, they didn't get online, but at least they had a head start. I was part of the Maryland Toy Run from approximately '87 forward, which is [where] they give money, collect money and toys for children, needy children. Toys for Tots. I have had a hand in part of that.
>
> My neighbors—a lot of my neighbors are handicapped senior citizens that are on fixed incomes, can't afford to pay a hundred dollars plus garages charge these days. I was a certified master automobile technician. Sometimes I work on their cars for nothing just

because they're neighbors. They needed a break. I spent a lot of time and effort cleaning up my neighborhood; trash, actual refrigerators, stuff like that thrown around . . .

I was told I was stupid, I was crazy, because people don't work for free, you know. Well, when your 88 year old neighbor can't afford to have her car fixed but she depends on that car, you fix it if you can. I'm not saying I bought the parts or anything. She would have to buy her parts or he would have to buy their parts, but I could do the labor for free, and I did a lot of that.

I'm not the bad guy that this report shows believe it or not. There's a lot of good I've been doing that's not in this report.

Steve DeBrota agreed that Loughry "may not be a fully one-dimensional character," but he put a sinister spin on Loughry's narrative. "The idea that he's participating in a program that confers a benefit, a computer on another child is scary," DeBrota told the judge. "That's not a good thing. I don't want anyone talking to this man who's under 18. And I don't really want him talking to anybody outside of a prison anymore because of the nature of his behavior. . . . There's no reason to think he is reformable at all."

But Loughry believed himself reformed—indeed, reborn—already. He traced his transformation back to a motorcycle accident on October 5, 1980 at 2:00 p.m. "It was a Sunday," he told the judge. "I remember it well. I died in that accident. . . . Right after I died in that motorcycle accident and came back to life—things changed for me. I tried as hard as I could. I tried to clean up my neighborhood, both physically and criminally and you name it. I tried to do the right things for a lot of people."

Yet, returned from the dead, Loughry could not deny that he had spent a fair chunk of his brand-new life on child porn websites, eventually coadministering the largest one discovered in the United States to that point. He expressed no remorse, accepted no responsibility.

When Loughry's speech concluded, Judge Lawrence told him, "Clearly the offenses you have been found guilty of are extremely serious and involve the exploitation of minor children who continue to be victimized each time a computer file or movie is downloaded, or a photograph is viewed or printed. There is no foreseeable end to their victimization." He sentenced Loughry to 360 months in jail.

The prison term is unlikely to be a placid one. Child abusers of all stripes face violence in prison; Loughry had already been beaten badly. "I would suspect that it's a difficult road ahead for Mr. Loughry," Cleary said at the end of the hearing, "given the crime."

/////

The resources spent cracking The Cache might seem almost despair-inducing; at tremendous expense leads appear, investigations develop, communities are infiltrated—yet most casual members simply melt away into the Internet's shadows, slipping into other closed networks not yet known or imagined by their pursuers.

But traditional policing didn't die with the Internet, and investigators have had lengthy experience in following gangsters, pornographers, and drug kingpins through a maze of social networks. Done correctly, the shutdown of a major child porn network doesn't mean that investigators are reduced to waiting for another Queensland police officer to discover a disturbing digital video; the original investigation should provide leads into new communities.

Operation Koala in Europe spawned Operation Joint Hammer in the United States. Joint Hammer spawned Operation Nest Egg, which took down The Cache. What would emerge when Nest Egg was cracked open?

We found out on August 3, 2011, when US Attorney General Eric Holder revealed Operation Delego. If The Cache was the largest child porn bust until that point, Operation Delego's target network—called Dreamboard—broke the record again.

"Operation Delego represents the largest prosecution to date in the United States of individuals who participated in an online bulletin board conceived and operated for the sole purpose of promoting child sexual abuse, disseminating child pornography, and evading law enforcement," said a DoJ announcement at the time.

Delego began back in December 2009, little more than a year after the raids that brought down The Cache. By June 2009, Cache members had started signing plea bargains with the government that appear to have given the feds their access to Dreamboard. Kevin "Spit4Branes" Harkless, for instance, told investigators all about The Cache and went on to describe, as the government put it, "other Internet forums dedicated to the advertisement and dissemination of child pornography." In addition, he "provided information concerning other individuals involved in similar offenses."

But if investigators learn something each time they shut down a site, the child pornographers take their own lessons from such raids. Dreamboard used the same system as The Cache, one in which content was posted off-site and encrypted with passwords shared only with Dreamboard members. But many users of The Cache had done little to protect their own identities; once the servers were seized, grabbing IP addresses and turning them into real names was a tedious but straightforward process. Even a coadmin like Loughry used no passwords on his computer and had installed no encryption software.

Dreamboard shored up these security weaknesses. Users routed their Internet connections through proxy servers that altered the apparent IP address of a connection, making it more difficult for people to be identified simply based on Dreamboard connection logs. Members also routinely encrypted material on their own computers to make it invisible in case of a search—encryption good enough to stymie most investigators.

Yet solid policing paid off. Dreamboard was infiltrated and seventy-two people were initially arrested in the United States; nineteen more were picked up in thirteen other countries ranging from Kenya to Ecuador to Denmark to Qatar.

Concerns that the "borderless Internet" makes anonymous crime simpler are well founded, but they only tell half the story. While Internet protocols know nothing of national borders, the Internet certainly exists within those borders even as its links extend across them. Its fiber-optic lines, switches, routers, cable modems, copper wiring, and servers all exist within geographic and political boundaries, each carrying with it layers of existing authority structures—and each authority has been happy enough to exert its coercive power upon the users sitting at the end of those connections.

The global reach and presumed anonymity of the Internet has been a boon to child pornographers by linking up far-flung people with perverse interests. But it provides similar advantages to investigators, who eventually learned how to harness their collective power to do these kinds of joint investigations that led from Queensland to Operation Delego.

"The Internet has connected all of us into one world without oceans and boundaries," said the FBI's Shawn Henry after Joint Hammer wrapped up. "As a result, cyber crimes present a challenge that can only be effectively confronted with strength and dedication exhibited daily by law enforcement agencies around the world working in close coordination."

Such coordination has been a concern for more than a decade. The Council of Europe's "Convention on Cybercrime" was concluded in 2001, though it took years for many states to sign on. (The United States ratified only in late 2006; the United Kingdom did not until 2011). The convention explicitly targets child pornography, among other things, and one of its innovations was Article 35's "24/7 Network." This created a full-time contact in each signing country who could "ensure the provision of immediate assistance for the purpose of investigations or proceedings concerning criminal offences related to computer systems and data, or for the collection of evidence in electronic form of a criminal offence."

Though this was by no means the only (or even the main) way police authorities exchanged cross-border information, the 24/7 network showed that governments saw the value in making it easier to follow individuals and messages as they hopped across existing borders. Rather than creating some new Internet Police, the existing police simply added Internet issues to their bailiwicks.

And the number of bailiwicks involved in taking down The Cache was impressive. A partial list of agencies involved includes the Australian police, the Belgian national police, Europol, European national police from at least nineteen countries, the FBI, US postal inspectors, ICE, the DoJ's CEOS unit, US attorneys, state task forces like the Indiana Internet Crimes Against Children Task Force, Virgina state and local police (who helped investigators during the week spent downloading all the linked material listed on The Cache), and local police in many cities who secured homes for search warrant raids and aided on arrests.

The sheer amount of police machinery put into place by a single Queensland video was staggering. While the Internet made criminals more agile, it did the same for their pursuers—who have continued the hunt. DeBrota told me that his team is "actually two operations after Nest Egg" now.

/////

Unlike most other offenses, where society shows a pragmatic willingness to tolerate low levels of illegal behavior, child porn has the distinction of being one of the few online activities condemned everywhere, by everyone. This has led to far more extreme remedies than we see with other Internet ills. Where citizens of liberal democracies would ordinarily not tolerate Internet censorship, child pornography has often been the thin end of the wedge that gets filtering in the door. "It simply cannot be tolerated that Internet users would accidentally be exposed to such horrific images," said European Union (EU) Commissioner Neelie Kroes when endorsing an annual report for the United Kingdom's main blacklist maker, the privately run Internet Watch Foundation.

Critics charge that, because of its horrific nature, child sex abuse is open to politicization by those who would prefer to see Internet censorship extended to things like copyright infringement but who have trouble making this argument directly. Rick Falkvinge founded the Pirate Party (Piratpartiet) in Sweden, a political party that eventually sent two representatives to the European Parliament after winning small but significant shares of the Swedish national vote. He has been a strong critic of this approach, which he sees as a threat to a free society. In a 2012 article, he recalled listening to Johan Schlüter, chief of the Danish Anti-Piracy Group, give a private speech in which Schlüter allegedly said, "Child pornography is great. Politicians do not understand file sharing, but they understand child pornography, and they want to filter that to score points with the public. Once we get them to filter child pornography, we can get them to extend the block to file sharing."

Though Falkvinge has extreme views on plenty of issues (he would also legalize the possession of child pornography, believing that the current approach makes it more difficult to catch child sex abusers), he's not manufacturing this view of the issue. European digital rights group EDRI got its hands on a 2011 "Single Secure European Cyberspace" presentation given to EU officials by an unnamed individual. On the slide "Characteristics of the Internet," the first bullet point was "borderless"—and the presenter explicitly advocated rebordering the Internet by creating "virtual 'border crossing points'" wherever Internet traffic enters the EU. This involved, among other things, Internet censorship, which would start with child sex abuse images. But the penultimate slide made clear that this was only a "first step." If the EU-wide system worked well and gained acceptance, it would then "be possible to broaden the cooperation of the blocking process by involving other types of crimes."

Once Internet providers have the technical infrastructure in place to block content, and once they have shown the willingness to use it against certain kinds of illegal material, their arguments against extending the system's use get weaker. When major movie studios, including Disney, Twentieth Century Fox, and Warner Bros., sued an online service called Newzbin in the United Kingdom for trafficking in copyrighted films, the judge noted that the site's operators had "moved offshore" and were thus "effectively beyond the reach of this court." Rather than attempt to unmask the people behind the site, or attempt to take the site itself down, the movie studios asked that UK Internet providers simply be ordered to block access to Newzbin instead. One of their key arguments: Internet providers already had the technology to do this, and made use of it for child pornography.

It convinced the judge. "In essence, what the Studios seek by their revised form of order is that [Internet providers] should implement the same measures with regard to the Newzbin2 website as it already operates with regard to URLs [Uniform Resource Locators, often website addresses] reported to it by the IWF [Internet Watch Foundation]," wrote the Hon. Mr. Justice Arnold in an order dated July 28, 2011—and then he gave them what they asked.

When US Internet companies voluntarily agreed to filter the Internet in 2008, the only content they agreed to block was child pornography. Andrew Cuomo, then the New York attorney general, helped put together the deal, and the recording industry wanted to find out how he had done it. After all, they had been pushing for years for more protections against illegal online file sharing, but broad resistance from both the public and from Internet providers had limited their technical options. So the recording industry's trade group went to Cuomo and, as they later told the *New York Times*, "pointed out to him that there are overlaps between the child porn problem and piracy."

When the Canadian government introduced a broad new Internet surveillance bill in February 2012, one giving police unprecedented powers to gather information without warrants and forcing Internet companies to build "backdoors" into their communications systems, child pornography was used as the rhetorical bludgeon to smash all critics. The law would have applied to all Internet communications—of which child pornography is a vanishingly small part—but critics were charged specifically with supporting sex abusers. Canadian Public Safety Minister Vic Toews took to Twitter to say that the law would "aid child porn investigations" and then called on the opposition New Democratic Party (NDP) to stop "making things easier for predators." During later parliamentary discussion of the bill, Toews returned to the same charge, telling another critic that he could "either stand with us or with the child pornographers."

Back in 2007, Australia's government proposed a mandatory "clean feed" system that would have blocked "illegal material" on all Internet connections in the country (and provided Internet subscribers with a second, voluntary filtering tier that would try to block pornography). American law professor Derek Bambauer noted that the plan was "the first time that a Western democracy will require, through formal statute, [Internet providers] to block users from accessing certain materials online" and that "the criteria by which sites will be designated for blocking remain opaque and uncertain." Local critics also raised questions about the secret blacklist that would power the scheme and about freedom-of-speech concerns. In response to these real concerns, Australian Telecommunications Minister Stephen Conroy went populist: "If people equate freedom of speech with watching child pornography, then the Rudd-Labor Government is going to disagree."

But the critics had good reason to ask their question. Whenever the lists leak, concerns mount. In 2009, WikiLeaks got hold of the Australian blacklist. According to the *Sydney Morning Herald*, the list "paints a harrowing picture of Australia's forthcoming Internet censorship regime" because it included not just child sex abuse but also "a slew of online poker sites, YouTube links, regular gay and straight porn sites, *Wikipedia* entries, euthanasia sites, websites of fringe religions such as satanic sites, fetish sites, Christian sites, the website of a tour operator and even a Queensland dentist."

That same year, WikiLeaks also obtained the list of 797 domains that it said were censored by the Finnish government; judging by the names alone, most look pornographic, though one Finnish security researcher argued that many of them contained only legal porn. In addition, the list contained a block for the website lapsiporno.info—not a pornographic site, but one that reported on secret blacklists.

WikiLeaks also obtained the purported block lists from Denmark, Norway, and Thailand. Of the latter, the site wrote, "Of the 1,203 Thai sites censored this year, all have the internally noted reason of lèse majesté—criticizing the royal family. Like Finland, the Thai censorship system was originally promoted as a mechanism to prevent the flow of child pornography. Cases such as Thailand demonstrate that once a secret censorship system is established for pornographic content, the same system can rapidly expand to cover other material, including political material, at the worst possible moment—when government needs exposure and reform."

The use of censorship to combat online ills can send free-speech diehards into fits. While legal scholars like Bambauer argue that such filtering is acceptable if used both sparingly and (more important) transparently, others take a more absolutist stance. Milton Mueller, a Syracuse professor, argues against *all* Internet content blocking. In his 2010 book *Networks and States*, Mueller lays out some key problems he has with blacklists:

1. They undermine transparency and due process because the lists are generally secret.
2. They often lead to structural overblocking, taking down entire websites instead of specific images.
3. They seem to shift law enforcement priorities toward simply stopping access to content and away from catching perpetrators responsible for creating it.

Critics like Mueller point out that blocking content doesn't eliminate it from the 'Net and the blocked material is still available to Internet users in other countries; far better, they argue, to make a stronger effort to remove it at the source and keep the Internet itself free of censorship, as we do in most areas of law. Mueller suggests more international cooperation to address the problem of child sex abuse in far-off countries. "The saving grace of this option, of course, is that it is only available when a strong international consensus about the status of the content exists," he writes, "such as those around the sexual exploitation of young children." The German group *MissbrauchsOpfer Gegen InternetSperren* (MOGiS), made up of "victims of sexual child abuse," was established back in 2009 to make the same points. The group's slogan is "Remove, don't block! Act, and don't look away." Thus, the continued infiltration and shutdown of major child porn operations seen in Joint Hammer, Nest Egg, and Delego become part of the argument in favor of more traditional police work and opposed to national filters.

Both sides of the debate show the limits of the more naive forms of Internet exceptionalism. The takedown of sites like The Cache, and the ease with which groups like the Internet Watch Foundation now say they can get content removed from foreign servers, both show just how far international cooperation can extend. The idea that evading legal and cultural limits is simple on the Internet has itself come to seem a bit simple.

Those who back filtering have also managed to make the same point about the Internet's "unexceptionalism" in a different way. While some once argued that the 'Net was literally unable to be filtered, they don't any longer. When the political will to filter exists, content that can't be taken down can be blocked. Whether it *should* be blocked—and how far that blocking should extend—remains contentious.

/////

Stories about Internet policing often focus on the tech—how a hacker exploited a particular operating system vulnerability to install malware inside a corporate firewall, how investigators used a new wireless sniffing device to spy on the hacker's Internet traffic. But technology is only the gun; human judgment pulls the trigger, and human judgment makes the same mistakes it always does.

As Roger Loughry's trial concluded, prosecutor Steve DeBrota called a postal inspector to the stand and walked through some of the material seized from Loughry's house. He questioned the inspector about it and established that several of the videos showed men having sex with girls who appeared to be younger than twelve. These videos had not come from The Cache, which tended to traffic in "lascivious exhibition of genitals" imagery as opposed to hard-core sex acts, and they were therefore not part of the conspiracy charges against Loughry in the case.

DeBrota had his reasons for focusing on the seized hard-core videos. During his initial interview with Agent Heath back in September 2008, Loughry had defined child pornography only as "images of young kids, male and female, naked, doing sexual acts, under the age of 18." The federal criminal definition covers far more than this, but DeBrota wanted to show the jury that Loughry possessed material that qualified as child porn—even under his own incorrect definition of the term.

Still images alone "are bad, Your Honor, but watching a video of that type is significantly greater in terms of its effect," DeBrota argued in seeking to play the videos to the jury. Loughry's lawyer, Joe Cleary, objected. Though the videos were illegal, he said, they weren't at issue in the case and could be improperly used to sway the jurors emotionally rather than to prove a specific charge. But the judge allowed them, and they were shown.

"The particular videos you are referring to were exceptionally graphic, much more so than the Cache material," Cleary told me after the trial. "You can imagine what it would be like to watch three to four minutes of a young girl having sex with an adult male. It was disturbing and difficult to watch. The Cache evidence, while disturbing, was principally limited to images of naked girls."

After sentencing, Loughry got a new lawyer and appealed his conviction; his key argument concerned these videos. Had they prejudiced the jury? The case moved three hours up the road from Indianapolis to the Seventh Circuit Court of Appeals in Chicago, where a three-judge panel considered the question. On October 11, 2011, the appeals court ruled that the videos had indeed been "highly inflammatory and had only minimal probative value. These errors were not harmless."

The entire case was overturned; Loughry was granted a whole new trial.

/////

The Cache leadership had been decimated and its servers seized, but no one could say with confidence that the site had died. "I am sure 'The Cache' is back up and running somewhere else that law enforcement is not aware of," said James Fottrell of the High Technology Investigation Unit at the DoJ's CEOS unit, during Loughry's trial. But "I don't have specific information as to where 'The Cache' is today."

For DeBrota, the Internet has made it easier to untangle child porn networks—but it has also made creating those networks so much simpler. "Before the Internet was easily searchable, back when it was just e-mail—we had these guys on the run," he told me. "Being able to find a like-minded individual easily and communicate about sexual fetishes wasn't very easy to do in 1992, but today is trivially easy."

Still, he wants the child pornographers to know that they can't act with impunity online. "Their arrogant assumption that they can do all this stuff on the Internet," he said, "is just an arrogant assumption."

3

"I FEEL THAT HE IS WATCHING ME": PRIVACY ON THE COMPUTER

THE HACKERS

In the spring of 2009, a college student named Amy received an instant message from a man claiming to know her. He supplied details about what her bedroom looked like and he had, improbably, nude photos of Amy. He sent them, then asked her to have "Web sex" with him.

Instead, Amy contacted her boyfriend Dave, who had stored those same photos on his own computer. The two exchanged instant messages about the incident, trying to figure out what had happened. Soon afterwards, each received a separate threat from the mysterious stranger. He knew what they had just chatted about and warned them not to take their story to anyone, including the police.

Amy, terrified by her stalker's eerie knowledge, contacted campus police. Officers were dispatched to her room and took down her story. Soon after, Dave received more threats—the stalker knew exactly what Amy had said to investigators, even though no electronic devices had been used in their face-to-face talk. The stalker appeared, impossibly, to be inside her dorm room. When the FBI interviewed Amy about the case, agents reported that she was "visibly upset and shaking during parts of the interview and had to stop at points to control her emotions and stop herself from crying." She was so afraid for her own safety that she did not leave her dorm room for a full week.

Dave too suffered increased fear, anxiety, and anger; he later told a court that the experience had been so intense that even his parents now "had a hard time trusting anyone or even feeling comfortable enough to use a computer."

Dave and Amy didn't know who the mysterious stalker had been, and neither could figure out how he had access both to the contents of Dave's computer and to discussions with police in Amy's room. The pair's privacy had not been so much invaded as obliterated.

The bizarre case wasn't an isolated incident. Around the same time, a Los Angeles–area juvenile named Sara received an instant message from a screen name that looked almost identical to her boyfriend's. The person behind it asked her for nude photos; thinking that it was in fact her boyfriend, she supplied them. Sara soon realized her mistake, but it was too late. Threats rolled in, saying that her mysterious interlocutor would post Sarah's photos on the Internet if she did not send more. When Sara e-mailed copies of these threats to her boyfriend, the stalker knew. He even called her on the phone to make the threats more personal.

"For the longest time I didn't know who this man was, why he was doing it or [if] he would come back," Sara wrote much later in a victim-impact statement, describing to a federal judge how the experience had affected her. "Not knowing is the worst, most dreaded feeling. It's always in the back of your mind. I moved away from the LA/OC [Los Angeles/Orange County] area but even here the thoughts never left me."

Another woman, Gloria, received an e-mail with the subject line "who hacked your account READ it!!!" from someone who claimed to have invaded her computer. The hacker said he had done so because Gloria's ex-boyfriend had hired him—a "particularly traumatic" move, as prosecutors later noted, because Gloria had actually taken out a restraining order against her ex-boyfriend. Gloria didn't reply to the e-mail and soon received another, this time containing a nude picture of her. Her hacker promised to post it across the Internet if Gloria didn't do as the message commanded.

It was one of the few cases where the attacker acted on his warning. After Gloria sent copies of these threats to a friend of hers, the hacker somehow knew. He e-mailed her, "You pissed me off now I'm going to show you." Gloria's nude photo was posted to MySpace—appearing on the account of the friend to whom Gloria had shown the stalker's threats.

The cases grew ever stranger. Women reported that the lights on their laptop webcams would pop on at times when the cameras weren't in use; one was so unnerved by the behavior that she covered her own computer's camera with a sticker to make sure no one was spying on her. But someone had been, and he went after so many people that Glendale, California, police finally recognized a broader pattern and alerted the FBI. On March 8, 2010, after six months of investigations and interviews, FBI agents obtained a search warrant for a small, neat home on Monica Lane in Santa Ana. Two days later, the feds descended.

Inside the home, they found thirty-two-year-old Luis "Guicho" Mijangos sitting in a wheelchair. Mijangos was an undocumented alien and a paraplegic who hadn't walked since he was around seventeen, when a drive-by gunshot had paralyzed him from the waist down and ended any possibility of a pro soccer career. He grew up—unhappily, in his telling—in Mexico, where his father was harassed by former police colleagues and died from a blood clot when Mijangos was young. Mijangos's mother took her son to the United States and eventually remarried.

Despite his injuries, Mijangos had prospects. He had taken computer classes at Orange Coast College in Costa Mesa and became proficient in programming languages such as Java and C++, and in Web design. He set up a home-based Web and computer consulting business and began clearing $1,000 per week for his work.

But when the FBI showed, Mijangos quickly admitted to much more. He worked with a few black-hat hackers, he said, helping them transfer money and make use of stolen credit cards. And he admitted that he did sometimes hack into other people's computers. A favorite trick was seeding peer-to-peer file-sharing networks like LimeWire with popular-sounding song titles that were actually malware; when unsuspecting teenagers went to download the newest pop confection and ended up with Mijangos's bogus file by accident, it infected their machines and opened the computers to external control. Mijangos claimed to have tried this trick only five times; agents were dubious.

When it came to the stalker-like behavior that so many women (and some men) had reported, Mijangos said that his work was being misconstrued. Instead of extorting his victims, Mijangos said he had hacked into women's computer after being recruited by their boyfriends or husbands; like a private detective, he said, he was simply trying to find out if they had been cheating. "Mijangos acknowledged he threatened to expose these pictures, and reckoned the threats might look like extortion, but stated that he did so to discourage anyone from contacting the authorities," the FBI report said. "Mijangos also acknowledged he asked for additional sexual videos but only to determine whether they would actually do it."

It didn't take long to punch a hole in these claims. The FBI recovered four laptops, a BlackBerry, and a clutch of USB drives from Mijangos's home; a "filter team" scoured the devices for anything that fit the parameters of the warrant, tossing out anything that wasn't relevant. After vetting, the material was turned over to the FBI case agents, who found evidence that Mijangos had actually gone after 129 different computers with a total of 230 victims. Forty-four of the victims were juveniles.

The Mijangos computers contained several kinds of malware, including key loggers that could record every keystroke a victim typed—including passwords and usernames for e-mail and social networking accounts. Agents also discovered software that could turn on the webcams and microphones built into infected computers and relay the information back to the hacker who controlled them. The women who suspected their computer's camera was flicking to life to catch them undressing were correct; the FBI found "dozens of videos" from those webcams, it said, most showing victims "getting out of the shower, dressing for the day, [or] having sex with a partner." In a file called "things importan" (sic), the FBI even found screen captures from victim machines that showed identifying information about them displayed on bank and financial websites.

On June 17, 2010, the FBI Cyber Squad operating out of Los Angeles swore out an arrest warrant against Mijangos. Five days later, at 6:10 a.m., Mijangos was arrested and charged with felony extortion—or, as the government has taken to calling it in cases like these, "sextortion."

Sextortion was Mijangos's calling card. Indeed, as the government later put it, he "dedicated considerable time to toying with victims." If he obtained access to a woman's computer, he searched for incriminating photos and video on the hard drive. After that, he might access the webcam and attempt to take some of his own. If he obtained access to a man's computer, he instead impersonated the male and reached out to the man's girlfriend to ask for nude photos. With photos in hand, Mijangos would approach the women electronically and threaten to post the images publicly unless they sent additional nude photos or videos of themselves. Some women did so.

Mijangos then spent significant time monitoring people's communications. In the case of his most spectacular hacks, Mijangos could watch the instant messaging and e-mail communications of both boyfriend and girlfriend, and could even listen in to conversations they had over the phone or in person by using the computer's built-in microphone, turning people's laptops into sophisticated electronic bugs that could be deployed against their owners. In isolation, each technique offered only a window into someone's life; combined—as they were against Dave and Amy—these techniques could turn a window into a full-fledged glass house. The omniscient effect this created unnerved his victims; during Mijangos's sentencing hearing on September 1, 2011, one of his victims took the witness stand and described how the hacks had affected her life:

> The minute that he attacked me, the very first minutes, I remember clearly as if it was yesterday because I got sick when I got the e-mail of him threatening me. I didn't know why someone would talk to me such way [sic] and how someone could know everything about me. It really scared me. I was working. I immediately went to the restroom. I started throwing up. I got a rash, developed a rash on my face, and I just couldn't continue to work. I had to leave the office, and I just got sick all over again. . . .
>
> I don't use my computer anymore, only for work purposes. It is restricted. I don't have access to a lot of stuff I did before just to be on the safe side. Any time that I get any type of e-mail, any spam, I freak out, I get anxiety. I think that it is someone else, or I think it is him. It is—I don't trust anybody. I always feel that he is still watching. Every time I turn on the computer, every time, I feel that he is watching me.

Mijangos may sound like some kind of hacker king, but in reality such digital voyeurism is easy. Entire tool kits exist that make it simple to infect "slave" computers with remote access tool (RAT) software, which can take control of the slave's webcam and provide full control over the machine. Only modest technical skills are needed to deploy such software—certainly, no coding is required.

As Mijangos's lawyer told the judge during sentencing for his client, "The malware that was used in this case is readily available on the Internet if anybody is looking for it. . . . The programs are already written. He is not writing the program. What he is doing is modifying the settings as to how many captures per how many seconds or how it is to be set up or what is to happen in terms of just the basic settings of the program. There is no code that has been demonstrated that has been written specifically by Mr. Mijangos."

Aspiring hackers can purchase a RAT toolkit for a few bucks and follow time-tested suggestions for getting it installed on victim machines; if even that is too difficult, it's possible just to pay for a list of already-compromised slaves. Whole Internet forums exist where men from around the world share information about techniques—and pictures of their targets.

"Some of these girls are disgusting but hey a slaves a slave," one poster in the RAT discussion area of Hackforums.net had written when I visited. "Wish I could get some more girls with webcams," he said. "It makes it more exciting when you can literally spy on someone. Even if they aren't getting undressed!"

The use of a RAT can scare people who notice odd behavior—their computer's camera light coming on, for instance, or software launching without apparent reason—but this is just part of the game to the people in the forum. "Will add more photos if she ever comes online again. I think I scared her lol," wrote one, while another said, "Unfortunately she asked her boyfriend why the light on her cam kept coming on, and he knew, she never came back :)."

Thousands of shared images show women of all ages (and a couple of men) from around the globe staring straight into monitors with no idea that their picture is being transmitted in real-time to some anonymous hacker. Frequently the bedrooms behind them are pedestrian, with posters on walls and clothes lying in disorganized piles, and the light is often unflattering. But the thrill isn't in the quality of the image; it's in the secret power of the voyeur.

Because many computers remain on continuously, some hackers use special RAT software with a motion-detection feature that sends pictures or video only after a certain amount of motion takes place in front of the camera. "While I was at work the motion detection picked up this girl and her boyfriend," one poster wrote after supplying pictures of the couple. "After watching a romantic movie she decides to climb up on him and pull down his pants. Use your imagination for what happened next and you probably won't be wrong."

To the hackers, this is terrific entertainment. "What a great way to spend a Sunday afternoon," one wrote. In addition to watching people through their webcams, hackers can look through every file on a slave's computer. One even "kept a couple of guys [as slaves] to browse their pron [sic] collections." Mijangos's decision to move beyond watching to toy with his victims made him unusual, but the tools that enabled him are available to anyone.

On March 21, 2011, Mijangos reached a plea deal with the government and copped to two felony charges: computer hacking and wiretapping. Federal judge George King sentenced Mijangos to seventy-two months in prison for his "psychological warfare" and "sustained effort to terrorize victims."

Shortly after his sentence, Mijangos agreed to an interview with GQ magazine. He talked about the opportunities being in a wheelchair had denied him and how he took his revenge on the whole and healthy. "These people were having fun," he told writer David Kushner. "They were making plans for prom, to go to parties. I never had that. So I decided to send those e-mails, thinking, Oh, you have all these wonderful things. Why don't you have a bad day just like me?"

"The FBI has seen a rise in similar cases based on the exploitation of emerging technologies by criminals," said Steven Martinez, assistant director in charge of the FBI's Los Angeles field office, in a statement after the sentencing, "and it's my hope that this sentence serves as a warning for victims of Internet predators to advise law enforcement or a trusted source when threatened, and always refrain from sending compromising photographs via cyberspace."

Good luck with that advice. Digital devices have made it so easy to point, shoot, and share that most people targeted in the Mijangos hacks already had provocative pictures on their computers—and had usually shared them with others. But although notions of privacy and propriety in the digital age have shifted, the Mijangos case reminds us that privacy itself remains deeply guarded.

While police forces are happy to protect private lives in Mijangos-style cases, their overall relationship with privacy remains conflicted. That's because techniques for entering people's personal computers over the Internet hold so much promise for law-enforcement investigations. The Internet police—which is to say, all police—want people like Mijangos shut down, but they also want to gather and make use of information gained via similar tools.

The Internet connects its users to everything "out there," but many users never think hard about the obvious converse: it connects everything "out there" to *them*. In the pre-Internet age, the only way someone could hear a conversation inside your bedroom was to break in and plant a bug, or to crouch in the bushes beneath the window. The sheer difficulty, risk, and expense of such methods deterred their use even in local cases—to say nothing of the simple impracticality of traveling halfway around the world to spy on a total stranger's life in China. Connect a laptop to the Internet, however, and you open a worldwide highway to your inner sanctum: stored photos, e-mail, webcam, microphone, keystrokes. Without proper precautions, any attacker—individual, corporate, or governmental—can stroll down that road with ease.

THE CORPORATIONS

Susan Clements-Jeffrey didn't wake up in June 2008 expecting police officers to arrive at her apartment carrying photos of her topless Internet chats and keystroke logs showing everything she had typed, from online passwords to a search for Boston airfares. The fifty-two-year-old widow and long-term substitute teacher in Springfield, Ohio, had a foot injury, self-diagnosed as a broken toe, and she had remained in her pajamas that morning as she lit some incense and called boyfriend Carlton "Butch" Smith on the telephone.

The knock was startling; Clements-Jeffrey wasn't expecting visitors, and the building was secured. She also believed that she was the victim of an unknown stalker who had once painted a flower on her garage. She had no plans to open the door.

"This is the police," said a male voice from out on the landing. "We can get a warrant."

The voice paused.

"You need to open this door or we will gain entry."

Clements-Jeffrey promised to call Butch back, hung up, and limped over to the door. Local cops Geoffrey Ashworth and Noel Lopez stood on the landing.

"Are you Susan?" said Ashworth.

"Yes, I am."

"Do you have a laptop?"

"Yes, I do."

"We need to see the laptop now."

The cops followed her into the apartment while Clements-Jeffrey went into her bedroom and retrieved a Hewlett Packard laptop. The officers took it, flipped it over, and noted the scratched-off serial number on the bottom. The machine had been stolen from the local school district. The cops asked Clements-Jeffrey how much she had paid for it. She told them she had purchased it for $60 from a student at the alternative school where she taught, though she said she had no idea the machine was stolen property. The price didn't make her suspicious, she said, because the computer was not working when she bought it.

Then the minor theft case took a surreal turn. One of the cops showed her a dossier; inside lay a printed screen capture from Clements-Jeffrey's private online video chats with Butch. She later described the moment during a sworn deposition. "[The officer] was laughing the whole time. He was laughing, having a good time, and then he flashed—he picked up that paperwork he had in his hand, I don't recall, and he flashed a paper, a picture, one of those pictures. . . . He said, 'We've had an officer in Milwaukee keeping you under surveillance over the last 16 days'. . . . At that point he was laughing and told me I should have known better, you know, than to, you know, be on my webcam."

The cops placed the substitute teacher under arrest, charged with receiving stolen property. They helped her down the stairs into a waiting car. Clements-Jeffrey was driven to the police station and sat there in handcuffs. The details of what happened at the station are disputed, but Clemtents-Jeffrey's own account at least brings home just how the secret surveillance disturbed her:

> [Officer Ashworth] sat down next to me, again lectured me, saying, "You're a school teacher; right?"
>
> "Yes, I am."
>
> "You're so stupid that you don't know better than what you got yourself into. Don't you know what happens on the Internet, on webcams on the Internet?" And I said no. And he said, "You don't get on a webcam doing what you're doing. You should know better than that."
>
> I said, "I am in the privacy of my own home. I am a grown woman. I should be able to do what I want in the privacy of my own home". . .
>
> He had the dossier sitting in his lap. Then he opened it up to show more pictures . . .
>
> And he goes, "The judge isn't going to be very happy looking at this kind of activity coming from a teacher."

And I said, "You are not going to show that to the judge. I know you can't."

And he said, "I don't know. It will all depend how you cooperate." We are back to cooperation again. "I might cut it out, but I'm leaving Butch's on there."

I really forget what Butch's was. Probably a risqué picture as well. I don't know. I was so shook I couldn't—at this point I couldn't think straight. Here it is more pictures, and then now he's flipping through the papers, he's talking to me and I'm really looking at everything now. I see I.M. [instant messaging] messages from Butch and I see e-mail stuff, because he's just kind of flipping . . . I was shocked. I'm just—I am almost hysterical now. Then he goes and sits back down again.

The arrest may have been a bit of police overreach; when the local prosecutor received the case, he quickly dropped it. Clements-Jeffrey did not. Traumatized by the experience, she entered both private and group psychological therapy. Her life began to change. She wasn't able to work. After bumping into one of the arresting officers at a gas station some time later, she became convinced that the police were watching her. Perhaps they were tapping her phone or her Internet connection? Profound anxiety set in.

"I cannot sleep," she said, describing the experience:

I feel worthless. I cannot socialize like I used to, and in the past I was a very social person. I was in many clubs, professional. I could leave the house, I could shop for food. I could do things that now I cannot do. I cannot necessarily shop, go out of the house. My heart's palpating [sic]. I can break out in a sweat when I see a police car. . . . My mind flashes back to the dehumanizing—what I call rape, when I can sit in the privacy of my own home and be spied on . . . I cannot work. I cannot obtain work. [My story is] in the public view. I don't want to necessarily see people. It's alarming to me. It's degrading to me. It's humiliating to me. It's anxiety ridden . . . I never had to lock my bedroom door or put a lock and do all these things before or call [the] cable [TV company] every two minutes because I'm assuming somebody's spying through my TV or listening to the clicks on my telephone thinking I'm wiretapped.

The ability of the police to reach so deeply into the most intimate communications from her computer—and thus into the most intimate chambers of her life—unnerved Clements-Jeffrey almost as much as it unnerved the Mijangos victims. Finding out that others could watch her keystrokes and video chats led Clements-Jeffrey to ascribe improbably godlike powers to her local Ohio police department. "I don't know what to believe," she testified later. "They stalked me in my house. They told me they were watching me surf on the net. They could be doing anything. Obviously they're capable of doing anything."

In 2010, she filed a federal lawsuit over the "grossly excessive search and seizure of sexually explicit images" from her computer. But how had the cops done it?

They hadn't. While we may hope that the Springfield police department exists only to "protect and serve" its citizens with the utmost competence, integrity, and professionalism, we might suspect that the department's property crimes investigator for the southwest—and part of the northwest—section of town is unlikely to be a wiretapping expert. Indeed, thirteen-year police veteran Geoffrey Ashworth, who led the visit to Clements-Jeffrey's apartment, knew little about the topic.

He did know about stolen laptops, though, and Ashworth already had a file on a stolen laptop from Springfield's Keifer Alternative School. The case had offered little to go on—until he received an unexpected call from Absolute Software on June 23, 2008. The company operated a service called Computrace that could help recover stolen computers; Keifer Alternative had spent around $30,000 for the service after fifty of the school-issued laptops had been stolen during the first year of the school's "laptop for every child" program.

Computrace was a small, stealthy piece of code that could be installed on Windows laptops. When connected to the Internet, each computer would ping Absolute at regular intervals and provide its current IP address. If the computer was reported stolen at any point, any subsequent ping would alert Absolute that it had contact with a hot laptop; an investigator would log these IP addresses and could turn the information over the local police.

This primitive functionality had a serious limitation: turning the IP address into a real-world location requires the cooperation of Internet providers, who generally don't hand out private information on their subscribers without a subpoena. Busy local police departments might not even bother doing that much work to hunt for a low-value laptop. Besides, so many people access the Internet wirelessly that after all this work, the various IP addresses might resolve only to the wireless network at the local Starbucks.

So Absolute's investigators tried to make things easy for local cops. When stolen machines connected to the Internet, Absolute could sometimes connect to them and remotely install its own set of RAT tools; an investigator sitting at his computer anywhere in the country could see exactly what was taking place on the stolen laptop's screen. He or she could also switch on a key capture tool that grabbed everything typed by the suspect. Reading someone's chat logs and watching their Web-browsing history might eventually reveal key information—a name, an address, even a photo—that could be used to identify the thief and to recover the laptop. Such identifications could take time to make, but Absolute occasionally got lucky, as it did here.

When the laptop Clements-Jeffrey purchased was first reported stolen, the case was taken by a former cop working for Absolute out of his home in Milwaukee, Wisconsin. After another teacher at Keifer Alternative helped Clements-Jeffrey get her newly purchased but nonfunctional machine working again, Clements-Jeffrey took it home and connected to the Internet—and Absolute connected to her.

The Milwaukee investigator logged the machine's IP address and later decided to gamble by using Absolute's own RAT software—usually a time sink that revealed little of value. But on the very first attempt to access Clements-Jeffrey's machine, he could see the laptop's new owner video chatting over the Internet with her boyfriend. He had never seen a video chat in progress while using the RAT, and he snapped a few quick screenshots to help police identify the woman. He later swore under oath that he had "never even looked at the screen shots. It was a matter of 30 seconds of taking them, and I had about four different files open."

The investigator also used the keystroke logger to grab passwords and several instant messaging conversations. (Sample: "Hope to see Your 'fine' ass son [backspace backspace backspace] sometime [backspace backspace backspace backspace] time sooner than later!!! If only for a short time [backspace backspace backspace backspace] period!!! Duty calls!!!") Again, he was incredibly lucky; the laptop's owner entered two names while he watched her use the computer, one of which was quite likely to be her own.

Few computers come preloaded with these sorts of backdoors; while such tools can help serve a useful purpose, general deployment would be a security and privacy catastrophe. One has only to look at the sorts of things that have happened in relatively small local deployments to realize just how quickly surveillance tools can be turned to bad ends.

For instance, 1,617 rent-to-own stores across the United States deployed software called PC Rental Agent on the laptops they rented in the late 2000s, ostensibly for recovery of the machines in the event of nonpayment. The software could report its location but also had a "Detective Mode" that could activate the computer's webcam, log all keystrokes on the machine, or take pictures of the computer's screen. What could possibly go wrong? How about a federal class action lawsuit and a Federal Trade Commission investigation, both of which claimed that rental company employees routinely used to software to spy on customers. (The case was set in motion by a family who opened their door one day to find a rental company employee bearing webcam shots of them using the computer; they sued.)

In a better-known case, a similar lost-laptop tool called TheftTrack was deployed in 2009 on computers handed out to students at the Lower Merion School District in Pennsylvania; it wasn't long before school officials were activating student webcams when the kids were at home and snapping thousands of photos in a bid to recover stolen machines. The school did use screenshots and webcam images to recover a few computers—one stolen laptop eventually journeyed to Pakistan and back to Pennsylvania before being located—but the temptation to activate such tools in inappropriate or trivial circumstances can be high.

A school administrator eventually showed a male student a webcam image of the student ingesting "pills" while seated before his computer at home in his bedroom. (The "pills" turned out to be chewy candies.) The student sued, as did several others, and the extent of the school's surveillance system became clear. It also explained the widespread phenomena noted by students and teachers alike: the slight flickering of the green "in use" light beside their laptop's built-in webcams, even when the cameras were not in use. According to the school's official report into the matter, some teachers had seen the lights and took to masking their webcams with tape—just as some of the Mijangos victims had done.

The scandal caused a national uproar, one finally resolved in late 2010 when the district agreed to pay $610,000 to the students and their lawyers. TheftTrack was eventually discontinued and the company behind it was purchased by Absolute.

In the Clements-Jeffrey case, the Absolute investigator gathered his information and then called the Springfield police department. He was directed to Ashworth, and the Absolute investigator quickly provided the detective with the collected IP addresses, keystroke data, and screen shots from the laptop—he even helpfully extracted possible suspect names from the captured data. One of the names was Clements-Jeffrey's. Ashworth ran it through the Ohio Bureau of Motor Vehicles database and obtained a photo and current address. He decided to pay Clements-Jeffrey a visit—and to take the complete set of printouts from Absolute along with him.

He knew the screenshots were a delicate matter. As he put it in a deposition much later, he roped Lieutenant Noel Lopez into coming along precisely because of the screenshots. Despite this precaution, he also claimed to have no idea that an armed officer showing private, top-less photos to the person depicted in them might not go well.

Q. [Clements-Jeffrey's lawyer] What was it about the sensitive nature of the photographs that caused you to want Lieutenant Lopez or some other person with you?
A. [Ashworth] Because one of the photos was explicit.

Q. What's that got to do with your investigation?
A. I wanted the lieutenant with me because of that.

Q. Did you intend to show these photographs to Mrs. Susan Clements-Jeffrey?
A. They were part of the investigation.

Q. That's not my question. Before you went out, did you intend to show the photographs to her?
A. If she needed to see them, yes.

Q. If she needed to see them for what reason?

A. Because that's what I used for identification purposes.

Q. I see. You didn't consider that it would potentially be an emotional trauma for this woman to be presented by you with photographs of her in sexually explicit positions that she had no intention that anybody else would see other than Mr. Smith?

A. No, sir.

Q. You didn't think about it?

A. No, sir....

Q. You don't think the very fact that you're a police officer and you have the authority and you got a badge, you don't think that's intimidating to some people?

A. It could be.

Q. But you don't think you've ever intimidated anybody?

A. I try not to. I may have, but that's not my intention.

When the two officers arrived at Clements-Jeffrey's apartment, they said they smelled marijuana wafting out from her door—replaced by the scent of incense after they made their presence known. Because Clements-Jeffrey admitted to them that she had the laptop they sought, the officers were allowed to enter without a search warrant. Once inside, Ashworth found the machine he was seeking. He disputed Clements-Jeffrey's claims that he mocked her or in any way mistreated or tried to make an example of her.

And yet—arresting a fifty-something substitute teacher simply for having purchased a stolen laptop from a student delinquent seems a bit unusual. Clements-Jeffrey was able to provide police with the name of the student who had sold her the machine; the young man was already suspected by police in other thefts. Still, it was Clements-Jeffrey who ended up in handcuffs. Ashworth's answers in later deposition testimony make the odd point clear:

> **Q.** But you tell us you have no interest in investigating to find out who actually committed the theft?
> **A.** Correct.
>
> **Q.** So then this initial theft report was closed without resolution, wasn't it?
> **A.** No, it was closed with an arrest.
>
> **Q.** It was closed with an arrest for receiving stolen property?
> **A.** Right.

This wasn't how all such cases were handled. Some time after the incident, Ashworth found another laptop located by Absolute. The machine had been stolen in New York, then traced to Florida and eventually to Springfield. A different Absolute investigator called Ashworth one day and provided the name of the suspected owner. Ashworth headed over in his car; a man at the address showed him the laptop in question but was not arrested.

> **Q.** He showed you the computer?
> **A.** Yes, sir.
>
> **Q.** Did you look for a serial number?
> **A.** Yes, sir.
>
> **Q.** Was there one on it?
> **A.** Yes, sir.
>
> **Q.** Did you tell him it was stolen?
> **A.** Yes, sir.

Q. Did you take the computer?
A. Yes, sir.

Q. Did you arrest him?
A. No, sir.

Q. Why not?
A. Because he bought it on eBay.

Q. What's that got to do with anything?
A. A lot.

Clements-Jeffrey's arrest wasn't a mere matter of an hour's angry discomfort at the Springfield police station. It led her boyfriend in Boston to confess the relationship to his own wife, out of a fear that the matter would now become public (thanks to the Internet, local news out of Springfield was simple to come by). The "very stressful" conversation that resulted led to talk of divorce—but Butch decided to join Clements-Jeffrey's lawsuit regardless.

"How does the fact that you and [Clements-Jeffrey] are bringing this lawsuit together go over with your wife?" he was asked by one of the lawyers in the case when he flew out to Ohio to offer testimony. "Not too well," he answered.

Though Clements-Jeffrey brought her lawsuit after a profound sense that her personal privacy had been illegally violated, the suit invaded her privacy more than the actual arrest ever had. (The suit was finally settled privately just before it would have gone to trial.) While the police dossier of her photos and keystrokes had been shocking, it was also locked up in a filing cabinet. The lawsuit made huge amounts of deeply personal material—driving records, employment history, counseling session summaries, financial statements, the photos themselves—part of the public record, all available through the US federal courts to anyone in the world with an Internet connection and the ability to pay ten cents a page.

THE GOVERNMENT

Imagine a man—let's make him a banker with a warped morality—suspected of bilking his clients out of their pensions through a complicated investment scheme involving the arbitrage of dwarf alpaca fur. The investigator working the case can't yet prove fraud, but he strongly suspects that the recently reported wave of dwarf alpaca brain fever that decimated the herd was a sham; indeed, he suspects that there never was a herd in the first place. To prove it, he needs access to records that only exist in the banker's home office.

In 1965, such records would have existed on paper. In 1995, the records would likely be digital, stored on a computer, a floppy disk, or compact disc. Despite the tremendous technological change between 1965 and 1995, however, the later investigator had essentially the same tool for getting access to the records: a search warrant. The warrant required the high standard of "probable cause," a trip to a judge, and plenty of paperwork. Once the warrant was issued, it was only useful at the tail end of the investigation, since the very act of executing it would reveal to the banker that he was a target.

But what else to do? Agencies like the FBI occasionally conducted "black-bag" jobs and broke into homes and offices to install bugs or to photograph documents, but such techniques remained rare (and in the first half of the last century were often done without any judicial authorization). And tapping a suspect's phone was never going to help much if what you really needed was a set of financial ledgers.

Then came the damnable, wonderful, information-drenched, hyperconnected Internet. Unlike the telephone, which opened point-to-point connections and could only be tapped by a listener, the Internet opened up an avenue to every other Internet-connected machine in the world. And the people behind those machines could do more than listen; they could act. By 2005, the government could reach our banker's digital records without his knowledge, by slipping court-approved software onto his computer through the Internet. The 'Net makes all kinds of crime easier, but it also creates the possibility of perfect surveillance. Everything an individual like Mijangos or a corporation like Absolute did, the police can do as well.

Such tools are cloaked in secrecy, but they do make occasional public appearances. One of the most famous involved bomb threats against Timberline High School just outside of Olympia, Washington. The threats began on May 30, 2007, with a handwritten note that led to the evacuation of the school.

On June 4, the threats migrated to e-mail. "I will be blowing up your school Monday, June 4, 2007," one said. "There are 4 bombs planted throughout timberline high school. One in the math hall, library hall, main office and one portable. The bombs will go off in 5 minute intervals at 9:15 AM." The school was evacuated again.

On June 5, another e-mail arrived. "Now that the school is scared from yesterdays [sic] fake bomb threat it's now time to get serious. One in a gym locker, the girls. It's in a locker hidden under a pile of clothes. The other four I will only say the general location.... They will all go off at 10:15AM. Through remote detonation. Good Luck. And if that fails, a failsafe of 5 minutes later." Yet another evacuation was ordered.

On June 6, the e-mailer wrote to say that "that school will blow up and that's final! There are 2 bombs this time (Iran [sic] short on money to buy things at [hardware store] home depot.)" Everyone out of the building!

On June 7, the school was emptied again after an e-mail warning that said, "Locking the doors is a good plan, but too late."

On June 8, not one but two threatening e-mails arrived. The school's response? Evacuate everyone once more.

The messages taunted authorities, who were, it said, "too stupid to trace the e-mail." Timberline students who had accounts on the social networking site MySpace began to receive invitations from "Timberlinebombinfo," another MySpace user purporting to be the person at the other end of the threats. Investigators subpoenaed MySpace and the e-mail services used to send the messages, hoping to find the source—but all they learned was that the attacker's missives had been routed through various Italian computers used to disguise his tracks. (Investigators even reached out to the FBI legate attaché in Rome to request help from Italian Internet providers and the country's national police, but such processes took time. With bomb threats rolling in daily, waiting was not an option.)

By June 12, the FBI was involved and ready to take more direct action. Special Agent Norman Sanders sought a warrant that would allow the FBI to target the "Timberlinebombinfo" MySpace account with a Computer & Internet Protocol Address Verifier (CIPAV), a small software program that would collect basic information about a computer, then relay that information over the Internet to an FBI-controlled computer somewhere in Virginia. It would reveal the computer's IP address to the FBI, and it would log the dates, times, and destinations of all e-mails sent from the machine (though it would not scan or record their contents). The initial warrant request was to run the CIPAV for ten days, and to do so without notifying the target of the search.

The plan was predicated on getting the CIPAV to run stealthily on the bomb threat–maker's computer. Agent Sanders remained cagey about how this would be accomplished. "The CIPAV will be deployed through an electronic messaging program from an account controlled by the FBI," was all his warrant affidavit said, and the CIPAV would only be targeted at the person who controlled the Timeberlinebombinfo account on MySpace.

Perhaps the FBI used MySpace's messaging functions, or perhaps it sent an e-mail with attached (and disguised) malware to the timberline. sucks@gmail.com e-mail address linked to the account. Perhaps the agency used a previously undisclosed flaw (called a "0-day" flaw in security circles, this is an attack vector for which no patch yet exists) in a common Web browser to insert its CIPAV into the target computer after tricking the bomb hoaxer to click on a specific Web-page link. Perhaps it made multiple attempts—the warrant request notes that "the FBI cannot predict whether any particular formulation . . . will cause person(s) controlling the activating computer to activate a CIPAV," and it asked for permission to roll out "additional CIPAVs" until it found an attack vector that worked.

The judge signed off on the request and the FBI had no trouble sneaking its CIPAV onto the target computer; the warrant was "executed" successfully the next day and the CIPAV quickly reported back. Investigators then went to Internet providers and asked them to turn an IP address into an actual subscriber name and address. Comcast turned the information around in about a day. At 2:00 a.m. on July 14, investigators arrived at the residence of a fifteen-year-old boy named Josh, who quickly confessed to the bomb threats. He also helped the local police clear up a matter they had once thought unrelated, confessing to a set of telephone death threats sent to teachers and to his own parents earlier in the year.

The bomb hoaxer turned out to be a student who had made a poor decision—when I asked several years later about the reason for the threats, he didn't want to share any details—and was terrified both of telling his parents and of going to school, where the consequences of that decision would be realized. His solution—bomb threats—led him to serve time in a juvenile facility, pay a fine, and perform community service.

One sad by-product of the whole case was that before the student was caught, he did what he could to make the Timberline community believe that *another* student was behind the threats. According to contemporary newspaper accounts, that innocent student endured so much abuse (his mother says he was spat on by those who blamed him for the threats) that he decided to change schools.

CIPAV-style software doesn't need to be so basic, and it's clear that the FBI has many different types of tools available. As one FBI agent admitted in a 2007 e-mail released under a public-records request, "We all know that there are IPAVs and then there are IPAVs." The full capabilities of these tools have never been revealed; as another 2007 e-mail noted after the Timberline case became public, "We want to ensure that the capabilities of the CIPAV are minimized, if discussed at all. This and many tools deployed by the FBI are law enforcement sensitive and, as such, we request that as little information as possible be provided to as few individuals as possible."

Plenty of people paid attention to CIPAV. E-mails show the FBI responding to requests from groups as diverse as the Air Force and the German government. "I am embarrassed to be approaching you again with a request from the Germans (after your previous help and offers of assistance that have not yet been followed up on by our German colleagues)," ran an e-mail from a US legal attaché in Frankfurt, "but they now have asked us about CIPAV... software."

And for good reason. The FBI certainly does more than dabble in off-the-shelf technologies when designing its electronic tool kit. The Bureau has an entire Data Intercept Technology Unit and a separate Cryptologic and Electronic Analysis Unit (CEAU), which design, build, and roll out electronic tools with advice from their own staff lawyers. (CEAU assisted with the Timberline case after a request from the FBI's Seattle field office.)

While the full capabilities of modern CIPAVs aren't known, Mijangos-style wiretapping, webcam control, and keystroke logging are certainly within the range of possibilities. In late 2011, the Chaos

Computer Club (CCC) in Germany gained access to a similar tool used by various German states and by the federal criminal investigators at the Bundeskriminalamt (BKA), the country's FBI equivalent. The tool had been built by a German company called DigiTask. Once installed on a user's computer, it could wiretap specific programs such as Skype, Web browsers like Firefox, and instant messaging programs like MSN Messenger.

Germany's own tortured twentieth-century history under both Nazism and (in part of the country) communism has created plenty of suspicion around police surveillance; in a 2008 decision, the country's highest court limited such computer incursions to "source wiretapping." Tapping at the source—in this case, a computer—rather than on the network enables investigators to bypass a thorny problem for all such surveillance systems: encryption. Instant messaging and Skype calls are routinely encrypted by default, while encrypting many other forms of communication can be done easily and with freely available tools. Tap the Internet connection itself and you might be able to tell that a call is taking place, but unscrambling the audio could prove impossible. But place the tap on someone's computer and you can listen to the audio in decrypted form as it is played back for the listener. The encryption might be truly unbreakable and yet—it hardly matters.

The code examined by CCC could do far more than monitor Internet-bound communications, though. According to the group, the software could spy on users through their webcams and microphones, it could install additional software, it could log keystrokes, it could search through a user's files, and it could snap screenshots.

Even worse, the CCC said the software was badly coded and could be easily commandeered by others over the Internet, providing a backdoor into one's machine that was left swinging wide open. "Not only can unauthorized third parties assume control of the infected system, but even attackers of mediocre skill level can connect to the authorities, claim to be a specific instance of the trojan, and upload fake data," said CCC in an English-language statement. "It is even conceivable that the law enforcement agencies' IT infrastructure could be attacked through this channel." A spokesperson for the group said that "the security level this trojan leaves the infected systems in is comparable to it setting all passwords to '1234.'"

A leaked presentation from DigiTask showed that its software could be custom-built to a specific court order, with all the "forbidden" features stripped out for that particular use. But CCC was able to build its own tool to take remote control of the surveillance tool, and the arbitrary update function meant that any capabilities stripped from the code could always be sent to the machine later.

A major scandal erupted. The software hadn't been used often—an official told a parliamentary committee that similar tools had only been used 100 times in Germany between 2007 and 2011. The police claimed that they had used source wiretapping only twenty-three times in total, which "shows how sensitive we are [when using] this tool," said BKA chief Jörg Ziercke. The BKA discontinued use of the tool while it investigated concerns about constitutionality.

The tool's power appeared to surprise the public. Many argued that its full functionality was illegal. The country's political Pirate Party, which advocates in part for the broad overhaul of digital copyright and online surveillance law, called for criminal charges against several officials; other people threatened private lawsuits against DigiTask.

The rule of law can (depending on the country) exert checks on such software, and misuse can carry a serious downside for investigators: tainted evidence puts years of casework at risk, as it has in both Germany and the United States when such concerns have come to light. Police insist that the consequences of overstepping proper surveillance boundaries are all they need to keep investigators on the straight and narrow. As an FBI official told Congress back in 2000, "FBI employees fully understand that the unlawful interception of the content of private communications will lead to the suppression of any and all tainted evidence and any evidence or fruits derived therefrom. In short, the penalties for violating the electronic surveillance laws are so severe as to dissuade any such unlawful behavior, even if someone were so inclined."

But overstepping the law's bounds still happens—and police routinely interpret those boundaries in the widest possible way when it comes to new technologies. In countries where the rule of law is weaker, or where the law allows the police far greater latitude, such tools may be deployed with a freer hand and the potential for abuse is huge. While the FBI and BKA have used expensive custom software in the past, there's little reason to do so today if you don't care about the niceties of court-ordered restrictions. As we've seen, tools to invade computers and monitor their webcams, keystrokes, and files can be had on the Internet for a few dollars; these RATs even come packaged in neat tool kits that make deployment simple for the aspiring hacker.

Governments no longer need a budget the size of the FBI's to reach into citizen computers. Neither do theft-recovery companies or the kid down the street. The Internet, which has democratized so much, has extended its leveling power to the most invasive forms of surveillance. Your home computer is a terrific place to deploy them.

4

A CARNIVORE GOES DARK: PRIVACY ON THE NETWORK

Government officials, on the whole, aren't known for flashy presentation, which is why the FBI surprised onlookers in the late 1990s by naming its second-generation Internet wiretapping system "Carnivore." The name terrified critics, who pictured the US government ripping into Internet communications and civil liberties, leaving privacy's battered corpse by the roadside.

Orin Kerr, a law professor who was at the Department of Justice while such tools were in use, noted in a 2003 law review article that "both commentators and the press have portrayed Carnivore as a frightening and mysterious beast that invades privacy willy-nilly. The menacing name itself probably accounts for much of this criticism." Carnivore had replaced a more primitive system known internally as "Omnivore" (thanks to how much data it slurped up), and was actually more protective of privacy; the name was chosen, FBI officials said, because the revised tool could get at the "meat" of the investigation more easily. Had the FBI called Carnivore something properly stultifying—such as the "DCS-1000" moniker used for later versions of the tool—the commentary on and congressional oversight of its use might both have been more muted.

But it wasn't just the name that raised concerns. Critics understood—correctly—that Carnivore was a sealed computer delivered by FBI technical agents to the offices of an Internet service provider, then installed in such a way that it could see much of the data passing over that provider's network. It might be looking for Joe X. Terrorist's e-mails in transit, or it might try to monitor his instant messages, but yours and mine might also pass through the same router.

In older "circuit-switched" networks like the telephone system, every call created a dedicated circuit between the two phones, tying up one specific line for the duration of the call. One of the Internet's great innovations was its move away from this model to a "packet-switched" network that instead breaks up every online communication into small "packets" of data, then jumbles everyone's packets together in transit. Packets get sent by the fastest path available, which can result in one e-mail attachment taking many different routes from the sender to the receiver, the packets arriving in a different order from the one in which they were sent; the computer on the receiving end sorts and reassembles them into an attachment. This approach produced huge gains in efficiency—in a phone conversation, much of the available bandwidth on the two wires of a phone line is wasted because only one person speaks at a time and the conversation has plenty of pauses, even if just the spaces between words. A packet-switched network can stuff its wires and fiber-optic cables full with bits of data running in both directions at all times. But the necessary corollary of this efficiency is that wiretaps deep inside the network can see the traffic of many people, nearly all of whom are not under surveillance and who are not allowed to be watched.

Was Carnivore logging everything that passed through? It had the technical ability to do so. Carnivore was a "packet sniffer," a class of devices that can watch every one of the billions of packets passing by on a network connection, then take action only on those packets that meet certain criteria. The FBI could program the system to find and log only those packets going to and coming from a specific IP address, for example.

Carnivore lived up to its name in one way—it was powerful for its time. Today, commercial packet sniffers are routinely sold as expensive boxes that can operate at "wire speed"—analyzing and acting upon every single electrical impulse rocketing along a provider's fat Internet connection in real time—but this was less common a decade ago. During congressional testimony in September 2000, the assistant director of the FBI's Laboratory Division broke down the feat for senators sitting on the Judiciary Committee, who had serious concerns about the limits of Carnivore's Internet wiretapping power.

"Carnivore's first action is to filter a portion of an ISP's high speed network traffic," said the FBI's Donald Kerr. "Specifically, it filters binary code—streams of 0s and 1s that flow through an ISP network, for example, at 40 megabits per second and often at much higher speeds. Carnivore operates in real time with these speeds. To visualize this, imagine a huge screen containing 40 million 0s and 1s flashing by on this screen for one second, and for one second only. Carnivore's first effort—entirely within the Carnivore box—is to identify within those 40 million 0s and 1s whether the particular identifying information of the criminal subject (for which a court order has been authorized) is there."

Even when Carnivore made this identification correctly, though, privacy concerns remained. The warrant authorizing a wiretap might not have covered a full content-based tap; the judge may have approved only a tap on "addressing information." In the telephonic world, this means access to a list of every number called by a suspect, but not to the audio of the calls themselves. Special "pen register" devices installed in phone company offices could log this addressing information with no chance of grabbing the call itself. The distinction was often analogized to the postal service: investigators needed a much lower standard of evidence to look at the address written on an envelope than they did to slit the envelope and read the letter inside.

On the Internet, the distinction between the envelope's address and the contents it carries gets trickier. Because of the way Internet protocols split up transmissions, the first few packets of an e-mail might contain the sender's and receiver's addresses—but they might also include bits of the subject line or even the start of the message itself. Even making a good-faith attempt to grab only a user's "addressing" information might result in the FBI accidentally "opening the envelope" and taking a peek at the first few lines of the letter inside.

Carnivore was custom code, written in part because commercial packet sniffers of the time couldn't make the proper cutoffs when logging surveillance data. This produced privacy concerns for the public, of course, but it also created more work for the FBI, which had to pass its captured data to a separate "minimization team" that scrubbed it of anything not approved by the court order before the actual case agents could see it. Carnivore's design emphasized precision—it could log specific "ports" belonging to a particular IP address in order to capture only e-mail traffic or Web browsing or some other specific use; it could capture data sent using specific Internet protocols, such as those belonging to specific online chat programs; it could log in the more limited "pen" (addressing only) or the wide-open "full" (addressing and content) modes. In other words, it was supposed to be better for everyone. But it didn't always work.

Months before the FBI had showed up on Capitol Hill to assure Congress that Carnivore devoured nothing but judicially authorized red meat, an angry e-mail arrived in the inbox of Marion "Spike" Bowman, the FBI's associate general counsel for national security affairs. The sender—whose name is redacted in the version of the note finally released in 2002—was facing pressure from various Department of Justice lawyers over the FBI's use of Carnivore.

"I just received a call from [REDACTED] at OIPR [Office of

Intelligence Policy and Review at the Department of Justice]," began the e-mail to Bowman. "To state that he is unhappy with ITOS [International Terrorism Operations Section] and the UBL [Usama bin Laden] Unit would be an understatement of incredible proportions."

The FBI had been brought in to help with the investigation linked to the hunt for al-Qaeda leader Osama bin Laden, and had apparently botched the job. As part of the investigation, the Carnivore team installed its system at an unidentified Internet provider on March 16, 2000, set up the software, and flipped the switch. Agents quickly realized they had made a mistake and that Carnivore was collecting too much data.

"The software was turned on and did not work correctly," continued the e-mail to Bowman. "The FBI software not only picked up the e-mails under the electronic surveillance of the FBI's target [REDACTED] but also picked up e-mails on non-covered targets. The FBI technical person was apparently so upset that he destroyed all the e-mail take, including the take on [REDACTED] . . . no one from the FBI [REDACTED] was present to supervise the FBI technical person at the time."

The good news, from a privacy perspective, was that the FBI technical agent handling the tap recognized the severity of the problem and—believing the captured data was now compromised—deleted it. The bad news was just how easy it was for a Carnivore misconfiguration to start gathering more than it was allowed to see. The mistake was part of a "pattern of occurrences" which spoke to an "inability on the part of the FBI to manage" the execution of such warrants, the e-mail concluded.

The FBI knew that such powerful surveillance tools raised public and Congressional interest like few other law enforcement techniques. In another high-level FBI e-mail on Carnivore from April 2000, the unidentified writer notes, "There are few, if any, investigative techniques that garner (and have garnered in the past) such vehement criticism when errant surveillances or missteps (be they intentional or unintentional) occur."

The FBI had plenty of surveillance-related snafus in its past, but the agency had been operating more cleanly since the Watergate scandal and valued its reputation for following the law. As Congress and the public both asked questions about Carnivore, the FBI opened the system to outside scrutiny.

In December 2000, the IIT Research Institute dug into Carnivore and published a lengthy technical report on how it worked. The system turned out to run a terrifically ugly Windows-based front end called Carnivore.exe. After putting version 1.3.4 of the Carnivore software through a battery of tests, IIT concluded that it largely behaved as expected and should satisfy court orders—when configured correctly.

But configuration was everything. Carnivore allowed agents to choose settings that "may not be appropriate or even technically feasible," said the report, including "all TCP [Transport Control Protocol] information that is available on the local area network." In other words, click one button and Carnivore would grab almost everything passing through the router to which it was attached. IIT also found that mistakes could be made too easily. The user interface had numerous quirks, and buttons with vastly different functions (such as "full" and "pen mode" collection) were only pixels apart.

The good news? Massive data collection was possible but impractical (at the time; no longer true today). Carnivore used 2 GB removable Jaz drives for storage, small enough that such "full-pipe" collection would fill the disc in a matter of minutes—after which an agent would have to drive out to the Carnivore location and swap in a new disc.

By the time the report appeared, little of this mattered. Carnivore was never used often, nor was its successor, the DCS-1000. By 2003, an FBI report to Congress revealed that the FBI had not used DCS-1000 to do court-ordered surveillance at all that year; the agency had already switched to "commercially available" products rather than custom work like Carnivore. The new, off-the-shelf tools were deployed eight times to investigate terrorism, obscene phone calls, weapons of mass destruction, and sexual exploitation of children. Carnivore had been devoured by a more powerful predator: the free market.

/////

If the Internet were a wheel, the rim at the edge would contain all the network "endpoints": desktop computers, iPads, smartphones. The hub would be the servers and services on the network that drive its use: the machines providing access to Netflix, Gmail, eBay, Amazon, and millions more. The spokes that link the center to the edge are the network itself, a fantastically complex set of global data centers, network interconnection points, business arrangements, fiber-optics, undersea cables, and massive routers that direct global traffic.

In the chaos of the Internet, digital surveillance can productively take place at all three places. We have already seen the power that comes from conducting surveillance right at the endpoints, on people's computers. This provides access to a user's broad set of data, but it has to be deployed on a machine-by-machine basis, making mass use impractical for most governments. It also comes with the risk inherent to breaking into someone's house: they may notice the intrusion.

Police can go instead to server operators in order to demand the Twitter posting history, or the Amazon purchase records, or the Hotmail login records of users. This provides a simple way to access the records of millions of people, but it returns only narrow pieces of data. It has the great advantage of not requiring a break-in, however, and it doesn't tip off users that they are targets of an investigation.

If the police conduct their surveillance inside the network itself, they can't grab data running on local machines or on Internet servers, but they can block traffic, view traffic in transit, and—most nefarious of all—silently modify traffic as it passes along the wire between source and destination. Put your taps at the right place and you can watch most of the Internet traffic flowing in and out of an entire country—as the US National Security Administration apparently did in the mid-2000s with the voluntary help of the largest network providers. It's a unique position to be in, and what government worthy of its name wouldn't want such tools?

Indeed, almost all of them did, and US, Canadian, and European companies took the worldwide lead in delivering them. By the early 2000s, the FBI's homegrown code couldn't keep up with the pace of private development, and those tools had become so advanced that it was cheaper simply to buy the "lawful intercept" gear the Bureau needed than to build it. A decade on, the newest generation of packet sniffers make Carnivore look more like a toy poodle; developers today publicly boast about handling wire speed traffic at 10 gigabits per second—looking at and acting on billions of 1s and 0s per second—or faster. Their tools can untangle and analyze long data "flows," extracting a complete record of individual Internet activity from the chaos of packets passing through core Internet routers. Such tools can piece Internet-based voice calls back together, reassemble e-mails, harvest user logins to Facebook or Yahoo, and break some Internet encryption. While Carnivore stored data on 2 GB removable drives, today's tools can access *petabytes* of storage (a petabyte is a million gigabytes).

While such tools aren't exactly secret, the companies that build them and the governments that put them to use rarely publicize their capabilities. But occasional stories break even into the mainstream to remind those who are paying attention just how powerful Internet surveillance technologies have become—and how "Western" tech gear has become the chief enforcer of Internet policies in the least liberal regimes in the world.

"There are few barriers that prevent Western producers of keystroke loggers or spyware from exporting their technologies to Syria, Saudi

Arabia, or China," writes Evgeny Morozov, who has worked hard to complicate easy narratives of the Internet's "democratizing" effects. "High demand for their products in the West ensures low costs and constant innovation. The sophistication of Egypt's security apparatus is directly proportional to the sophistication of methods pursued by the NSA and FBI. The failure to recognize these spillovers—a failure that underpins much of Hillary Clinton's 'Internet freedom' agenda, which focuses on empowering bloggers, not restraining US technology firms—guarantees that dictators have easy access to Western surveillance tools."

A leaked 2002 internal presentation from Cisco, one of the largest Internet router builders in the world, showed the company considering whether to help China build a countrywide "Great Firewall" known as Golden Shield. China didn't hide its goals for the project. Though much of the talk was about "security" and "network-related crimes," a Chinese government official also made clear that Golden Shield would help to "combat 'Falun Gong' evil religion and other hostiles"—a quote printed right in the Cisco slide deck. The very next slide was headed "Cisco opportunities"; these included planning, construction, technical training, and ongoing maintenance and security work. As *Wired* reported at the time, "Cisco went on to sell about $100,000 of routers and switches that became part of the Golden Shield project."

The torrent of criticism over the standard corporate line—that once they sell the hardware, companies cannot control what their customers do with it—has led to some minimal restrictions on the sale of such gear to the worst regimes on the planet. But the restrictions don't appear to stop such regimes from acquiring it.

In 2011, a free-speech-focused hacker who went by the handle Punkbob was scanning various Internet-connected routers and servers in Syria for vulnerabilities, then penetrating the machines as he found openings. In the course of his hacking, Punkbob stumbled across a server filled with log files from an Internet appliance made by a California company, Blue Coat. The logs tracked thousands of Syrians' online behavior in great detail.

"At first we were just poking around, but when I saw that, I had this feeling of dread," Punkbob told *Forbes*, describing the moment. "To see exactly what Syria was tracking and who was providing the technology to do it.... That was when it felt real."

The revelation that—once again—Western gear was serving the cause of political oppression caused a huge controversy in the United States. Blue Coat responded with a public statement saying it wasn't responsible, and that the "appliances were transferred illegally to Syria after being sold to a channel distribution partner for a seemingly appropriate designated end user." The US Commerce Department opened a probe of the company, but that did not appear to scare off investors; a group of them purchased Blue Coat a few weeks after the news broke, taking it private for $1.1 billion.

The restriction on selling directly to Syria wasn't a corporate one; it was US government policy. In most cases, security firms have broad latitude to sell to slightly less repressive regimes. In such cases, Blue Coat said, it would not dictate approved and unapproved uses of its gear. As the company noted in a December 2011 statement, it simply created the tool and then allowed purchasing governments to "create their own policies and decide how to use the product."

One of the more creative uses of packet-sniffing technology took place in Tunisia during early 2011 when popular protests targeted (and eventually took down) the authoritarian Ben Ali regime. The Tunisian government, in an apparent attempt to control electronic coordination of the protests, used the technology to scan for Internet users who were requesting Facebook's login page. Web pages are simply collections of code, and many security appliances can be programmed to alter that code as it flows past from Facebook's servers to a Tunisian computer.

In this case, the government transparently injected a few lines of additional code into each copy of the targeted page in real time. All the user saw was the standard Facebook login screen, but the page secretly harbored a tiny program that the Web browser ran in the background. It watched for usernames and passwords being entered on the page, then passed them back to whoever was watching; the code's key function was named "hAAAQ3d" (hacked). Tunisian activists complained that the passwords on their Facebook pages were being changed to lock them out.

Facebook itself wasn't hacked, not were the individual Tunisian users. Because Tunisia required all Internet providers to connect through the Ministry of Communications for international connectivity, the government simply used its national choke hold over the Internet to do something more sophisticated than outright blocking—capturing an entire country's worth of passwords.

"We've had to deal with ISPs in the past who have tried to filter or block our site," Facebook security officer Joe Sullivan told *The Atlantic* in January 2011. "In this case, we were confronted by ISPs that were doing something unprecedented in that they were being very active in their attempts to intercept user information."

Such techniques only work easily when Web pages are unencrypted; even the basic Secure Sockets Layer (SSL) encryption included by default in all modern browsers can make life far more difficult for would-be watchers. (Five days after it learned about the code injection, Facebook encrypted its entire login page when the page was requested by a Tunisian IP address.) Privacy-conscious citizens and criminals both know about SSL, of course, and so the private packet-sniffing industry has been hard at work on solutions. The *Wall Street Journal* and the secrets-sharing website WikiLeaks have each published huge troves of marketing material from these companies, much of which is not public information.

Even a cursory skim through the marketing documents shows a concern with bypassing encryption (actually cracking the encryption is much more difficult and in many cases practically impossible). Packet Forensics builds gear that can sit between an Internet user and a Web server, for instance, engaging in "man-in-the-middle" attacks in which both sides believe that they have created an encrypted channel with the other party. In reality, each side has unknowingly been tricked into creating an encrypted link with the security gear, which decrypts and stores the communications from each side before re-encrypting them for the other party and forwarding them along.

"Your investigative staff will likely collect its best evidence while users are lulled into a false sense of security afforded by Web, e-mail, or VoIP [Voice over Internet Protocol] encryption," a Packet Forensics newsletter cheerfully notes.

Such talk alarms Internet wiretapping critics, who worry that companies looking to sell expensive and powerful hardware to a limited set of customers—generally government and large corporations—might not ask many questions about its intended uses. Or perhaps they know the client's intended use but don't believe that it's their business to weigh in on the ethics of particular deployments. After all, every country has different laws; how is any particular company in a place to judge whether one country's wiretap laws are "just" while another's are "repressive"? When might a system sold for "lawful intercept" be put to unlawful use, or turned over to intelligence agencies, or resold to a third country where it results in a dissident arrested and tortured?

These are questions worth wrestling over, though WikiLeaks doesn't believe they are being wrestled over much by the companies involved. "International surveillance companies are based in the more technologically sophisticated countries, and they sell their technology on to every country of the world," said the site in an unsigned introduction to its "Spy Files" document collection. "This industry is, in practice, unregulated."

The group believes that we have entered a new era, one characterized by near total, automated surveillance of digital communications.

In traditional spy stories, intelligence agencies like MI5 bug the phone of one or two people of interest. In the last ten years systems for indiscriminate, mass surveillance have become the norm. Intelligence companies such as VASTech secretly sell equipment to permanently record the phone calls of entire nations. Others record the location of every mobile phone in a city, down to 50 meters. Systems to infect every Facebook user, or smart-phone owner of an entire population group are on the intelligence market.

What has been created in the last decade—in large part by the private sector—is a kind of online surveillance industry, so different in scale from telephonic wiretapping and even early Internet systems like Carnivore as to be something entirely new. Still, marketing materials are never where one turns to find hard truths, and online surveillance in practice isn't always as godlike or effortless as those selling products would like you to believe. In fact, despite all the advances, agencies like the FBI claim their ability to do surveillance online is quite literally "going dark."

/////

The FBI didn't want to be in the business of maintaining its own packet-inspection gear, hauling it out to remote switching sites, installing it, removing it. The Carnivore approach put investigators in control, but it cost a huge amount of money for the software, gear, and personnel needed to run it. Installing packet-sniffing systems into unfamiliar networks also posed technical problems and, even when it worked, could provide the government with access to far too much information. Besides, wholesale Internet taps weren't usually wanted; increasingly, authorities wanted specific bits of information rather than gigabytes of packets—real-time access to a suspect's every Facebook activity, for instance, or e-mails sent from a specific account, or Skype calls from a certain username.

The easiest way to do this would simply be to require companies like Facebook—who know their own systems better than investigators ever could—to perform the wiretap and send the court-authorized data back to police. Sounds simple enough, but what happens when an Internet company can't comply?

This happened in 2009 when the FBI investigated a pimp who was trafficking minor girls into prostitution. The Bureau had plenty of evidence about the pimp's activities, but it also learned that he found girls to entice into prostitution using an online social networking site. The FBI wanted to intercept all of his communications on the site, as they happened, as a way of identifying more victims and to sniff out any coconspirators.

The social networking site had never built such a real-time intercept capability, however. Investigators believed they had the evidence needed to secure a judicially ordered wiretap—a "last resort" measure that involves plenty of paperwork and oversight—but they didn't bother to seek one. The site couldn't comply, and the FBI wasn't going to spend its time and money trying make its own solution work.

"In this case, the FBI was able to build a case against the target and secure his conviction using other investigative techniques," said Valerie Caproni, the FBI's general counsel, in 2011 testimony to Congress, "but our inability to intercept certain electronic communications resulted in a weaker case and a lighter sentence than might otherwise have occurred." The question that lingered was whether criminals would soon go dark on the Internet as new digital communications services were increasingly built without the wiretap capabilities that had existed for decades in the phone network. As the 2000s rolled on, addressing the issue became one of the FBI's top priorities.

Back in the not-so-good old days, telephone companies like AT&T had total control of their lines—so total that customers could only attach "company-approved" gear. In the United States, this sort of control was finally shattered by the famous "Carterfone" decision from the Federal Communications Commission (FCC) in 1968. Henceforth, users could attach any device to the network so long as it caused no harm, paving the way first for fax machines and then for the data modems that connected so many people to the Internet in the 1990s.

Until this point telephones had been "dumb" devices where all the intelligence was provided by a "smart" network. To tap a line, police could go to the network operator and demand access to network traffic. In the United States, the 1994 Communications Assistance for Law Enforcement Act (CALEA) extended the requirement to all digital call-switching systems, which were harder to tap than the old analog phone lines had been. But CALEA's real innovation was its architectural approach; phone company gear would now have to be designed with "lawful intercept" backdoor capabilities in mind. CALEA didn't contemplate Internet surveillance, but the FBI did push successfully to have the law extended to Internet-based (or "VoIP") calling services in 2003.

The CALEA approach was complicated by the 'Net, since so much of the network intelligence had moved to the edges—into people's computers and smartphones. The network operator didn't control the applications or protocols running over its network, so demands to a network operator for a tap had limited utility; all sorts of encryption and obfuscation could be employed by user devices in ways that were difficult or impossible on the old phone network. The basic framework of CALEA quickly became outdated.

In the era of instant messages, Skype calls, Facebook wall posts, encrypted e-mail, and even video games with in-game audio chat features, criminals can always find a way to communicate that bypasses any law targeting specific technologies. Law enforcement didn't want to spend the time and money needed to capture and crack every communications program on the planet; just contemplating the scale of the job revealed its impossibility. What law enforcement really wanted was a more general principle: all communications providers should simply turn over the unencrypted result—the "plain text"—of the suspect communication. Why not, that is, extend CALEA's architectural requirement to the Internet? The government could order software developers to build systems with wiretapping in mind, just as it had ordered makers of telephone hardware do the same.

Russia already has such a CALEA-style system for the Internet, called the "System for Operative Investigative Activities." Internet-based companies in the country must, at their own expense, build in government access to their systems—and make it remotely available to investigators from the federal security service (the FSB, by its Russian initials). As for a court order, it's not even required. Government investigators can pull data directly from social networking servers without a warrant, without having to tap (and then filter) all the traffic flowing through an Internet service provider's pipes, and without having to leave the office. They don't even need to involve the companies they are tapping.

Two Russian security journalists interviewed state investigators in late 2011. As one investigator put it, "Why should we hassle the social networks when we can use the System for Operative Investigative Activities to take stuff off their servers behind their backs?"

US officials have never proposed such an obviously problematic approach, but the idea of extending CALEA to Internet companies has percolated for years. It reappeared in late 2010 after a *New York Times* article exposed the detailed planning for just such a law. "Essentially, officials want Congress to require all services that enable communications—including encrypted e-mail transmitters like BlackBerry, social networking Web sites like Facebook and software that allows direct 'peer to peer' messaging like Skype—to be technically capable of complying if served with a wiretap order," said the article. "The mandate would include being able to intercept and unscramble encrypted messages." Without such a system, investigators worried, electronic surveillance would gradually become impractical or even impossible.

Given the Internet's global reach, such a requirement would be hugely unpopular with American Internet companies, whose products would suddenly be viewed with much more suspicion throughout the rest of the world. Applying mandatory decryption provisions to international open-source projects that might have no company behind them would present huge practical problems. Developers based in other countries would be unlikely to comply with the law. Even defining which Internet software might be covered by such a law posed problems; would a game developer who allowed in-game voice and text chatting be required to build a real-time intercept solution for the feds? Would the law essentially make it illegal for one guy coding after work from his den to build online chat tools, even in rudimentary form, without first making the tool wiretap capable? No one knew, because there was no public proposal.

Even the FBI wasn't quite sure what it wanted. In part as a reaction to the *Times* article, the House Judiciary Committee called in the FBI and local police in 2011 to testify about what the FBI now officially calls the "Going Dark" problem. The FBI backed away from some of the material in the *Times* article, saying that it had no actual solutions to propose yet. This didn't go over well with Henry Johnson, a Georgia Democrat not excited about the idea of extending CALEA. He pressed FBI General Counsel Valerie Caproni for her plan:

Mr. Johnson: What is it exactly that you would want Congress to do, or are you asking Congress for anything?

Ms. Caproni: Not yet.

Mr. Johnson: Or did we just simply invite you here to tell us about this?

Ms. Caproni: You invited me, and we came. But we don't have a specific request yet. We are still—the Administration is considering—I am really here today to talk about the problem. And I think if everyone understands that we have a problem, that is the first step, and then figuring out how we fix it is the second step. The Administration does not yet have a proposal. It is something that is actively being discussed within the Administration, and I am optimistic that we will have a proposal in the near future.

Mr. Johnson: So you mean I have been worried for the last 24 hours about some legislation or some issue that I could have worried about later, I guess?

But Caproni did use her appearance to bang the drum for something to be done at some point soon. "Over the past several years," she said, "the FBI and other law enforcement agencies have increasingly found themselves serving wiretap orders on providers that are not covered by CALEA and, therefore, under no pre-existing legal obligation to design into their systems a wiretap capability. Such providers may or may not have intercept capabilities in place for all of their services. If they have no capability or only limited capability, it takes time to engineer a solution—sometimes days, sometimes months, and sometimes longer." Sometimes, as in the 2009 child prostitution case, no solution might be found.

Mark Marshall, chief of police in Smithfield, Virginia, and head of the International Association of Chiefs of Police, laid down the same message. "The lawful interception of voice and data communications is one of the most valuable techniques available to law enforcement in identifying and crippling criminal and terrorist organizations," he said. The Going Dark problem "often undercuts state, local, and tribal law enforcement agencies' efforts to investigate criminal activity such as organized crime, drug-related offenses, child abduction, child exploitation, prison escape, and other threats to public safety. This must change."

The government continued crafting its plans in silence, working to blunt behind-the-scenes opposition from the Internet companies and encouraging them to cooperate voluntarily. It saw some successes; as the *Washington Post* reported in July 2012, Skype, after its acquisition by Microsoft, made it possible for investigators to get access to text-based chats (though listening in on the encrypted audio calls remained difficult or impossible).

When the FBI's associate deputy director trekked over to Congress two months later to deliver a status update, the Going Dark program was a top-line item—and cooperation was a theme. "Because of this gap between technology and the law," he said, "law enforcement is increasingly unable to access the information it needs to protect public safety and the evidence it need to bring criminals to justice. It is only by working together—within the law enforcement and intelligence communities, and with our private sector partners—that we will find a long-term solution to this growing problem."

Actual Internet wiretaps remain rare. In 2010, the US government's own public report on wiretaps showed that 2,311 tap orders had been granted to federal, state, and local investigators. Of these, 2,253 covered telephones, both landlines and mobiles, and a mere sixteen were pure "electronic" wiretaps (another twenty-seven were "combination" taps that may have included some electronic component). The report doesn't include national security wiretaps, which are overseen by a separate and secret court, but it's clear that full Internet wiretaps are rarely used for common crimes. The FBI says that its agents often don't even bother seeking wiretaps on systems that they know are encrypted or that don't have intercept capability. With an easier way to access that data, it's reasonable to assume electronic wiretaps would go up.

Too often discussions paint the "going dark" problem as one that affects only investigators, but solutions impose their own costs. Demanding architectural changes to the way innovation happens on the Internet will cost developers money and could slow progress. Those companies who comply will be able to aid the FBI—but they will also be able to help any government who comes asking for user data, and they will have no technical reason to say no. Making wiretap capability the US default will go quite some ways to making it the world default. As Derek Bambauer puts it, "America requires telecommunications companies to build wiretapping capabilities into their products and services; once spying is part of the core functionality of, say, Internet telephony, it's available to countries whose snoops are far less restrained than the FBI."

But beyond the possibility of lawful abuse of such a system, there's the very real chance that a built-in capability to wiretap will lead to illegal use of the function. Though designed for lawful government access, such backdoors provide opportunities to anyone able to access them. This was seen most famously in Greece, where a high-level wiretap scandal in 2004–2005 led to taps on at least 100 top officials, including the country's prime minister.

Vodafone Greece had purchased some large cell-phone switches from hardware provider Ericsson; these came without Ericsson's "interception management system" (IMS) software, which Vodafone had not purchased. But hardware functions are never static in the Internet age, and new features are only a software update away. In 2003, Ericsson rolled out a new version of the software that powered its switches, and it included low-level wiretap code without the high-level IMS suite used for setting up taps. Some months later, hackers were able to infiltrate the switches and activate the dormant tapping features—and to hide their tracks. Their custom code monitored the switches for calls to and from specific phone numbers; when one was detected, a copy of the call stream was made and sent to the eavesdropper's phone. Location information on the targeted cell phones was also sent separately to eavesdroppers as text messages.

After some odd error messages, the rogue code was eventually located; the perpetrators never were. The remarkable sophistication of the hack shocked observers. In 2007, the magazine *IEEE Spectrum* published a detailed technical account of the hack by two Greek computer science professors, who called it "the most bizarre and embarrassing scandal ever to engulf a major cellphone service provider." They concluded with a call for better security measures, so that "such systems are developed and operated safely," but they didn't question the basic security problem inherent in built-in backdoors.

Others have. Susan Landau was for a decade a Sun Microsystems mathematician and engineer who specialized in Internet security; she has recently authored several seminal books on wiretapping and the Internet. "Wiretaps are a risky business," she writes. "They are an architected security breach that can be subverted and put to nefarious use."

Landau testified at the "Going Dark" congressional hearing in 2011. She brought up both the Greek example and a similar case in Italy. "When you build wiretapping capability into an application, when you build it into a switch, you are creating a serious security risk," she said. "I would say in light of the cyber exploitations we have been seeing nationally the last half dozen years, that is not a risk we can afford."

One of Landau's favorite examples is an IBM security researcher named Tom Cross, who gave a talk at the Black Hat 2010 hacker conference called "Exploiting Lawful Intercept to Wiretap the Internet." Cross had looked deeply at the lawful intercept features built into Cisco's routers—some of the most important pieces of Internet infrastructure in the world. The paper he presented explained how vulnerabilities in Cisco's approach "could enable a malicious person to access the interface and spy on communications without leaving a trace." Such an attack wouldn't be trivial to implement, but someone with the proper knowledge could gain tremendous power to "capture any traffic on the device and route that traffic to any destination IP and port on the global Internet."

Such vulnerabilities exist in all software and are routinely patched when pointed out, but the very existence of government-mandated backdoors creates a permanent vulnerability that is left unpatched by design. The Internet Engineering Task Force (IETF), which oversees the technical standards behind the Internet's most important protocols, was asked years ago to start designing protocols with wiretapping features in mind. In a 2000 policy document, the group decided not to do so, because wiretap functionality would "conflict with the goal of freedom from security loopholes.... Wiretapping, even when it is not being exercised, therefore lowers the security of the system."

So what's a cop to do?

/////

Going Dark is a real problem for investigators, but when digital technologies take away with one hand, they offer generously with the other. Internet applications may provide no simple way to wiretap their users, and they may be under no (current) obligation to do so, but the information that they do have is still extraordinary. The government can already force companies like Google to turn over Gmail archives or to help unlock a seized Android phone; it can demand that wireless operators like Verizon hand over detailed data about whom someone called, when, for how long, and where the caller was located; it can get Twitter or Facebook to turn over private messages and contact lists. Almost every Internet service can provide a list of IP addresses from which a particular user connected at particular times.

And then there's the even more basic information from telephones, which has become an astonishingly effective tracking tool as mobile phones have taken over from landlines. An example Landau often makes in her writing is that the US Marshals Service has reduced its average time to catch a fugitive from forty-two days to just two—a remarkable decrease. They don't do it by listening in to calls, waiting for a fugitive to give away his location; instead, they simply get mobile-phone tracking information from phone companies, which shows where the phones have been and what numbers have been dialed. Data from 2011 revealed by the US Marshals after a lawsuit showed that they only filed 409 requests for transactional data with Internet companies—but 14,568 with telephone companies. This sort of "transactional" data can't offer up a suspect's actual words, but in many cases, it hardly matters if your goal is simply to locate a person, and all cell phone providers are equipped to turn over such information. And it's much easier to get than a search warrant or a wiretap order.

With such a wealth of stored data to sift, investigators don't need real-time taps the way they once did. When electronic wiretaps are truly needed, though, investigators routinely run into a second going-dark problem: strong encryption. Such encryption, when used correctly, is believed to be unbreakable without the key. Law enforcement has long worried about a future in which communications are encrypted by default, even as the geeks have welcomed it.

"Privacy in an open society also requires cryptography," wrote activist Eric Hughes in his 1993 "Cypherpunk's Manifesto," which was typical of the strong encryption movement. "If the content of my speech is available to the world, I have no privacy. To encrypt is to indicate the desire for privacy, and to encrypt with weak cryptography is to indicate not too much desire for privacy. Furthermore, to reveal one's identity with assurance when the default is anonymity requires the cryptographic signature."

Faith in strong crypto has been a hallmark of privacy activists for decades; it certainly motivated those behind HavenCo, who believed that unbreakable encryption could eventually make the need to stick servers in places like Sealand unnecessary. In 2000, the IETF stated its belief that "both commercial development of the Internet and adequate privacy for its users against illegal intrusion requires the wide availability of strong cryptographic technology."

But most people still have trouble using cryptography securely. Even among those who know what they're doing, crypto hasn't been an impenetrable shield; instead of halting investigations altogether, it has forced investigators to get creative. Cops can get the key, for instance. They can simply ask for it, as they often do in computer investigations involving encrypted computers. Suspects sometimes turn it over; when they don't, a bit of subterfuge can get the job done, as we saw in the raids that brought down The Cache. Failing that, investigators can go to court and ask a judge to order a defendant to provide the key or face contempt charges. (Courts are currently weighing the situations in which this is appropriate and whether it amounts to forced self-incrimination.)

When investigators require the key but also need to get it secretly, they can do so by—among other methods—breaking into a suspect's computer. In 2001, FBI agents executing a search warrant surreptitiously installed key-logging software on a computer belonging to gambling and loan shark suspect Nicodemo Scarfo. While they couldn't decrypt his files (in particular, one file called "Factors"), they *could* seize the decryption key as it was typed into the machine in order to use it later. Today, such tools could be remotely deployed through RAT/CIPAV software. Rather than making the locks less secure, as in the case of expanding CALEA-style laws, the government can focus on finding the keys when it needs them.

Even this isn't always required. To be useful to their owner, encrypted documents at some point must be decrypted, encrypted video chats must be descrambled, and encrypted instant messages must be translated into clear text. Instead of looking for passwords, investigators can use a RAT to view the information after decryption. They can interview the other party to a conversation. They can rifle through a suspect's trash looking for printed copies of encrypted documents—software can even rebuild shredded documents from their strips.

Matt Blaze, who writes widely about cryptography, points out that police have become better than their own doomsday hype sometimes suggests. "Periodically, government eavesdroppers in law enforcement and intelligence agencies, worried that their ability to intercept will soon 'go dark' because of some technological advance on the horizon, sound the alarm to urge that new technology be designed to accommodate their wiretapping needs," he says. "And, to be sure, their concerns are as genuine as the work they do is vital. But as we saw from the 1990's crypto debate, the eavesdroppers proved far more resilient than they themselves predicted."

If investigators can find ways around crypto, were the cypherpunks simply wrong about its value? No. Few want cryptography to provide a shield for all manner of illegal dealings; what they want is a higher level of privacy. Cryptography provides that privacy by keeping transmissions out of the hands of most private eavesdroppers on the Internet, essential to building robust systems of commerce and communications. As for government, crypto forces investigators to expend significant effort to overcome encryption—which is a feature, not a bug. If used properly, crypto can prevent the government from engaging in mass automated surveillance of our digital lives without necessarily giving free rein to the worst impulses of the human heart.

As Blaze puts it, "While traffic encryption is highly effective at preventing wholesale, un-targeted interception, it does surprisingly little to prevent targeted government eavesdropping in the complex architectures of modern computing and communication technologies."

The government's own wiretapping report notes the success that investigators have had against crypto. "In 2010, encryption was reported during six state wiretaps," says the 2010 report, "but did not prevent officials from obtaining the plain text of the communications."

5
NATURAL MALE ENHANCE-MENT: PRIVACY ON THE SERVER

This being the Internet, it was perhaps fitting that one of the seminal online privacy cases involved penis pills. And not just *any* penis pills—no, the case was about Enzyte, the tablet promising "natural male enhancement." Enzyte was once such a staple of late-night TV advertising in the United States that its unspeaking spokesman Smilin' Bob became not only the "envy of his neighborhood" but a cultural icon. The reason for Bob's unsettling grin wasn't spelled out directly in the ad, but the admiring housewives of his neighborhood clearly sensed that something extraordinary had taken place inside Bob's pants.

Something extraordinary was also taking place at Berkeley Nutraceuticals, the Cincinnati, Ohio, startup behind Enzyte. The company, founded by Steven Warshak, eventually sold thirteen different herbal products with vaguely medical-sounding names like Rovicid (allegedly enhanced sex), Ogoplex (allegedly intensified orgasms), and Keflex (allegedly masked drug traces in urine), but it was Enzyte that became the corporate gold mine.

Readers of this book aren't the sort of people who purchase sex concoctions from online retailers, of course. Readers of this book have finely tuned senses for snake oil and secretly suspect that no one actually buys herbal penis supplements from TV pitchmen. But readers of this book live in a rarefied world.

In the real world, Enzyte proved a massive hit with late-night TV watchers and men's-magazine readers. At the Enzyte launch in 2001, Berkeley Nutraceuticals employed some fifteen people, mostly friends and family of Steven Warshak; Warshak's septuagenarian mother Harriet even helped out in the business. By 2004, Berkeley had grown to 1,500 employees and ran a twenty-four-hour call center to process orders. That year, it sold $250 million of supplements—most of it Enzyte.

Berkeley became an entrepreneurial success story and a major Cincinnati employer. Smilin' Bob's grin grew so big it looked as though it was about to split his face in two, but the grin hid a secret. Though Berkeley bragged in ads that Enzyte had a 96 percent customer-satisfaction rate, huge numbers of customers had actually complained. The complaints grew loud enough that the head of the Better Business Bureau wrote a letter to Warshak in mid-2004 to announce "serious concerns about the number of complaints" it had received. Those complaints had a single focus: Berkeley's "auto-ship" program.

Berkeley didn't make most of its cash from people looking to try a single box of Enzyte tablets; it made most of its cash from putting callers into a renewal program that sent them a $70 supply of Enzyte every two months until canceled. Many customers had no idea that they had even signed up for such a renewal program, however, and canceling was (purposely) difficult.

The FBI and the Federal Trade Commission both began sniffing around Berkeley and soon unearthed a set of shocking corporate practices. In 2001 and 2002, Berkeley customers were "were simply added to the [auto-ship] program at the time of the initial sale without any indication that they would be on the hook for additional charges," wrote one federal judge, summing up the evidence amassed against Warshak and his firm. When asked why customers weren't told about auto-shipping until their orders actually arrived in the mail, Berkeley chief operating officer James Teegarden eventually testified in court that "nobody would sign up."

Apparently realizing that the auto-ship program might attract unwanted attention, Berkeley began making disclosures during the initial customer phone call—but only *after* the order had been placed. The disclosure immediately followed the line, "This product is not a contraceptive nor will it prevent any sexual disease." Teegarden admitted that this placement was deliberate. The company believed that "if we started off with a statement about a contraceptive, something other than what it was, that people wouldn't really listen to what we were disclosing to them," he testified.

Not that the "disclosure" always meant much. In November 2003, Berkeley outsourced some of its Enzyte sales calls to another firm. That firm actually asked customers outright if they wanted to join auto-ship; not surprisingly, 80 percent declined. Warshak wouldn't stand for this. "Take those customers, even if they decline[d], even if they said no to the Auto-Ship program, go ahead and put them on the Auto-Ship program," he ordered his employees in an e-mail. Another Berkeley e-mail showed that "all customers, whether they know it or not, are going on [auto-ship]."

Surprised customers routinely demanded an end to auto-ship, and they wanted refunds. In late 2003, Warshak told his staff to remove the company's return shipping address from the label on its own products. "Let's make them call—work some deals," he said, telling call-center staff to convince unhappy customers to accept other "nutraceuticals" in lieu of cash refunds or credit.

The resistance to refunds reached comic extremes. The dry

description of Sixth Circuit Appeals Court Judge Danny Boggs illus-
trated the lengths to which Berkeley would go to avoid returning cash:
"At one point, Enzyte customers seeking a refund were told they needed
to obtain a notarized document indicating that they had experienced
'no size increase.' The admittedly ingenious idea behind the policy was
that nobody 'would actually go and have anything notarized that said
that they had a small penis.' In 2002, 'there was really no refund policy.
It was: Sorry, you got it, you keep it, and we'll cancel you off of future
shipments.'"

This led to short-terms gains but long-term problems. Angry customers, unable to get satisfaction from Berkeley, went to their credit
card companies instead. Berkeley's "chargeback" ratio went through the
roof as customers disputed charges and banks took money back from
Berkeley, putting the company's very ability to accept credit cards in
jeopardy. (Payment processors would have cut off Berkeley if more than
one percent of its transactions were chargebacks).

Berkeley went frantic in its attempt to keep the chargeback ratio low.
The company "double-dinged" on charges, splitting transactions into
two parts (one for the product, one for shipping), billing each separately.
By 2003, it was triple-dinging charges to make the volume of "good"
transactions appear higher. If Berkeley thought its chargeback ratio was
too poor in any given month, employees would bill Warshak's personal
credit cards with a host of one-dollar transactions until his card limits
were reached; Warshak would then be reimbursed by the company.

When even more good transactions were needed, Berkeley simply
plucked random customers from its database, charged their credit cards,
then immediately refunded the money. In April 2002, for instance, 2,482
customer credit cards were billed $19.95 each, after which the charges
were reversed. If people called to complain, Berkeley blamed a "computer
glitch."

What customers got for their money was a supply of herbal

supplements designed to look as much like a pharmaceutical as possible, right down the shape and color of the tablets. Berkeley lacked scientific evidence that Enzyte worked, but it's fair to say that efficacy wasn't one of the company's chief concerns. For instance, Berkeley at some point reformulated Rovicid, its prostate-health/sex-enhancing supplement, as a "heart-health dietary supplement" instead. Rather than throw out the old Rovicid, Berkeley simply slapped new labels on the old containers— even though the new ingredient list didn't match what was in the tablets. In 2004, when Food and Drug Administration (FDA) inspectors came through the company's warehouse, the second shift manager went to the "sick aisle" of mislabeled products, packed the relabeled Rovicid into a rental truck, and drove it to the parking lot of another Berkeley-owned building. He restocked it after the inspectors left.

An early magazine ad for Enzyte claimed that the product had been developed by "Dr. Fredrick Thomkins, a physician with a biology degree from Stanford; and Dr. Michael Moore, a leading urologist from Harvard." But as Teegarden would later admit on the witness stand in the federal case against the company, "Those two doctors did not exist."

The 96 percent satisfaction rate too was illusory. After receiving an e-mail from Warshak, Teegarden simply created a spreadsheet of 500 people drawn from the Enzyte customer database, then marked 480 of them as either "satisfied" or "very satisfied." Voilà—instant customer survey.

Berkeley's approach to marketing its products was perhaps best summed up by a February 2005 e-mail from Warshak that explained the secrets of his advertising success. "GET 3–4 BOTTLES OF WINE . . . THEN SIT AROUND AND MAKE SHIT UP!!" he wrote. "THAT'S WHAT I DO . . . BUT WRITE IT ALL DOWN OR YOU'LL FORGET IT THE NEXT DAY."

Warshak argued that his company was simply the victim of its own success, overwhelmed with orders and run by people with no real experience in business at this scale. Berkeley's "operational deficiencies," as Warshak's lawyers called them, were simply "a byproduct of unsophisticated business practices in Berkeley's formative years and Berkeley's virtually unprecedented growth, rather than the result of criminal fraud." As evidence, they noted that the company had finally abandoned its undisclosed auto-ship program after several years and had installed an automated system to record all calls with customers. It even set up a compliance department, which at one point had nearly fifty employees, to ensure that customer interactions were aboveboard.

As for the government's negative spin on Berkeley's business practices—well, this was merely normal corporate behavior, went the defense argument. "Negotiating with customers to try to save sales, implementing strategies to recover credit card transactions that were declined, and continuously revising corporate polices regarding refund and guarantee programs—all of which the government sought to criminalize—are standard American business practices," wrote Warshak's lawyers.

They didn't convince either a jury or a set of appeals court judges. (As Judge Boggs eventually wrote of the company, "A reasonable juror could easily conclude that Berkeley's sales operation was, for the entire duration of its existence, little more than a colossal fraud.") After a six-week federal trial in early 2008, Warshak was sentenced to twenty-five years in prison, and he had to surrender $459 million in proceeds from the sale of Berkeley products and another $44 million for money laundering. His mother, Harriet, got two years in jail. Berkeley eventually entered bankruptcy.

The case had been made partly on the back of Warshak's private e-mails, even though he had taken numerous precautions to secure these. Somehow the feds got their hands on those messages even before they obtained a search warrant. How had it happened? The answer to that question made the Enzyte case a pivotal piece of Internet law—and revealed how investigators had learned to lean on another key pressure point in the Internet ecosystem: third-party servers.

/////

Warshak's e-mails had helped to secure the 112-count indictment against him from an Ohio grand jury in 2006. But when the government finally turned over its evidence against Warshak in the run-up to his 2008 trial, his lawyers noticed something strange: the government had grabbed 27,000 of Warshak's e-mails even *before* executing a 2005 search warrant on Berkeley's corporate headquarters.

This didn't seem possible. Warshak's e-mail provider, NuVox, deleted his messages from its servers after Warshak's computer grabbed a copy of them. To get access to the messages, the feds should have had to (1) infiltrate Warshak's computer or (2) wiretap Warshak's Internet connection to look for e-mail on the wire. But there had been no software subterfuge and no Internet wiretap. Instead, government lawyers had sent NuVox a letter on October 25, 2004, demanding that the company "preserve" copies of Warshak's future e-mails. The company complied without notifying Warshak, maintaining a private cache of all his messages rather than deleting them when his computer downloaded copies. The feds then returned twice in 2005 with court orders—but not with the much-harder-to-get warrants—to collect the e-mails that had been "preserved" for them.

Warshak's lawyers were furious. The Stored Communications Act (SCA) covers situations like this one in which user data is held by a third-party service like NuVox or Google or Yahoo and is stored on that company's servers, and it makes that data fairly simple to get. Full warrants are often not required, in part because such surveillance is "retrospective"; the government gets access only to messages already stored on the server by a suspect. Even the name of the act makes this distinction clear—it was meant to cover "stored" material.

"Prospective" surveillance is generally covered by a different law, the Wiretap Act, and by the much more stringent requirement to obtain a "probable cause" warrant first. Orin Kerr, a leading Internet privacy scholar, notes that "prospective surveillance tends to raise difficult questions of how the communications should be filtered down to the evidence the government seeks" and that "retrospective surveillance usually presents a less severe filtering challenge."

In Warshak's case, the government had used a retrospective process to gain access to prospective messages. The SCA does allow the government to issue "preservation" requests, but these apply only to existing records that might be at risk of deletion; they do not apply to future messages. The Department of Justice's own surveillance manual made this clear even at the time, reminding agents that preservation requests "have no prospective effect.... [Preservation] letters can order a provider to preserve records that have already been created, but cannot order providers to preserve records not yet made."

The fundamental issue went deeper than the improper preservation request, however, and struck at the heart of the SCA. If the government had to get warrants to open a suspect's postal mail or to search his home, why didn't the government need a warrant to seize e-mail stored on a third-party server? Wasn't this an "unreasonable search and seizure" under the Fourth Amendment?

Warshak appealed his 2008 conviction to the Sixth Circuit Court of Appeals, saying that "the issue of whether the government's secret *ex parte* [one-sided] acquisition of private e-mails without the consent of either the sender or recipient, without a showing of probable cause, without a warrant, and without limits on the scope of the privacy invasion authorized is one of grave importance in an age where e-mail communications have largely replaced letters as the universal means of written communication and have made substantial inroads on the use of the telephone."

The Electronic Frontier Foundation, the organization cofounded by John Perry Barlow, weighed in on Warshak's side during the appeal. "Put simply," it wrote, "the government misused the SCA to conduct a 'back door wiretap' of Warshak's e-mails and bypass the Wiretap Act's strict requirements, including its requirement of probable cause."

A three-judge panel of Sixth Circuit appellate judges took up the question in a lengthy opinion handed down on December 14, 2010. To address the Fourth Amendment issue, the judges first had to decide if taking the e-mails from NuVox constituted a "search" at all—with "search" in this case defined as the government infringing upon "an expectation of privacy" that "society is prepared to consider reasonable."

The first part of the definition proved simple to answer. Warshak clearly expected his messages to remain private. As the judges wrote, "Given the often sensitive and sometimes damning substance of his e-mails, we think it highly unlikely that Warshak expected them to be made public, for people seldom unfurl their dirty laundry in plain view."

Did society concur that this expectation was reasonable? That depended on how literally the judges interpreted the Fourth Amendment—and whether they sided more with a famous bootlegger or a famous gambler.

/////

The Fourth Amendment to the US constitution wasn't written with e-mail in mind. It protects "the right of the people to be secure in their persons, houses, papers, and effects, against unreasonable searches and seizures" and says that this security "shall not be violated, and no Warrants shall issue, but upon probable cause." Read literally, this applies much more obviously to tangible items than to electrical signals on a wire.

In 1928, former President William Howard Taft confronted this issue as a Supreme Court justice. The court had taken the case of famous

Seattle bootlegger Roy Olmstead, a onetime police lieutenant who set up a thriving trade in alcohol during Prohibition. Olmstead operated quite openly in Seattle, eventually becoming one of the area's largest employers. He had an office downtown complete with six telephone lines to take orders for booze.

Prohibition agents wiretapped these lines without a warrant and used the taps in their case against Olmstead and his crew. Police eventually arrested ninety people, including Olmstead and his wife—who were accused of doing $2 million in prohibited sales per year.

The government obtained convictions, but the case was appealed to the Ninth Circuit in San Francisco and then to the Supreme Court in Washington, DC. Olmstead's key contention was that his Fourth Amendment rights had been violated by the warrantless wiretaps. The government argued, however, that its phone taps had occurred outside Olmstead's office building; therefore, it had not "searched" his person, property, or possessions. No warrant was needed.

Taft wrote the majority decision in the case, one woodenly literal in its interpretation. "The reasonable view is that one who installs in his house a telephone instrument with connecting wires intends to project his voice to those quite outside, and that the wires beyond his house and messages while passing over them are not within the protection of the Fourth Amendment," he wrote. "There was no searching. There was no seizure. The evidence was secured by the use of the sense of hearing and that only. There was no entry of the houses or offices of the defendants."

But as the telephone became ubiquitous, the Olmstead ruling became more difficult to defend. US law had protected the security and privacy of the postal service since the republic's early days, but the police were now free to listen to anyone, anywhere, so long as they resorted to an outside-the-home phone tap. Could it really be the case that the privacy of a conversation depended solely on the medium used to hold it?

This was untenable, and in 1967 the Olmstead decision collapsed as another Supreme Court articulated a wildly different privacy standard. The justices were this time dealing with small-time gambler Charles Katz, who had been arrested in Los Angeles after another warrantless wiretap. Katz routinely left his home and walked down to a group of three public pay phones, where he placed a series of calls at the same time each day. FBI agents investigating Katz for interstate gambling placed microphones on the outside of two phone booths; the phone company put an "out of order" sign on the third. A recording device on top of the booths captured Katz's conversation, which consisted of cryptic phrases like "give me Duquesne minus 7 for a nickel!" No warrant had even been sought.

Katz objected to these recordings being played at his trial. An appellate court allowed the recordings to be played, writing that—as in the Olmstead case—no Fourth Amendment violation had occurred because the FBI microphones had been outside the private space of the phone booth.

But when the Supreme Court took the case, it gutted this logic. "The Fourth Amendment protects people, not places," wrote Justice Potter Stewart for the majority. "What a person knowingly exposes to the public, even in his own home or office, is not a subject of Fourth Amendment protection. But what he seeks to preserve as private, even in an area accessible to the public, may be constitutionally protected." He went on: "No less than an individual in a business office, in a friend's apartment, or in a taxicab, a person in a telephone booth may rely upon the protection of the Fourth Amendment. One who occupies it, shuts the door behind him, and pays the toll that permits him to place a call is surely entitled to assume that the words he utters into the mouthpiece will not be broadcast to the world. To read the Constitution more narrowly is to ignore the vital role that the public telephone has come to play in private communication."

Though the court recognized that the agents had acted with restraint, capturing only Katz's gambling-related calls and tossing out the rest, it refused to leave this restraint to the sole judgment of the investigators conducting the surveillance. The supervision of a judge, exerted through the warrant process, was essential. The opinion continued:

> [Agents] were not required, before commencing the search, to present their estimate of probable cause for detached scrutiny by a neutral magistrate. They were not compelled, during the conduct of the search itself, to observe precise limits established in advance by a specific court order. Nor were they directed, after the search had been completed, to notify the authorizing magistrate in detail of all that had been seized. In the absence of such safeguards, this Court has never sustained a search upon the sole ground that officers reasonably expected to find evidence of a particular crime and voluntarily confined their activities to the least intrusive means consistent with that end.

After Katz, tapping phone calls would require a warrant.

/////

Before the Warshak case, e-mail on third-party servers was treated much as phone calls had been a century before—and the policy suffered from the same clear inconsistencies. The government needed a warrant to grab e-mail from people's personal computers, it needed a warrant to wiretap their Internet connections in real time, it needed a warrant to read their postal mail, and it needed a warrant to tap their phone calls. But when a person's e-mail was stored off-site on a third-party server—suddenly, no warrant was needed.

The government had an argument to defend this position, the so-called "third-party doctrine." Once the target of surveillance had voluntarily revealed information to someone else, the idea went, it was no longer quite so private and so could be obtained from that third party with a mere subpoena, which didn't require the high "probable cause" standard of evidence. This doctrine explained why remotely stored e-mail was so easy to access under the SCA, despite the fact that no one "reveals" the contents of their e-mail to their e-mail provider in the same way they might show a letter to a friend. Not surprisingly, the third party doctrine has been roundly criticized.

Whatever the intellectual oddities of this position, seizing e-mail from Internet servers quickly became a practical boon for investigators. "Even just five years ago, if the government wanted to get access to potentially incriminating evidence from the home computers of ten different suspects, investigators had to convince a judge that they had probable cause in order to obtain a search warrant for each person," wrote security researcher Chris Soghoian in a 2009 paper. "The investigating agency would then send agents to raid the homes of the individuals, remove the computers, and later perform labor-intensive forensic analysis in order to get the files."

Data stored on remote Internet servers made this process much easier. No longer did agents need to raid someone's home or obtain a wiretap order; they could peek at the e-mail evidence first before going to those greater lengths. A whole host of such e-mail orders targeted at Google's Gmail, for instance, could be executed at once—and executed cheaply.

If the appellate judges handling Warshak followed Katz rather than Olmstead, however, e-mail could become substantially more difficult for investigators to access. The Warshak ruling, the judges knew, would be a pivotal one, and they issued an expansive opinion that focused on the Fourth Amendment and its relationship to e-mail.

Citing Katz, the court ripped into the Stored Communications Act and its low level of protection for e-mail. Judge Danny Boggs wrote:

If we accept that an e-mail is analogous to a letter or a phone call, it is manifest that agents of the government cannot compel a commercial ISP [Internet Service Provider] to turn over the contents of an e-mail without triggering the Fourth Amendment. An ISP is the intermediary that makes e-mail communication possible. E-mails must pass through an ISP's servers to reach their intended recipient. Thus, the ISP is the functional equivalent of a post office or a telephone company. As we have discussed above, the police may not storm the post office and intercept a letter, and they are likewise forbidden from using the phone system to make a clandestine recording of a telephone call—unless they get a warrant, that is.

It only stands to reason that, if government agents compel an ISP to surrender the contents of a subscriber's e-mails, those agents have thereby conducted a Fourth Amendment search, which necessitates compliance with the warrant requirement absent some exception.

The court then dropped its bombshell: "To the extent that the SCA purports to permit the government to obtain such e-mails warrantlessly, the SCA is unconstitutional." E-mail—at least in the Sixth Circuit—was entitled to the same warrant protections as phone calls and letters.

Lawyers at the Electronic Frontier Foundation were jubilant. "Today's decision is the only federal appellate decision currently on the books that squarely rules on this critically important privacy issue," wrote EFF lawyer Kevin Bankston. "When the government secretly demands someone's e-mail without probable cause, the e-mail provider can confidently say: 'Come back with a warrant.'"

Paul Ohm, a former Justice Department lawyer turned law professor, called the ruling "a very big deal" that "marks the first time a federal court of appeals has extended the Fourth Amendment to e-mail with such care and detail."

The ruling was good for e-mail users; Warshak hoped it would be good for him, too. But although his constitutional rights had indeed been violated by the investigation, the court declined to overturn the verdict. Noting that most of the evidence actually presented at trial came from the physical raid on Berkeley headquarters rather than from the e-mails, and that the search warrant application had not used the e-mails as evidence, the court called the violation in Warshak's specific case "mostly harmless."

/////

Berkeley Nutraceuticals entered bankruptcy as a result of the investigation, but it was rescued by its local landlord, Pristine Bay, which said it didn't want to lose an anchor tenant. Berkeley's name was changed to Vianda. The company now sells a "new" Enzyte blend that includes horny goat weed, ginseng, and ginkgo biloba—though it says it has ditched the shady sales practices. As for Smilin' Bob, he's still smiling his way through TV commercials; devotees can even order "Livin' Large" T-shirts adorned with the character's face.

Warshak now resides in an Ohio federal prison (his mother Harriet was eventually given five years probation instead of jail time, and due to ill health was released from community service obligations). He forfeited homes, numerous bank accounts, several vehicles, annuities, college savings plans, a $10,000 membership to the La Costa Resort and Spa, two grand pianos, and even a Segway scooter as part of the judgment against him.

The US marshal for the Southern District of Ohio, which collected and sold Warshak's valuables to pay his judgment, did a thorough job of tracking down his property—but the marshals couldn't find the Segway, which Warshak's family had reported stolen. Three years later, the Segway resurfaced in the abandoned property room of the local sheriff's office. Someone had found it by the side of a highway back in 2008; it took until 2011 for police to realize that it was the missing Warshak scooter. In May 2012, after the gear had all been sold, the Department of Justice released $24 million to repay Berkeley victims.

With that, the case wound to an almost farcical close—but not before it set a powerful privacy precedent for the digital age. The next time you check your e-mail, remember that its privacy was secured, in at least some small way, by a penis pill.

6
TICK/TOCK: SPAM I

Twenty-four-year-old Oleg Nikolaenko knew cold-weather life, having already purchased a fine house in a wealthy Moscow suburb. So the mop-haired young man wasn't surprised to find himself spending the winter of 2010 in the grip of an arctic chill—he just hadn't planned on doing so in a Wisconsin jail cell.

Nikolaenko had been arrested while attending the massive Specialty Equipment Market Association (SEMA) auto show in Las Vegas. A car buff, he had also attended the event in 2009 and displayed no obvious reluctance to apply for a US visa on either occasion. He landed at JFK airport in New York on October 30, boarded a connecting flight to Las Vegas, and checked into the Bellagio hotel for a planned six-night stay.

But Nikolaenko's passage through US Customs in New York had alerted FBI agent Brett Banner to his presence. Working out of the FBI's Milwaukee office, Banner was on the Cyber Crimes Squad that had pursued Nikolaenko for more than a year. Banner believed that the young man—later described by his attorney as the kind of kid "you find in a basement munching nachos and playing Wii [video games]"—had actually created and now controlled a massive botnet named Mega-D.

Botnets work by infecting thousands or even millions of computers around the globe with small pieces of malicious software. The code runs silently in the background—most users have no idea of its presence—turning a computer into a "bot" that sits listening over the Internet for any instructions from its controller. The botnet controller can take this massive network of machines and pass them specific pieces of spam, along with lists of e-mail addresses to contact. As the computer owner surfs the Web or watches an online video, her computer could be firing off thousands of messages silently in the background, all of them untraceable to the actual botnet owner. Rather than develop spam pitches themselves, botnet owners often rent out their networks to the highest bidder as a high-tech delivery mechanism for other people's payloads.

The Mega-D botnet had infected more than 500,000 computers around the globe; they were pressed into service as spambots. At its high point, Mega-D's spam output was estimated to account for 32 percent of all spam in the world. If you were on the Internet and checking e-mail between 2007 and 2009, you probably received many, many messages sent by Mega-D, usually advertising pharmaceuticals.

This earned Mega-D the title of "world's largest botnet," which suggested that quite a bit of money was behind the operation. Indeed, the botnet's mysterious owner earned so much cash that, according to records taken from an Australian spam broker who coordinated deals between spammers and the botnets who delivered their messages, Mega-D's owner had made $464,967.12 in just six months during 2007. And that was just the money from one client; Mega-D's firepower was so great that the botnet was used to spam for multiple high-volume pitchmen. The sheer volume of the operation brought Mega-D to the attention of US and Australian authorities. In a coordinated process that took years to unfold, agents painstakingly traced one particular spam operation from its America creator to its Australian broker to its Russian Mega-D distributor.

The man—it always seems to be a man—behind Mega-D had

remained inscrutable for several years, but in November 2009, FBI agents were able to trace money paid by the Australian spam broker to the Russian spammer. Google also turned over the Russian's e-mail account; he had unwisely used a Gmail address subject to simple US subpoena power. Both the money trail and the e-mail pointed to Oleg Nikolaenko, then living in a fine home on Spasskiy Proezd, Vidnoe 2, Russian Federation.

Nikolaenko had actually been in the United States only weeks before this discovery, attending the 2009 SEMA auto show. He could have been arrested then, had his identity been known, but after returning to Russia, he was hard to get; Russia's constitution forbids the extradition of its citizens. Banner and the FBI bided their time.

Situations like Nikolaenko's pose a sticky problem for Internet policing. Grabbing a domestic resident is easy enough, and international police cooperation makes arrests possible in "friendly" countries. But how to reach those who live in countries with enough infrastructure to make Internet work possible, but with limited interest in helping foreign police agencies arrest its citizens? No wonder that, facing such a situation, copyright holders and police agencies around the world have repeatedly proposed Internet site blocking or filtering; if you can't reach someone, you can at least stop them from reaching you. A blockade doesn't work against botnet spam, however, because it originates with hundreds of thousands of separate machines around the world.

The Nikolaenko case is a reminder that nothing so dramatic is usually needed. The United States, Western Europe, Australia, Japan, and other advanced economies exert extraordinary soft power even on spammers. They host many of the towns and cities those with money most want to visit; they host the world's best financial institutions; they host the world's best Internet companies; they host the most people with both Internet access and ready money who might be convinced to spring for an unvetted erection aid. Even cybercrooks who want to take a vacation in some remote Asian country often end up connecting on flights through places like Germany, which has shown itself ready to arrest them on behalf of US authorities when they step off the plane.

Nikolaenko had a number of US connections. He needed to receive cash from those he spammed for, he needed a good e-mail client, and he loved cars and Vegas. In the end, he settled on what was easy over what was smart, using a US-based Gmail account, signing up for a nonanonymous ePassporte account to receive cash transfers, and traveling to car shows in Las Vegas on two occasions. Had he limited himself only to the first two indiscretions, his identity would have been revealed to Banner's team, but he was unlikely to face immediate arrest in Russia. How long he might have lived in comfort, visiting only Black Sea resorts instead of Vegas, we can only guess. But Nikolaenko couldn't stay away.

When he entered the United States on October 30, 2010, it took Banner several days to receive the information and then to swear out a criminal complaint. He knew that he was racing against time; the Bellagio hotel informed him that Nikolaenko was only scheduled to stay until November 5.

On November 3, Banner took a two-count criminal complaint to US Magistrate Judge Aaron Goodstein in Milwaukee. The complaint accused Nikolaenko of violating the federal CAN-SPAM Act by sending e-mails with forged header information. It also charged him with "aiding and abetting" mail fraud; an FBI agent had ordered Viagra from one of the spam messages Nikolaenko sent, but only "VPXL" male enhancement pills had arrived. Judge Goodstein signed off on an arrest warrant.

FBI agents arrested Nikolaenko in Las Vegas on November 4. They took him before a federal judge there, who shipped him off to Wisconsin in the custody of the US marshals. Denied bail by a Milwaukee judge, who noted that he carried two passports and a large quantity of cash, Nikolaenko spent Christmas staring at the inside of a cell.

/////

Spam has been an unavoidable side effect of e-mail's popularity for more than a decade now; nothing about its existence seems strange or even particularly unusual anymore. But for those who dutifully delete from their inboxes electronic pitches for Rolex knockoffs, cheap mortgages, and sexual satisfaction, paying no closer attention to the Spam Wars being fought across the Internet, the Mega-D case certainly ought to raise some questions. Chief among them: how did this whole business get so *serious*? Why did Mega-D's creator have to create a purpose-built infection tool capable of invading 500,000 home and office computers around the world, then lying silent to await further instructions—all to send out e-mails hawking pharmaceuticals? Why did the larger operation he was a part of need people on three continents, complete with middlemen and a robust affiliate system? Why did everyone go to such great lengths to maintain their anonymity?

Spam didn't begin this way. While early users of the noncommercial, US government–controlled Internet in the 1980s and early 1990s were not strangers to unsolicited e-mail and newsgroup comments, the first overtly commercial spamming operation is generally traced back to a pair of married immigration lawyers, Laurence Canter and Martha Siegel. The duo, living in Arizona at the time, hired a local programmer to write a special script in the text processing language Perl. On April 12, 1994, Canter and Siegel unleashed their new advertising weapon on the Internet. Their script accessed more than 5,000 Usenet newsgroups, popular text-based discussion forums at the time, and posted a simple message to each. That message read in part:

> Green Card Lottery 1994 May Be The Last One! THE DEAD-LINE HAS BEEN ANNOUNCED.
> The Green Card Lottery is a completely legal program giving away a certain allotment of Green Cards to persons born in certain countries. The lottery program was scheduled to continue on a

permanent basis. However, recently, Senator Alan J. Simpson introduced a bill into the U.S. Congress which could end any future lotteries. THE 1994 LOTTERY IS SCHEDULED TO TAKE PLACE SOON, BUT IT MAY BE THE VERY LAST ONE...

For the next FREE, information via Email, send request to cslaw@indirect.com

Canter & Siegel, Immigration Attorneys

3333 E Camelback Road, Ste 250, Phoenix AZ 85019 USA

cslaw@indirect.com telephone (602) 661-3911 Fax (602) 451-7617.

By today's standards, the message looks tame. It advertised an actual, if overpriced, service related to a real event, the US government's Green Card lottery that grants winners permanent residency in the country. It contained no pornographic images. It provided real names and correct contact information for the people behind the message. Nothing about its transmission information was forged.

In the noncommercial ethos that dominated Usenet at the time, however, the message was an abomination—made even worse by the fact that it appeared in thousands of forums with no connection to immigration issues. Readers who *were* involved with immigration got even angrier. The government's Green Card lottery required nothing more than a postcard containing a name and address; Canter and Siegel were seen to be pitching an overpriced legal service for a straightforward process. Fellow lawyers complained immediately to the American Immigration Lawyers Association (AILA) in Washington, DC.

Ray Everett-Church worked in the AILA office at the time. On the day after the message appeared, he walked into the office and "the receptionist handed me a stack of angry faxes and forwarded a voice mailbox full of furious calls," he recalled for *Wired* in 1999. "All the messages were about the Internet, the Green Card lottery, and a pair of Arizona lawyers.

By the time I stumbled to my cubicle, I had met the enemy. Their names were Laurence Canter and Martha Siegel."

But AILA had only limited power to address the issue. "As a voluntary association, AILA's only recourse was to throw them out of the association," Everett-Church added. "However, when I went to AILA's senior staff to ask what that procedure entailed, a director of the organization asked: 'Canter and Siegel? What did they do this time?'" The pair, it turns out, had been suspended from AILA before.

It took several years for the case to wind its way through the official complaints process of the Tennessee bar, one of the states where the two were licensed to practice law. In 1997, the state of Tennessee revoked their law licenses and highlighted the seriousness of what it called the "Internet issue." Legal advertising is tightly regulated, and the Tennessee Supreme Court noted that Canter and Siegel had not included the disclaimer "This Is An Advertisement" on their messages. More generally, said the court, "The posting appeared on computer screens unsolicited, and each reader was required to read at least the introduction of each message. The posting appeared on Bulletin Boards having no relevance to immigration law. It was, therefore, an improper intrusion into the privacy of the recipient."

Perhaps—but it was lucrative. Canter later recalled that he had made between $100,000 and $200,000 from the ads, adding that the scheme could have been far more profitable had his Arizona Internet provider not cut off his account in the days following the posting.

He didn't really see the harm in what he had done. "The Usenet, to my way of thinking, is very different than e-mail because it's not something that's just coming to you," he told the computer news site CNET in a 2002 interview. "You're going to these message boards for whatever reason, and although it may be true that mass posting to every Usenet group in sight wasn't good, I still don't see how it is nearly as intrusive as receiving 300 pornographic e-mail solicitations every day.... Somebody would have done it, if we hadn't done it."

The combination of easy money and profound Internet outrage paved the way for the two decades of back-and-forth that have followed. For the spammers, the money remains too good—and the cost too low—to lay off; for opponents, the power of the Internet as a cheap international communications tool has proven so profound that they will not tolerate people who seem bent on making it less usable. But e-mail was built for a very different Internet, and all attempts to impose order on the medium have met with only mixed success. (Even Hormel, which owns the trademark on the canned meat product SPAM, gave up its battle long ago; the company now acknowledges that spam is the common term for junk e-mail. "Also, if the term is to be used," Hormel says, "it should be used in all lower-case letters to distinguish it from our trademark SPAM, which should be used with all uppercase letters.")

How chaotic was e-mail in the early years of the Internet's public popularity? One evening in 1995, I logged into my school's Unix server to check my e-mail. The collegiate modem pool at the time was a small one, supporting only eight concurrent users—and each user could see what programs the others were running and what files they were downloading. In a moment of terrible decision making, I thought it might be funny to let another student know that I could see the tawdry image he was (very slowly!) loading. And what better way to do it than with a friendly e-mail from God Almighty?

Using a networking program called Telnet, I connected to our college's mail server on port 25, the usual port for e-mail. The system had no way to verify who I was; it would accept messages from just about any other computer, and it did nothing to check that the sender's claimed e-mail address was valid. When I connected, the server provided a line of text announcing itself and then offered a prompt for my input. I told it what network I was connecting from:

HELO heaven.org

The server happily responded, "Hello, heaven.org" and left me at another prompt. I then pecked out my particular return address for the message I wanted to send:

MAIL FROM:god@heaven.org

The server was just fine with this. "OK" it responded, ready to deliver a message from god@heaven.org. I then told it which local user should receive the message, and then I typed:

DATA

The server responded with "354 End data with <CR><LF>. <CR><LF>"—a cryptic-looking command that was really just telling me to end my message by placing a period on its own line and hitting return. I entered my message, ended with the period, the return, and the final command:

QUIT

With that, the word of God was on its way.

If the whole system sounds shockingly insecure, well—you're getting a sense for why spam has been so hard to curtail. E-mail is built around SMTP, the Simple Mail Transfer Protocol, which was first devised in 1982, a decade before Canter and Siegel's newsgroup spamming. SMTP was built as a fast and easy method for networks to accept and to send e-mail messages to other networks. The protocol's original documentation described its goal as transferring mail "reliably and efficiently"; security was not a priority on the nascent Internet, which still largely connected universities and government agencies and was used mostly by the research community.

As the Internet grew, especially in the days after the last "noncommercial" limitations were removed in 1995, SMTP spread with it—what network wouldn't want to support e-mail? It worked fine for years until the general public discovered the Internet in the mid-1990s and formed a critical mass of users that marketers could not resist. By the time the problem became apparent, SMTP was so embedded in so many servers around the world that a wholesale replacement for the protocol simply wasn't feasible. Like many things about the Internet, early protocol decisions set the stage for both the benefits and problems that the network would encounter later as it went global.

After Canter and Siegel, spam spread quickly out from newsgroups and wormed its way into inboxes. And why not? People received unsolicited postal mail all the time, and that had yet to send the general public into a collective spasm of rage. For a time, it looked as though reputable companies might even get into the bulk e-mail marketing business, pumping out annoying but legitimate pitches.

But people hated spam. In the postal system, mail cost money, it was more easily traceable to a real sender, and it was policed by postal inspectors, which kept a lid on fraudulent pitches and limited the scale of legitimate ones. E-mail wasn't free—Internet connections cost money, and serious spammers could ring up quite a bill—but it was *nearly* free in comparison to postal mail. That opened up all sorts of possibilities for pitching dubious products; even a minuscule "buy rate" could still make spam insanely profitable. With the upfront costs so low and with almost no policing, spam quickly devolved into hucksterism—and porn, porn, porn. Unlike the mail, where pornography was disguised and rarely went right to children, spam brought porn to the inboxes of men, women, and even children everywhere.

Working for a major Internet provider did nothing to stem the tide. In 2003, Dr. William Hancock of Cable & Wireless told a government antispam summit that the biggest spam problem back in 1998 would have been "the announcement of a seminar at Bell Labs or something like that." In the years since, pitches for penis pills had been coming to his young son—and Hancock couldn't stop it. "My son has grown up very, very good in the geeky lifestyle," he told the audience. "He has the proper 2.3 computers in his bedroom, and of course with a T3 [dedicated Internet line] connected in the house, my son is well equipped to go back and deal with Internet capability. It helps to work for a carrier."

The audience chuckled.

"The situation is, folks, that my son also came in at the ripe age of six and said, 'Daddy, what is a penis?' And I said why? And he said, 'Someone sent me an e-mail where I can make mine bigger,' and I thought great, this is what I need to hear right now."

The audience laughed again. But Hancock wasn't kidding.

"Although lately he's been asking about breasts and it bothers me a bit," he continued. "The situation is that these kids get this stuff.... Well, to adults, it's somewhat of an irritant; to kids, it really sociologically causes them some very serious problems. And, so my major reason why I am very much anti-spam and why I spend a great deal of my time worrying about it, stopping it, scanning for it and finding it and killing it dead, is because of my son."

Legislators were angry, too. New York Senator Chuck Schumer, speaking of his then fourteen-year-old daughter, told the same conference that he wanted the Internet's educational and recreational benefits for his daughter. "But you can imagine my anger and dismay when I discovered that not only was she a victim of spam like myself, but like all e-mail users, much of the junk mail she was receiving advertised pornographic websites," he said. "I was and remain powerless to prevent such garbage from reaching my daughter's inbox."

Spam became so noxious so quickly that legitimate companies stayed away, leaving it almost wholly to less-than-scrupulous operators. Spammers weren't about to stop simply because they were enraging people, but Internet providers were determined to tackle the problem. It wasn't just a customer nuisance for the Internet companies; it cost them serious money. A small Internet provider called Lava.net, for instance, spent nearly $200,000 in 2002 upgrading its mail servers, moving spam-ridden customers to new e-mail addresses, and developing e-mail filtering technology that didn't kill important messages. For larger providers, costs stretched into the millions of dollars.

But SMTP's basic limitations meant the spam battle could only become an arms race. The Internet community deployed antispam measures; spammers unveiled countermeasures. For every tick, the spammers found a tock.

/////

In the earliest days, spammers blasted out e-mail through their own Internet connections without much effort to disguise themselves. They might have paid the local phone company for a dedicated T1 or T3 line, hooked it up to a computer, and simply fired out messages from a fixed IP address. Internet providers who saw their systems being deluged by this junk mail would block the IP address from which it was originating.

Spammers responded by learning to hop between fixed addresses. One particular scheme, popular in 1995–96, involved a spammer who shipped servers around the United States to people with access to serious Internet bandwidth. The servers would be hooked up and turned on but sat mostly unused; checks would arrive every month from the spammer as a sort of contingency fee. When one of the spammer's servers had its IP address blocked in too many places, he simply cycled his spam operation to the next server on the list. When that too was blocked, he moved on.

The countermeasure to this countermeasure? A faster method of creating and sharing spam blacklists with Internet providers and large companies, who would use the blacklists to ignore messages coming from suspected spammer IP addresses. Michael Rathbun of Allegiance

Telecom in Texas witnessed the struggle and later described how Internet engineer Paul Vixie created the first real-time black-hole list for spam. "Whenever Paul would make an update to his list as to where [noted spammer] Sanford Wallace or one of his other counterparts was sending from today, suddenly that IP address would vanish all over the place where anybody else who was accepting that feed was able to block those essentially in real time, as soon as Paul saw them coming in," said Rathbun during a panel discussion at an antispam conference. "Within half an hour, anybody who subscribed to that list was also protected. That was sort of the death knell for that particular round of what I would call fixed-address spamming."

So spammers took greater caution to conceal themselves. One popular technique beginning around 1996 was to use an "open relay"—a mail server that would accept messages from any machine on the Internet to any other machine on the Internet (these servers should generally have accepted only mail bound to or coming from registered users of their network). Thanks largely to ignorance and poor configuration, open relays were rampant in the 1990s, and they existed all over the world. US spammers would routinely connect to a Chinese server misconfigured as an open relay and dump thousands of spam e-mails into it (with bogus return addresses, of course), just as I had done on my college computer— but using automated software that went thousands of times faster. The spammers could then sit back and watch as the target machine dutifully sent those messages back to US spam targets for delivery. Using this technique, the original sender of the spam remained obscure.

The antispammers then launched a worldwide effort to shut down open relays, but their automated scans of servers around the Internet revealed the scale of the challenge: hundreds of thousands of open relays, many hosted by businesses new to the Internet and unaware of the problems they were causing. Language barriers made notification tricky, and Internet providers were loath to cut off customers who couldn't be bothered to fix the problem or who didn't know how; after all, blocking a mail server meant that the organization that controlled it would be suddenly unable to send or receive e-mail. As late as 2003, 250,000 open relays were still on the active list—and some experts believed that only half of all such relays had even been found.

Antispam crusaders eventually added open relays to their blacklists, which provided a wake-up call to many of the firms running open relays. Alongside a worldwide education effort on their dangers, open relays were gradually closed or blocked. As they became more difficult to find and then to make productive use of, spammers moved on to an easier target: open proxies.

Open proxies are machines that sit between user computers and the worldwide Internet. A business, for instance, might run a proxy server that connects directly to the Internet, but all computers in the office connect to the proxy. The approach can create a single firewall point against Internet intrusions, making it much easier for a business to update security settings and control corporate Internet access. Unfortunately, many proxies with incorrect setups would allow connections not just from a corporate computer but from any computer, even those outside the company. Because of the way proxies work, all communications passing through them appear to issue from the proxy itself. This provided yet another convenient way for spammers to send e-mail; angry responses to the spamming would be directed back toward the innocent proxy owner.

A whole ecosystem developed around spam. Software developers built bulk e-mail tools easy enough for nontechies to use; others harvested and sold lists of open relays and proxies, even offering monthly subscription plans that kept the lists up to date.

Antispammers then added the open proxies to their blacklists and mounted a new education campaign, but progress was slow. In 2003, antispam company MessageLabs issued a press release announcing its belief that more than two-thirds of all spam was sent through open proxies.

The pushback against fixed IP addresses, then against open relays, and finally against open proxies gradually forced spammers deep underground, but it didn't silence their output. For their next move, spammers eventually hit on the unholy marriage of a computer virus with their customized spam-sending "ratware"—and botnets were born.

Around 2003, coders developed custom computer-invasion software that could take advantage of security flaws in common computer operating systems—usually Microsoft Windows. Attached to software downloaded from the Internet or sometimes installed through a security hole in a Web browser, such software infiltrated the host operating system, hid itself from view (a user would certainly not see any obvious sign that unknown code was running), and then waited for instructions from its controller. Thousands of such machines, chained together over the Internet into a distributed spam-sending monster that took instructions from a central source, were known first as "zombies" and later as "botnets." By making it appear as though the messages were coming from tens or hundreds of thousands of individual users, spammers had further hidden themselves and made their messages far more difficult for blacklists to halt. In 2004, AOL announced during congressional testimony that most of the spam it saw now came from botnets.

Spam fighters—largely Internet providers trying to protect their customers—at first tried their luck in court, but this was easier in the early days when spammers didn't hide themselves well. In the late 1990s, for instance, a dozen antispammers sued Sanford "Spamford" Wallace—a true character we'll meet again—for openly running one of the Internet's top spam operations from his base in Pennsylvania. Most of the plaintiffs settled out of court with Wallace, who agreed to stop spamming their networks, but the experience of litigating taught most Internet providers a lesson: lawsuits against individuals were not going to scale. Sure, one could go after a few of the top US-based spammers, but broader legal action wasn't feasible or affordable.

Merely identifying the spammer in question became difficult. One major Internet provider reported confidentially to the US government that it had collected 45 million pieces of spam from "honeypot" e-mail accounts it set up just for this purpose. After a major investigation, it found that only 2.6 million spam messages could even be linked back to a responsible party. Some 271 spammers were identified, but teams of lawyers could only find actual contact information for 91 of them. Simply identifying these took 12,100 hours—133 hours for each spammer found. Another Internet provider told the government that filing one lawsuit required one thousand hours of work by an eight-person team, thanks largely to the effectiveness of the various techniques spammers had adopted to hide their identities.

As the government noted when summing up these reports, "Not surprisingly, some ISPs believe that lawsuits against spammers are an expensive and often fruitless way to stop spam."

The antispammers turned from the source of the messages—now diversified by botnets across tens of thousands of machines—to the actual content of spam, and they developed their own ecosystem of software developers and filter designers. Sophisticated Bayesian filtering schemes analyzed billions of pieces of spam, "learning" what made up a spammer's pitch and then routing such messages into spam folders instead of user inboxes. The spammers responded, of course, building automated tools that inserted blocks of random text within each e-mail to confuse the filter. Filter designers flagged huge sets of keywords likely to be spam, words like "Viagra"; spammers began spelling it "V!@gr@." And every time a filter was tightened in response to some new spam development, more legitimate mail was caught accidentally—and, as any e-mail user can tell you, losing a single important message is much worse than seeing a bit of spam.

As the problem seemed to grow beyond the capabilities of private actors, hopes turned to an entity with even more resources—and the power to throw spammers in jail. It was time to see what government could accomplish.

/////

For years, both Republican and Democratic legislators were skeptical that federal power was needed against to clean up people's inboxes. Rep. Zoe Lofgren, a California lawyer who represented Silicon Valley in Congress, had publicly rejected a legislative approach for years. "We have a delete button, that's all we need," she was fond of saying. In the Senate, Conrad Burns admitted that none of his colleagues "really thought that this was a very serious problem" back in 1998. By 2003, however, the tone had changed, and Lofgren and Burns both supported a federal remedy for the "toxic sea of spam," in Burns's phrase, that was engulfing e-mail and threatening the increasingly important medium.

While Lofgren backed legislation in the House, Burns partnered with Senator Ron Wyden of Oregon to introduce the CAN-SPAM (Controlling the Assault of Non-Solicited Pornography And Marketing) Act in the Senate. Wyden was convinced the law could help. "Let me say that the spammers may not be quaking in their shoes this morning because a Montana cowboy [Burns] and a Jewish guy [Wyden] who wanted to be in the NBA are coming after them—but they sure ought to be," he told a conference.

This wasn't mere wishful thinking; the federal government had recently launched its Do Not Call list over the howls of the telemarketing industry and had achieved phenomenal success. Millions of Americans signed up instantly; unsolicited commercial calls to those numbers dried up. Why not just extend this winning idea to spam, the telemarketing of the Internet?

Proponents of legislation at first believed they might get the spam problem under control by launching a Do Not E-mail list. Others believed they could convince spammers to stick an "ADV" tag in the subject line of their e-mails, announcing the advertising content within. Some suggested further refinements, such as requiring more specific tags like "ADV 5 percent mortgages." It made a certain amount of sense— marketers could reach those actually looking for 5 percent mortgages, while everyone else could easily block the messages. Everyone wins!

The ideas got increasingly unlikely. At one point, Congress considered handing out bounties on spammers in an early federal attempt to crowdsource a solution to the problem. While only the government could actually sue spammers under this proposal, it would offer a percentage of any eventual court-ordered fine to whoever had helped the government find and prosecute a particular spammer. Lofgren was particularly boosterish. "Now, I'm busy, I will probably not participate in this bounty scheme, but I have an 18-year-old son who will," she said at the FTC's 2003 spam conference. "And, so, I really think of this structurally as unleashing the 18-year-olds to go after the spammers, and I have confidence that American 18-year-olds are up to the task."

None of this would happen. Unsolicited commercial e-mail had been tainted for so many years by outright scams and dubious products that the legitimate businesses who might comply with such laws didn't want to be lumped in with everything else arriving unasked for in user inboxes. They stayed out of the business altogether. The spammers who remained knew that most people would simply block every message with "ADV" in the subject line and so had no intention of adding it.

Bounties also posed huge problems. The idea proceeded far enough that Congress actually ordered the Federal Trade Commission (FTC) to investigate its feasibility. When the FTC submitted its "CAN-SPAM Informant Reward System" report to Congress, the language was mild— but the commission's unhappiness was evident. The agency warned that the hoped-for army of eighteen-year-olds wasn't equipped to provide good evidence. "Much of this sleuthing is based on intuition or other inadmissible perceptions, does not definitively identify the spammer, and would not constitute admissible evidence in an enforcement action," it said. The FTC saw huge problems just tracking all the tips, judging who deserved payment, and fighting off lawsuits from those who thought the cash was theirs. Fifty pages of such warnings were enough to deter Congress; the idea died a silent death.

As for a Do Not E-mail registry, it too earned an FTC feasibility study; when the report arrived, negativity dripped from its pages. Telephone calls could be tracked and authenticated—a by-product of the need to bill every call. But spam couldn't be tracked with any reliability. Without any idea of who was sending the spam, a centralized registry of millions of e-mail addresses might instead be used by spammers "as a mechanism for verifying the validity of e-mail addresses and, without authentication, the Commission would be largely powerless to identify those responsible for misusing the Registry," said the report. "The risk that spammers would misuse a Registry is so high that Consumers Union has stated that if the Commission were to adopt an individual e-mail address Registry and distribute the Registry to marketers, it 'would emphatically tell all 42 million subscribers [of the magazine *Consumer Reports*] not to sign up for it.'"

So that was that. What survived was the mild CAN-SPAM Act, which went into effect on January 1, 2004. How mild was it? Instead of outlawing spam, the law legalized it; critics called it the "You CAN SPAM Act." Spammers just had to follow a few basic rules for their messages:

1. refrain from advertising anything fraudulent;
2. include proper routing information (and avoid open relays and proxies);

3. avoid "deceptive subject headings";

4. label "adult" messages clearly in the subject line; and

5. provide an easy method to opt-out of future mailings.

If they did so, they could send unsolicited e-mail with impunity. CAN-SPAM's passage also overrode existing state laws, some of which had already criminalized spam or required the use of the "ADV" tag. No wonder that at a 2004 conference on spam and the law, noted law professor Lawrence Lessig called CAN-SPAM an "an abomination at the federal level."

The ability to send bulk e-mail was the law's carrot, designed to make spam at least more manageable and less overtly fraudulent by luring it into the open. The stick was increased civil penalties for violating CAN-SPAM's rules—and felony charges if the spam helped further fraudulent activity. Enforcing the law fell largely on the FTC, which gamely brought its first CAN-SPAM case in April 2004. It worked with postal inspectors and the US attorney in Detroit to shut down a Michigan-based outfit that was selling bogus diet patches and earning $100,000 a month doing so. The agency has done heroic work on spam in the last decade in a hundred or so cases against spammers. It has secured huge fines (though getting the spammers to pay them remains a problem), and its work has led to imprisonment of various spammers across the country.

But spam poses a scale problem. The FTC, US attorneys, state attorneys general, and the FBI all have now waged effective campaigns against particular spammers, but not even the combined resources of the US government can police the entire world. Botnets, the new spam-delivery mechanism of choice, have often been controlled from Eastern Europe, for instance. If CAN-SPAM had helped to push spammers out of the United States and into harder-to-reach jurisdictions, had the law achieved much?

"Once we pass a tough national law, let's understand what the spammers are likely to do," said Ron Wyden when he backed CAN-SPAM in 2003. "I think that the first thing they're going to do is try to move off-shore." Steps were taken to make this movement harder. Within a year of CAN-SPAM's passage, for instance, the FTC partnered with the UK's Office of Fair Trading to hold an international conference on spam that featured nineteen agencies from fifteen countries. But the spam continued to flow.

Two years after the law came into effect, the best the FTC could conclude was that "the Act has provided law enforcement agencies and ISPs with an additional tool to use when bringing suit against spammers." Spam itself had not declined—the agency suggested it was "leveling off." As for spammers, they hadn't stopped—they just made their businesses even more opaque. "Spammers have also sought to frustrate law enforcement by using increasingly complex multi-layered business arrangements," the FTC concluded.

A 2009 study published in the *International Journal of Cyber Criminology* by Portland State graduate student Alex Kigerl looked specifically at the effectiveness of CAN-SPAM. Kigerl used a sample of two million e-mails for his work; after examining them, he concluded that the "CAN-SPAM Act had no observable impact on the amount of spam sent." And the spam wasn't even following the minimal CAN-SPAM requirements; in fact, he wrote, "compliance with the accurate subject requirement was significantly decreased after CAN-SPAM."

I caught up with Kigerl to ask if anything over the last few years had changed his view on laws like CAN-SPAM; nothing had. "Even if we apprehended all spammers within the United States, there's still the whole rest of the world full of spammers with almost zero barriers to having their spam e-mails sent to America," he said.

Instead, he advocated a different approach to spam control, one relying on a new set of pressure points. "I think a better solution might be to target some of the banks that allow recipients of spam to purchase the fraudulently advertised goods," he added. "Apparently something like 80 percent of the spam-related transactions are handled by just a few banks."

Despite new laws in many countries, global spam levels have remained high throughout the second half of the decade. MessageLabs, which provides antispam services, has tracked spam volumes for years. Consider its global spam estimates between 2005 and 2010:

2005: 86.2 percent of all e-mail
2006: 85.3 percent of all e-mail
2007: 84.1 percent of all e-mail
2008: 81.2 percent of all e-mail
2009: 87.7 percent of all e-mail
2010: 89.1 percent of all e-mail

Particular spam operations can be tackled—a graph of spam volumes shows sharp declines whenever a major botnet is shuttered—but spam itself has proven resilient even to government action.

/////

Oleg Nikolaenko spent his teen years watching the spam wars play out as botnet kingpins and spam brokers made fortunes around him. Few suffered any consequences except wealth. In 2007—the year Nikolaenko turned twenty—Mega-D took pride of place in the botnet community and became a serious contributor to the spam problem worldwide. Everything about the network's operations revealed it as a quintessential product of the decade-long war on spam.

The complex business model. The FTC warned back in 2005 that the spamming business was becoming multilayered, and Mega-D was part of the overall trend toward specialization. The botnet's controller had the technical chops to build a 500,000-strong army of zombie spam computers around the globe—and that's what he apparently stuck to. Finding the products to hawk, writing the pitch messages, arranging payment and shipping solutions—it was all left to others. Mega-D was sold as a pure spam-delivery vehicle to anyone who could pay.

And it was treated as a business. Chat logs between spammers, leaked in late 2011 and translated into English by security researcher Brian Krebs, show a person known as "Docent" (alleged to be Nikolaenko) selling botnet services to a huge Russian operation known as SpamIt, which lined up delivery mechanisms for spammers. Docent promises that he can deliver 500 million messages a day and says that, "according to US laws, even spam can lead to 1,000 years of imprisonment. Especially in large volumes. And from bots." But most of the conversation would sound legitimate in any other context: commissions, percentages, chargebacks. The Mega-D operator even complains about getting ripped off, writing, "I do not like my current partner. He screwed me over $50k. And he does not admit it, bastard."

It was a business that made plenty of cash. According to these chat logs, Mega-D was paid $325,000 between 2007 and 2010 by SpamIt alone.

The delivery mechanism. It was a botnet, of course, and one of the world's largest for a time. Internet hosting providers were too centralized; it was simple to find those spewing out huge volumes of spam and have them disconnect the spammer. "Bulletproof" hosting—which refused to disconnect customers and could withstand technical and legal attacks—continued in places like China, but was now largely used for the actual websites spammers directed recipients to visit. Private spam blacklists could cut off any centralized delivery service in the event that Internet providers weren't helpful. So sending the messages was now the job of botnets, and Mega-D's operator knew to how to play the game.

The location. Internet crime has flourished in Eastern European states such as Russia and Ukraine; in early 2012, seven of the ten most important spamming operations identified by the UK antispam group Spam-Haus were believed to be in Eastern Europe. As the *Christian Science Monitor* put it in 2010, "The pursuit of Internet fraud is often a cat-and-mouse game between international authorities and criminal organizations located mostly in Eastern Europe, where immunity laws are weak and foreign governments do not consider Internet crime as a serious threat." And why should they? Most of those targeted by spam live in places like Western Europe and the United States.

The anonymity. Unlike early spammers, the Mega-D owner covered his tracks better, at least in public. He sent messages composed by others, which pointed to websites that were managed by others and distributed from hundreds of thousands of machines not linked personally to the botnet owner. The domain names publicly registered as command-and-control servers, which sent instructions to all the machines in the botnet, all featured inaccurate contact information. Even Mega-D's spam clients didn't know the operator's real name; to both SpamIt and Affking, two of the largest clients, he was known only by the screen name Docent. Such protection did not ultimately help, but it was certainly several steps beyond what an earlier generation of spammers had even bothered doing.

/////

The tick/tock of measures and countermeasures has produced a spamming situation that is, to put it mildly, suboptimal. But the success of the spammers isn't some law of nature; it's possible that the legal or technical pressure eventually will squeeze spam tightly enough to bring the problem under control. Fifteen years of enforcement have pushed spammers toward botnets, and botnet owners to Eastern Europe. Prosecutions of people like Nikolaenko take time to realize, but they send a message:

Yes, you can earn piles of money spamming, but you can't come to the United States and spend it. Continued FTC civil actions against domestic spammers make overseeing a worldwide spam operation from within the United States a risky venture.

If countries like Russia decide to push back hard on spam, they could raise the "hassle factor" for spammers even further, and Russia has been more cooperative on spam of late. At the end of 2010, it announced a major investigation of SpamIt; the operation shut down and its owner is believed to have left the country. But the *New York Times* account of the SpamIt investigation is a reminder of just how unusual this reaction was. "The officials' actions were a departure from Russia's usual laissez faire approach to online crime," said the paper. "Why, after years of ignoring spammers, Russian authorities have now acted has left online security experts puzzled."

SpamHaus estimates that only 100 people in the world now are hard-core spammers, so it wouldn't take many prosecutions to shrink the community. Technical measures to better authenticate e-mail are always being developed. Spam filters have improved, so even when spam is sent, most of it is not delivered. Private companies like Microsoft are increasingly suppressing entire botnets by cutting off their command-and-control servers (thus preventing any new spam instructions from being sent) or by removing the malware on user computers that powers the botnet. New calls to "follow the money" have led to increasing pressure on the few key banks in the world that handle the spammers' cash. And the historical insecurity of the Windows operating system—which made botnets so simple to build for so many years—has been tightened dramatically in recent years.

But botnet creators continue to learn from the example of people like Nikolaenko and from the demise of Mega-D. Back in 2009, a year before Nikolaenko's arrest, the online security company FireEye decided to mount its own attack on Mega-D after studying how the botnet's code operated. Most botnets require regular instructions from a controller, telling them what to do or updating their security settings or providing new spam to send. Mechanisms to share these instructions with each machine in the botnet can be complex, featuring multiple fallback approaches to establish contact with the botnet owner in case the authorities disrupt one. Mega-D featured such fallbacks, but FireEye decided to try for a knockout blow anyway.

The first line of control for Mega-D was a defined set of command-and-control servers, most located within the United States. They could be reached at odd domains such as foodcaters.info, gondolfrazrv3.com, and zavaretalies.com—but if researchers couldn't shut them all down simultaneously, the Mega-D operator could use any one of the still-functioning domains to pass a new set of contact instructions to the botnet, including an entire new set of command-and-control domain names. FireEye researchers shared their evidence package with Internet hosting companies and the domain name registrars who controlled these servers and domain names; most were quickly taken offline.

With these hard-coded command-and-control servers out of action, Mega-D resorted to a common fallback technique in which each machine in the botnet used a custom algorithm to generate an identical string of letters that were calculated based on the current date. If unable to reach the hard-coded servers, the botnet would reach out to this new domain name (the random domain name generated for November 4, 2009, was "dfcznu9q.biz," for instance), looking for new instructions each day.

This put a tremendous strain on anyone trying to take Mega-D down. Every one of these random domains had to be registered in advance by the "good guys" to keep it out of the hands of Mega-D's owner; missing even one day's domain name meant that the botnet could potentially reach a command-and-control server and therefore download new bits of code and new instructions. "Unless someone is committed enough to pre-register those domains," FireEye researchers wrote, "the bot herders can always come forward and register those domains and take botnet control back." Even a "dead" botnet could be instantly resurrected whenever the good guys gave up grabbing new domains.

"After seeing all these fallback mechanisms, it doesn't look very easy to kill [Mega-D] in one go, but hurting this beast might not be that difficult," wrote FireEye's Atif Mushtaq in the days after the company's attack on Mega-D. At the very least, the attack "will be another gesture to show the bad guys that the security industry is awake and keeping a close eye on them."

FireEye worked with domain registrars to set the future domains aside, making them off-limits to the botnet controller, and then disrupted the hard-coded domains. The work had an immediate effect. Mega-D's spam deliveries nearly disappeared, dropping from 11.8 percent of all worldwide spam sent on November 1 to under 0.1 percent three days later. Mega-D was down.

FireEye's researchers had done more than irritate the botnet's owner—they may have interrupted his vacation. Nikolaenko was in Las Vegas at the 2009 SEMA auto show when the takedown happened. Although his visa application said he would remain in the United States until November 11, he flew back to Russia on November 9.

"Based on the timing of the FireEye attack on the Mega-D botnet," wrote the FBI's Brett Banner in his complaint against Nikolaenko, "I believe that Nikolaenko left the US early to repair the damage caused by FireEye." Mega-D's owner was successful at reviving his creation—by November 22, the operator had again found ways to make contact with the machines in his botnet and provided them with new instructions. Soon, Mega-D was actually exceeding its pretakedown spam levels and accounted for 17 percent of all worldwide spam. When Nikolaenko ended up in jail a year later, Mega-D traffic died down, too.

Other botnet takedowns followed. Microsoft in particular took an aggressive stance toward botnet operators and sought court orders allowing its own investigators to seize key servers, and it pursued suspects overseas. But the success of these takedowns produced an inevitable response: botnet operators found ways to code around the weaknesses that made them vulnerable.

For instance, while Mega-D was taken down in large part because of its reliance on centralized command-and-control servers, the later Alureon botnet eliminated such servers altogether. Instead, it relied on a serverless, peer-to-peer command scheme in which each machine in the botnet could pass control information on to other machines rather than having to make contact with a centralized server. In 2011, researchers described Alureon as "practically indestructible." Tick, tock.

A decade from now, we may look back at the spam wars as a historical artifact, curious to recall but with little daily impact on our lives. But it's more likely that spam will still be with us. Chaos, like water, digs out new channels when old ones are blocked.

7

SLIPPERY FISH: SPAM II

ATTACK OF THE STATES

In 2003, spam was posing real problems for the then-largest Internet provider in the United States, AOL. Not that AOL was itself a stranger to unsolicited mass mail. Derided by the tech elite as the home of hopeless Internet "newbs," the company was still widely remembered at the time for the astonishing way it had blasted the nation with sign-up CDs in the late 1990s. So brutal was the rain of discs that at times it appeared AOL was single-handedly keeping the US Postal Service afloat.

The company's marketing plan had involved the actual mailing of physical objects. It cost money to stamp the CDs, it cost money to ship them. But freed from such constraints as "physicality," bulk e-mailers were positioned to absolutely eclipse legitimate companies like AOL when it came to blanketing people with unsolicited messages.

AOL had its headquarters in Loudon County, Virginia, where it was part of the burgeoning tech scene around Washington, DC, and an important piece of the state's economy. As the spam problem escalated from "torrent" to "deluge," AOL executives went to the Virginia legislature for help. In 2003, Virginia became the first state in the country to make spamming a felony, beating the federal government to action.

The Virginia law set a high threshold for prosecution. To qualify, spammers had to send more than 12,000 unsolicited e-mails in a day, or 100,000 in a month, or a million in a year. In addition, the law applied only when e-mail header information was forged to disguise the sender. Want to spam AOL under your real name? The law didn't care, and it didn't need to care—unforged mass e-mails would have been trivial to block.

So spammers routinely forged everything they could in a bid to get their messages through, and AOL had no trouble finding a spammer who qualified for action under the law. Indeed, the company was then being assaulted by one of the top ten spammers in the world, a man whose messages pitched everything from a "Penny Stock Picker" to "Internet history erasers" to a FedEx refund claims product. He wasn't a hard-to-reach foreigner; most of his messages asked people to mail $29.95 to a North Carolina address. AOL had traced the many IP addresses he used to an area around the state capitol, Raleigh.

The company turned its information over to the Virginia attorney general's office, where it ended up in the hands of Assistant Attorney General Gene Fishel, head of the state's Computer Crimes Section. As the first felony spam prosecution in the entire nation, whatever case he began with would set a precedent, and Fishel was determined to hit his mark once he took aim. The AOL spammer's volume was so high and his location so close—only 2.5 hours away by car—that Fishel decided to proceed.

With limited state-level resources to pursue computer crimes, Fishel put three-quarters of his own work time into the case for an entire year. His office tried to run down the source of the spam by tracing it backward along its electronic journey, but as with countless other spammers, this at first proved difficult. The headers had been forged and were useless, but the perpetrator had actually blasted out the spam using his own computers on lines belonging to his own Internet account.

The search also showed investigators that "follow the money" was a reliable way to track down shadowy spammers, who have a hard time remaining truly anonymous if they want to get paid. This spammer certainly did want to get paid, so Virginia investigators trekked down to Raleigh and found the mailing address named in the spam: a Mailboxes, Etc. location offering rental mailboxes. The store's records named the box as belonging to one Jeremy Jaynes, a well-off resident of the well-off Raleigh suburb of Cary.

But where, exactly, did he live? Jaynes had multiple expensive homes in Cary, and some of the addresses linked to his websites were actually vacant lots. A bit more digging revealed one key fact, courtesy of phone company AT&T: one of Jaynes's homes had an almost unimaginable number of number of fat Internet pipes in the form of dedicated T1 lines.

The Virginia attorney general's office, with its 300 employees, had a few T1 lines of its own. But this single Jaynes home had sixteen. Phone company trucks showed up at the address so often to add or maintain lines that even the neighbors took notice. Jaynes was spending tens of thousands of dollars each month to wire the home for Internet access, and Fishel suspected that he had found both the spammer and his den.

In December 2003, half a year after the Virginia spam law had taken effect, investigators headed down to North Carolina and obtained a search warrant from a Raleigh judge. Local Wake County police came along for muscle, as did a few federal agents intrigued by the allegations of Jaynes's wrongdoing.

A few days later, the warrant team convened in the 5:00 a.m. dark outside the $400,000 brick home with the T1 lines. They swarmed up to the door and pounded hard, demanding that Jaynes open. The team didn't expect him to be there—Jaynes actually resided in a million-dollar house across town—but after a minute, the door opened. Before them stood Jeremy Jaynes, a puffy-faced guy in his early thirties, in nothing more than his boxers and a T-shirt.

Police poured in. One snapped a picture of Jaynes—who did not look pleased—while most fanned out to search the house. It held little of interest. The house was empty apart from a single bed in one bedroom, but agents hit the jackpot when they walked into the attic. Jaynes's base of operations was spread out before them, a knot of desktop computers and servers and monitors. In the corner sat discs containing more than 176 million e-mail addresses and 1.3 billion more usernames, many stolen from AOL by that company's rogue employee. One computer was actually running an AOL spam script as agents entered the room. Small checks were everywhere; during Jaynes's trial, Fishel would spend two hours simply listing every one found in the attic.

The dummy house served as Jaynes's office, with the added benefit of keeping angry spam victims from showing up at his actual front door; still, Jaynes and his wife did spend at least some time there. As Fishel later described the scene during a 2007 "spam summit" at the Federal Trade Commission, investigators "found cases and cases of hundred dollar bottles of wine, twelve in each case, and the night before these guys apparently have so much money that they were drinking the wine out of wine glasses, throwing the wine glasses away, not washing them, and then grabbing a new wine glass to drink more wine. So, these guys were living the high life."

Jaynes was arrested and taken back to Virginia, where he was prosecuted as a spam felon. At trial, Fishel argued that Jaynes had become the top spammer on AOL's network by raking in $10 million from victims and passing it through at least six dummy corporations—and that he had provided nothing in return. The spammer was also a fraudster.

In Virginia, juries both convict and sentence defendants. Though

Jaynes faced up to fifteen years in prison, the jury convicted and sentenced him to just nine years. Brian McWilliams, author of the book *Spam Kings*, argues that Jaynes was unsavory but that he didn't deserve nearly a decade behind bars. "For this violation of Virginia's spam law, Jaynes faces a prison sentence comparable to that of people convicted of violent crimes such as rape," McWilliams wrote in 2005. "Is forging headers on par with heinous crimes such as armed robbery, kidnapping, and child molestation?"

I put the question to the Virginia attorney general's office. Caroline Gibson, a spokesperson, noted that although Jaynes was convicted for forging e-mail headers, this had actually been a "major, major fraud case." She pointed out that many white-collar criminals do more than nine years in jail for nonviolent offenses and added, "We obviously didn't think [the sentence] was disproportionate."

In the end, the question of proportionality hardly mattered; Jaynes would have his convictions overturned.

/////

By limiting their law to high-volume unsolicited e-mailers who also disguised the source of their messages, the Virginia legislature thought it was on solid constitutional ground. But e-mail, being "speech," can only be limited in certain tightly defined ways, and Jaynes's lawyers wasted no time in claiming that the law infringed on their client's freedom of speech.

The Virginia Court of Appeals thought not and affirmed Jaynes's conviction. The case then went to the state Supreme Court, where the conviction was again upheld in early 2008. Then, in an unusual step, the court appeared to have doubts; it asked to rehear oral arguments in the case. On September 12, 2008, the court withdrew its original order and replaced it with a new one—and it agreed that the law had not carved out enough space for speech. As written, the law "would prohibit all bulk e-mail containing anonymous political, religious, or other expressive speech," wrote Justice Steven Agee. "For example, were the Federalist Papers just being published today via e-mail, that transmission by Publius would violate the statute."

Virginia legislators had missed a single, crucial provision when drafting their bill: the law needed to target only "commercial" speech, which receives less protection than expressive speech, to avoid the Publius problem. But because it did not, the state Supreme Court ruled that the law was "unconstitutionally overbroad on its face because it prohibits the anonymous transmission of all unsolicited bulk e-mails including those containing political, religious, or other speech protected by the First Amendment to the United States Constitution."

The Virginia attorney general at the time, Bob McConnell, claimed that the state law wasn't about speech at all; it was about trespassing on someone else's computer network. He vowed to take the case to the US Supreme Court but was refused a hearing. Jaynes's convictions for spamming were vacated.

But it wasn't back to a life of one-time-use wine glasses and spare houses. The Virginia investigation brought Jaynes to the attention of federal authorities, who found a host of things with which to charge him. He was soon accused of joining a group that had obtained large blocks of shares in publicly traded companies through "forged corporate documents" and "fake attorney opinion letters," according to a federal complaint. With share ownership hidden by offshore entities, the group tried to manipulate the stock price of the companies in question through e-mail spam, junk faxing, voice-mail spamming, and search-engine advertising.

Those who don't respond to spam will always find it incredible that such schemes work, yet they seem to have some effect. In a single February 2004 incident, Jaynes was accused of spamming promotional information on a company called BodyScan to a huge number of randomly chosen office fax machines. BodyScan's stock price rose a bit afterward; when Jaynes and his fellow conspirators then sold 1.5 million shares in the company, they made $2.6 million.

Jaynes was convicted of securities fraud in North Carolina even as his spam appeals were winding their way through the state courts in Virginia. He served time in an Oklahoma federal prison, from which he was released just before Valentine's Day 2010. Two months after his release, the Virginia state legislature finally amended its troubled antispam bill. Rather than targeting all "unsolicited bulk e-mail" with forged headers, the amended law targeted "unsolicited commercial electronic mail" with forged headers. Though the law remains on the books, no one else has been prosecuted in Virginia.

Despite its outcome, the Jaynes prosecution was "absolutely worth it," Caroline Gibson insists. The initial spam arrest took a major fraudster off the streets for a while, and the case eventually led to a successful federal conviction on other charges.

The state Supreme Court also answered the crucial question of jurisdiction: did Virginia have the right to grab a spammer from another state and put him on trial? The court quoted with approval an early twentieth-century ruling: "It has long been a commonplace of criminal liability that a person may be charged in the place where the evil results, though he is beyond the jurisdiction when he starts the train of events of which the evil is the fruit." The principle remains alive and well in the Internet era. If you cause a local harm, you can face a local trial.

/////

But the case also illustrates why more spammers aren't prosecuted. Even at a time when people like Jaynes were brazen, spamming directly from their own machines out of wealthy suburban homes, the cases against them can be labor intensive. Though nearly any state may prosecute a mass spammer—since at least some people in the state no doubt are targets—few do anything about the problem.

"We are not the biggest unit in the world," Gene Fishel explained to the FTC's 2007 spam summit, "and one of the problems with state enforcement of this is—as opposed to federal enforcement, who has a ton more resources—is that these are very resource-intensive cases, and this tied up our unit for months. It tied up our unit investigating this for six to eight months, maybe, trying to develop this case to bring it to fruition."

Resource-constrained state and local prosecutors tend to pursue cases with a stronger local nexus and with more obvious harms; child pornography and sex abuse are staples of such investigative activity. Over time, antispam laws and prosecutions have worked just well enough to push many top spammers and their botnets offshore. These far-off spammers create problems for the whole country and the world; why should any one state spend resources to build a case against someone they can never arrest by themselves, anyway? Gibson told me, "We just don't have enough people to make a conscious effort" on the spam problem. "We have a lot of things on our plate; our hands are full and these cases never stop."

The Jaynes case was relatively straightforward; when cases get more complicated, the investigation takes even more work. For instance, in the early 2000s, the Washington State attorney general went after an out-of-state spammer, one operating out of Minnesota. His spam advertised the services of a real debt-adjustment company, so Paula Selis of the Washington attorney general's High-Tech Unit figured it couldn't be too hard to locate the man. But she was wrong. Here's how she described the hunt:

> We figured, well, we'll just contact the debt-adjustment company and find out who the spammer is, you know, how do they get their leads. Well, we contacted them and they said, well, we

don't know, we contract with a company in New York who gives us the leads. So, we contacted them with a pre-suit subpoena. We'd already sent one to the company in Florida. And the company in New York said, well, we contract with another company in Chicago. We sent a CID [civil investigative demand—like a subpoena, a way to get documents for an investigation] to the company in Chicago, and so on and so on and so on. We found out that really ultimately we couldn't trace the spammer that way. What we wound up doing was finding out where the spammer was hooked up at the time the ad was run, what the IP address was. We found out that it belonged to Microsoft. We CIDed Microsoft, who in fact had leased out that line to another company. We had to CID that ISP [and] found out who the line was leased to. Of course it wasn't leased to the spammer; it was leased to somebody who used a fake identify.

The only way her office found its target was by tracing the credit card used to pay the Internet provider bill. "That's a lot of steps," Selis concluded. "That's 14 pre-suit subpoenas, and that gives you an idea of how difficult it is."

Laws struggle to keep up with the spam tick/tock. In trying to make its law narrow, Virginia only criminalized unsolicited mass commercial e-mail with false headers. In the years that followed, some spammers developed techniques to spam using unforged headers. Others simply moved on from e-mail, spamming instant messaging accounts and social networks like Facebook instead.

Legislators might respond by crafting broader laws, but this can be tricky. When it comes to speech, breadth always threatens to sweep in protected content, and no prosecutor wants to invest years in a case only to have the law that undergirds it overturned by a court. Busting spammers under the usual fraud statutes is another approach, one used regularly by the FTC—but what if the spam advertises a legitimate product?

Even when prosecutors win, they can't seem to squeeze much money from defendants. In the Washington State case, the entire operation netted a judgment of $10,000; prosecutors had spent far, far more in pressing their case. "So, you know, a sort of happy ending, but, you know, not exactly an economical one," Selis concluded when she told the story. As for putting the spammers in jail, that has been even more difficult, as the Jaynes case in Virginia showed.

Investigation and prosecution of spammers has become such a hassle that it is today more often pursued by better-funded federal agencies, and often as a civil rather than criminal matter. But the feds have learned the hard way that finding a spammer and winning a court case against him is often not the end of the matter. Stopping a spammer who doesn't want to quit remains hugely difficult.

A FEDERAL CASE

On a warm April 2007 morning, one of the world's most notorious spammers walked through the doors of the Lloyd D. George Federal Courthouse in Las Vegas. Though the Federal Trade Commission was attempting to collect a $4 million judgment against him, Sanford "Spamford" Wallace showed up to his sworn deposition without a lawyer—and without any of the documents required of him.

Wallace, though nominally cooperative, had been nearly impossible to reach. When attorneys from the social network MySpace had sued him weeks before, the process server tasked with delivering legal documents couldn't make contact with Wallace and eventually went to the OPM Nightclub where Wallace worked weekends as a $400-a-week disc jockey under the name "DJ MasterWeb." The process server claimed to have approached Wallace at the club before being intercepted by security guards; the lawsuit papers were literally thrown at Wallace in an attempt to get good service on him.

FTC lawyer David Frankel, who was overseeing Wallace's courthouse questioning as part of a separate spam case brought by the government, had resorted to telephone calls, FedEx packages, and e-mails to contact Wallace; he even sent a personal messenger on occasion. Despite the extraordinary measures, Frankel didn't know when he showed up to court that April morning whether Wallace would actually arrive.

Wallace did arrive. After swearing to tell the truth in his testimony, he explained to Frankel that the problems weren't the result of malice but were instead caused by utter disorganization. "Let me just state, for the record, that I am chronically disorganized and that's one of the reasons it's so difficult to communicate with me, and some of the things that would appear to the normal person to be uncooperative, it's actually possible and very often related to the fact that I'm a very disorganized person," he said at the beginning of his testimony. "I think you'll see that as we continue this conversation that as a lot of documents haven't been filed or organized in a very efficient manner by myself, I want to just state for the record that that is something that I could probably have a psychiatrist to verify if I had to."

Yet Wallace had been organized enough to become a massive spammer. Born in 1968, he attended high school in Maplewood, New Jersey, but realized the academic world wasn't for him. He tried attending college twice, first at SUNY-Buffalo and then at New Jersey's Ramapo College; he didn't last a semester at either. He later described himself as "not a good student."

That didn't stop him from finding monetary success—and public notoriety—during the mid-1990s with his Pennsylvania company Cyber Promotions. As a heavyset twentysomething with close-cropped hair and glasses, Wallace first spammed fax machines and then moved on to e-mail, believing that he had a legal right to market his wares as he saw fit. Dubbed "Spamford" by opponents, he eventually embraced the nickname and even registered the domain spamford.com. (In 1997, Hormel sent him a letter objecting to the name on the grounds that it used the company's potted meat SPAM trademark). Unlike other spammers who hid their identities, Wallace regularly tangled in public with antispam crusaders.

Cyber Promotions quickly became so hated that a dozen Internet service providers, including AOL, sued Wallace in the late 1990s, each hoping to halt his flood of junk e-mail despite the lack of antispam laws at the time. Wallace pressed on, but the lawsuits did cramp his business. He settled several of them by agreeing not to spam the particular network at issue, which gradually whittled down the list of places he could send spam without getting into more trouble.

Antispam vigilantes were also after him and his company. They hacked his website, replacing its homepage, and went after the Michigan Internet provider that served Cyber Promotions. Wallace was angry enough about the hacking to offer a $15,000 reward and claimed he was alerting the FBI.

By 1998, the pressure was so intense that Wallace had trouble finding an Internet provider to offer service to his company. A local Philadelphia paper reported that Wallace had returned to his roots in junk faxing despite the fact that federal law now prohibited the practice. Local residents were furious; one managed to get Cyber Promotions delisted from the Better Business Bureau.

In April 1998, Wallace publicly announced his "retirement" from spamming. After several more failed ventures and a failed marriage, he moved to New Hampshire and in January 2002 bought a nightclub called Plum Crazy from Walter Rines, a former spam partner. The club, just outside of Rochester, proved popular; few visitors knew that club owner DJ MasterWeb had such a colorful past.

When *Wired* magazine visited Plum Crazy in 2003, Wallace appeared to be a changed man. Those lawsuits from Internet providers hadn't killed his business; "they put me into business—a business that worked," he said at the time. Even top antispam lawyers were pleased to see the change of heart. The *Wired* story included a line that at the time seemed perfectly sane: "I think the world of Sanford," said Pete Wellborn, an Atlanta attorney who won a $2 million judgment against Wallace on behalf of EarthLink in 1998. "He really is a man of his word, unlike the spammers we see now who are either ignorant or common criminals."

But Wallace soon needed money. Plum Crazy went bankrupt; Wallace sold his house and moved to Las Vegas. He revived an older business of his called SmartBot and soon began a scheme in which he infected computers with spyware that then popped up messages selling an "antispyware program" to clean the infection. This finally moved the feds to action. The Federal Trade Commission filed suit against Wallace in 2004 to halt his SpamBot practices. FTC lawyers worked the case for two years and in March 2006 obtained a default judgment of $4 million when Wallace didn't show up in court to contest the charges.

In October of that year, Wallace's friend Rines was also hit with an injunction in an online marketing case. While this might have seemed like a good time for each man to lie low, the pair instead partnered again. They were soon at work on a new plan to make money marketing through the newly hot social networks. (The two "wasted little time in violating the Court's Order" is how FTC lawyers later put it.) Their plan targeted the hugely popular MySpace site with the ultimate goal of directing MySpace users to websites advertising such things as ring tones and adult dating services.

Few people would click such low-quality links if they were clearly presented as ads. The beauty of the Wallace/Rines approach was that because their links appeared as messages from a MySpace user's actual friends rather than as ads, clickthrough rates were high—as were profits. The FTC estimated that the scheme raked in at least $555,850.04 (the actual tally was probably higher).

The project showed real, if devious, creativity. In order to access people's MySpace accounts, Wallace and Rines devised a plan to get people to hand over their account information. No subject was off limits. Could the resurrection of Jesus somehow be used to generate money from sex sites? Yes, it could. In one memorable exploit, the pair used MySpace accounts they had created to send 392,726 unsolicited messages pitching Easter e-cards to other MySpace users. When the recipients clicked the link to view the online card, they were asked if they would like to "forward" the card to their own friends. They did so by entering their MySpace password and username into a form that looked a lot like the actual MySpace login page; Wallace and Rines would then add the accounts to their database. Later, they would log into these accounts and spam links to people's friends, advertising whatever websites were willing to pay them. Visitors to the Easter e-card site who tried to leave the page without divulging their MySpace credentials were simply redirected to the advertising sites.

Even for a network the size of MySpace, which had 50 million registered users in early 2006, Wallace quickly became a serious problem. As the technical side of the operation, he used automated tools to log in to more than 300,000 MySpace accounts and send more than 890,000 messages with links. The MySpace abuse team received more than 800 complaints about this behavior. In early 2007, the company filed a lawsuit against Wallace, and the FTC soon went after both men for violating the injunctions against more spamming. But Wallace defended his actions.

During his deposition with Frankel, the FTC lawyer, Wallace insisted that the messages he sent to other MySpace users weren't "unsolicited" at all. This was the beauty of sending links from one MySpace user to the user's friends. "A message between two friends is not defined as 'unsolicited' by several standards," Wallace said. "If I call you up tomorrow and ask you if you'd like me to send you a document, is that an unsolicited phone call, or do we have an existing relationship?"

Besides, this wasn't e-mail in the traditional technical sense, he said. "It's not something coming from a stranger with a fake return address like the CAN-SPAM act is apparently trying to address.... This is friend to friend communication, and we don't evade any type of friend to friend blocking techniques. We don't trick in any way. We don't trick people into getting messages from their friends. It's based solely on their friend's action [in giving login information to Wallace]." Wallace insisted that he had found a novel, legal way to market websites. "I've just been working with [Rines] on MySpace-related activities, advertising and Internet traffic and things of that sort, nothing in violation of your order," he said.

Frankel let it go and turned to the question of the money. Why hadn't Wallace paid the millions he owed the FTC? After all, Wallace had pulled in more than $4 million from SmartBot alone and was earning hundreds of thousands from his work on MySpace. Wallace insisted he was in debt, that he no longer had a credit card because "I basically could not pay off some of my credit card bills," and that he had made big payments to six casinos for gambling debts—including $350,000 to the MGM Grand Mirage. But beyond that, he was maddeningly vague.

He said he could not recall the amounts he had paid to other casinos. He claimed to have no real idea of the total income he had made over the years. And he could not explain what had happened to all of his money:

Q. [Frankel] Well, here's the kicker with all that. What happened to all this money? What happened to the $4 million plus, where is it today?

A. [Wallace] Most of it was spent, I had debts and all this has to be—all this has to be reconciled through the use of this bank account which I would like to get cleared and taken care of with you, so that you can see exactly where the monies went. It's all pretty much a pretty obvious story if you look at the bank.

Q. What's your—give me the general answer. What happened to the money? Right now you're saying you have to show me documents, but where did the money go? Where is it? It's a lot of money.

A. Yeah. I mean I had a lot of debt, and honestly I don't know exactly where the money went. I would have to look at my bank account with you, and I'm not evading your question. I just don't know how to give a general answer to that. And monies went out and came in for three years.

Q. I'm not a rich guy, but if I had $4 million and I have nothing now, I would have at least some sense as to where the money went.

A. I had over a million dollars in casino debts.

Q. Okay. Grant that. Now, where did the other $3 million go?

A. Again, this is a very impossible question for me to answer without having actual paperwork in front of me to go over specific itemization of what happened to the money and what didn't happen to the money.

Although he claimed that he currently had only $20,000 in a checking account, Wallace drove a $30,000 car with only 1,500 miles on it, had a $1,100-a-month apartment, and had just purchased a $1,400 watch. How did he afford it all, Frankel asked, on his $400-a-week DJ income? "I could not afford my rent if I did not have the other business," Wallace admitted, referring to his MySpace activities. When the money got tight, he went back to what he knew.

Frankel was resigned. "I'm trying to help you reform," he said, as the day of sparring drew to a close, "which is probably not going to happen, but I'm trying."

/////

The hoped-for reformation was not to be. In the MySpace civil lawsuit, the one where the process server had allegedly thrown the papers at Wallace in an attempt to serve him, Wallace refused to comply with court orders. He offered the same set of excuses about total disorganization that he had given Frankel. As a 2008 CNET article put it, "Each time, MySpace waited and each time Wallace failed to comply. Early on, Wallace informed MySpace he was having a hard time finding legal counsel. Soon after, he said he couldn't comply because he was unaware of his court dates; he wasn't accepting mail or signing for packages and that's why he missed receiving notifications."

The judge, fed up with all the delays, eventually ruled Wallace in contempt and awarded MySpace $230 million dollars to be paid jointly by Wallace and Rines. Several months later, in September 2008, the FTC successfully convinced the chief federal judge in New Hampshire to hold both Wallace and Rines in contempt for their MySpace activities. They were ordered to "disgorge" the $555,850.04 in cash that the FTC had been able to track.

In early 2009, Facebook filed suit against Wallace after he tried his MySpace-style "marketing" on a new social network. Wallace failed to comply with court orders in the case and a default judgment hearing was scheduled for June 12. The day before the hearing, Facebook found out that Wallace had filed for bankruptcy in Las Vegas, which granted him an automatic stay on the default proceedings. But Wallace had not filed all the required documents with the bankruptcy court—perhaps he truly was pathologically disorganized, or perhaps the bankruptcy filing was just a delay tactic. The bankruptcy court threw his case out in late July, making Wallace again a viable target for Facebook. Company lawyers asked the judge to find Wallace in default and argued that, by their calculations, he owed them $7 billion.

The judge wasn't about to hand out $7 billion antispam awards but in October he did award Facebook $711 million in damages when Wallace still refused to appear. ("The Court is not persuaded that an award of statutory damages in excess of seven billion dollars is proportionate to Wallace's offenses," wrote the judge.) Facebook rather optimistically declared victory. "While we don't expect to receive the vast majority of the award, we hope that this will act as a continued deterrent against these criminals," said a post on the company's blog.

To summarize the absurd situation as it stood at the start of 2011: Wallace had been targeted by a major federal agency and now owed it $4,555,850.04 ($4 million for SpamBot plus a separate $555,850.04 for his MySpace antics); he had been sued by MySpace and hit with a $230-million judgment; he was the subject of several court-ordered injunctions against his behavior; and he owed Facebook $711 million.

Yet no one seemed able to squeeze any cash out of him, nor could they get him to stop spamming. According to the judge in the Facebook case, Wallace had spent a good bit of 2009 ignoring the court's initial temporary restraining order and continued his Facebook account harvesting and link spamming.

Perhaps what Wallace said was all true: he was a big-spending, boom-and-bust guy who paid no real attention to his finances, who missed court dates and didn't produce documents because he was supremely disorganized. Perhaps he really had moved from one venture to the next with good intentions, always believing that he had tweaked his approach just enough to remain legal. But increasingly, no one cared about the reasons; they just wanted Wallace to stop.

Pete Wellborn, the lawyer who had tangled with Wallace in the 1990s and who believed that Wallace had gone straight, told me in late 2012, "I absolutely believed Sanford when I made that statement nearly 15 years ago." Without personal knowledge of Wallace, Wellborn ventured no comment on the recent spamming charges. But "if any of the more recent charges against Sanford are true, it is a sad and disappointing state of affairs," he told me. "Like him or not, Sanford is crazy smart and could have been ultra-successful in any variety of legitimate technology ventures."

/////

"I was reminded of a quote by LBJ [US President Lyndon Baines Johnson]," said veteran FTC attorney Joshua Millard when I asked him about the difficulty of stopping a devoted spammer. "It's one thing to tell a fellow to go to hell; it's another thing to actually make him go there." Millard had led the FTC prosecution of Wallace during one of the spammer's many brushes with the agency. Though Millard believed that fines were generally "persuasive" deterrents, he acknowledged that the FTC sees "a small but hearty number of defendants who can be highly resistant to persuasion. A fellow like Wallace, somebody who's engaged in that much spamming over the years—that's very unusual—it really speaks to the degree that for him it's almost force of habit."

Finally, one judge had enough. Convinced that Wallace had "willfully violated" his initial restraining order in the Facebook case, Judge Jeremy Fogel at last referred Wallace to the local US attorney's office and requested that Wallace be prosecuted for criminal contempt.

After the criminal contempt referral, breaking Wallace of his habit became the job of the US attorney for the Northern District of California. No longer limited to fines, criminal contempt charges carried the threat of real jail time—the only absolutely surefire way to stop a spammer. The FBI investigated Wallace's Facebook activities for two years before the government finally filed its case, charging that that Wallace had connected to Facebook from 143 different, proxied IP addresses "in order to deceive Facebook" and had sent 27 million pieces of spam through 500,000 compromised Facebook accounts. On August 4, 2011,

Wallace—then forty-three years old—surrendered to FBI agents. "Interesting day to say the least," he wrote the next day on social network Google+ after posting a $100,000 bail.

The government's indictment suggests just how committed to spamming Wallace had become. In March 2009, he had been ordered to stop all contact with Facebook; he allegedly held out only until the middle of April, when he logged into his Facebook account from a Virgin Airlines flight to New York. Despite the $711 million judgment against him in the case and the knowledge that criminal contempt charges were likely in the works, Wallace maintained a Facebook profile for "David Sinful-Saturdays Fredericks" until at least February 2011.

Wallace's long case history illustrates an obvious fact: not even the powerful word of the US government is self-executing. Those who have grown up with respect for judicial and police authority and those with a strong stake in the existing system of law and order need little more than a judge's word or an FTC consent order to comply. For civil matters, the government does have mechanisms in place to ultimately compel behavior, but each mechanism requires renewed, and significant, human effort. FTC lawyers can go to court and obtain default judgments when their targets don't show up, but every move to enforce those judgments requires more trips to the judge, more evidence collection, more legal documents, and the eventual involvement of US marshals. If lawyers for a defendant start challenging these steps, the amount of effort needed to collect a fine grows more quickly than a Vegas air-conditioning bill.

The FTC's Frankel reminded Wallace of this government power when grilling him about money during their day together in Las Vegas. "I mean if we got to it, we could get to the point where we literally have a US Marshal—you understand, where collection actions go—US Marshals come to your apartment knocking on your door," he said. "If you don't answer, they can literally go in—I'm not saying we're going to do this—go in and say, 'We understand you have money in your kitchen cabinet somewhere.' I want to know approximately where it is and approximately how much it is."

Not that bringing in the US marshals solves the collections problem. They might be directed to seize a bank account in payment of a huge court judgment, for instance, only to find that it holds less than $1,000. What happened to the rest of the money? It's not their job to find out, which means the problem goes back to the lawyers to solve. The lawyers collect more evidence, hold debtors' hearings, investigate bank account records. That level of effort can only be expended for certain cases. If a lawyer suspects that his target really is out of cash, what's to be gained by spending another month in a fruitless attempt to secure payment?

For the most determined spammers and scammers, fines—if paid at all—may be little more than a cost of doing business. The FTC regularly requires bad actors to disgorge their ill-gotten gains, but in some cases these have already been spent or cannot be fully located. This procedure, one common complaint argues, creates a cold calculus of costs. Say you're a spammer with a hot new idea to try out on a new social network. The worst-case scenario is that you are (1) found out, (2) actually pursued in court, and (3) eventually forced to pay back the money. The best case is that the government gives up and you end up with all the cash. In neither case are you in jail, and in neither case have you paid huge additional fines.

This process sometimes riles up consumer advocates, who want scammers to lose more than their misgotten gains. At the *Scam Times* blog, for instance, writer Matt Jezorek complains that "the FTC needs to step up and quit being sissy's [*sic*] and start putting people where they belong either in jail or out of business, these types of people seem to think the fines are the cost of doing business and they are making enough money to pay the fines and continue with the same deceptive practices they are getting in trouble for."

Agencies like the FTC recognize the issue, of course, but insist that their enforcement actions stop all but the most devoted spammers—and that civil enforcement is not the country club operation that some critics suggest. As Millard put it, "I have yet to have anyone be cheered by the prospect of a Federal Trade Commission suit."

How do you make a fellow go to hell? Sticking him in a federal prison is a good start down that broad road—but it's also an admission of just how ineffective all lesser remedies have been.

8
GROUNDHOG DAY: PRIVATE POLICING AT INTERNET SCALE

From across the country, they arrived in Minnesota's October sunshine to defend "November Rain"—the legal team from Denver, the trade-group suits from DC, the music label executives from Los Angeles and New York. The chain of lawsuits that the US recording industry began forging in 2003 led link by link to this spot, the steps of the Duluth federal courthouse in 2007. Here, the declining-but-still-mighty recording industry would exert its collective legal power against the first Internet file-sharer ever to take her case all the way to trial.

Who did the industry get for a target? An obstinate single mother from Brainerd named Jammie Thomas, who worked for the Mille Lacs Band of Ojibwe in their Department of Natural Resources and made a (very) modest salary as a brownfield coordinator who helped redevelop environmentally contaminated property.

The optics of the situation weren't great—faceless coastal corporations against small-town midwestern mom—but neither side was prepared to yield. Thomas, angry about the suit against her for file sharing, refused to pay anything on principle; the labels couldn't walk away without jeopardizing the ten thousand other cases they had already filed against individuals all over the country.

The Thomas case began on February 21, 2005, when the recording industry's hired investigators saw an IP address sharing 1,700 songs through the online file-sharing network Kazaa. By filing a "John Doe" lawsuit against the anonymous holder of that IP address, the music labels received permission to send subpoenas seeking the information needed to tie the IP address to a name. Their search led them to Minnesota, and then to Thomas. But unlike almost everyone else caught up in file-sharing suits, she refused to settle.

In the four years between the start of the industry's lawsuit campaign and the Thomas trial, no one else had taken a case so far. Copyright cases, being a federal matter, are heard in federal court. A full federal trial can mean hundreds of thousands of dollars in legal fees—and that's just to pay your *own* lawyer. US law also gave the music labels the right to ask for damages of up to $150,000 per song if they could prove "willful" copyright infringement, even if the labels couldn't prove that the infringement had cost them a single cent in revenues. Thomas was sued over just twenty-four of the 1,700 songs seen by investigators, but those twenty-four songs could have cost her $3.75 million.

By the time the Thomas trial rolled around in late 2007, the music labels were confident in their legal arguments. They had by this time racked up thousands of settlements from accused online file-swappers, usually a couple thousand bucks each, with the "educational" goal of reminding people that sharing songs online without permission was illegal.

But the labels were losing the broader war for public opinion, and in spectacular fashion, targeting with their lawsuits the occasional child in public housing, the baffled grandmother, and even the dead. In the early days of the campaign, a recording industry spokeswoman copped to the mistakes, saying, "When you fish with a net, you sometimes are going to catch a few dolphin."

This displeased the fish and positively outraged the dolphins. A noted newspaper columnist from Pittsburgh wrote that the lawsuit campaign had "brought the music industry some of the most favorable headlines since Mussolini visited Ethiopia."

Thomas's Minneapolis-based lawyer, Brian Toder, knew this history well and planned to lean on it heavily. In the final run-up to trial, he summarized Thomas's case with this memorable paragraph to the judge: "Defendant is a single mother, residing in greater Minnesota who did not download anything from Kazaa or any other peer to peer network. Ironically, defendant is one of plaintiffs' best customers having bought hundreds of dollars worth of their CDs, yet she has shared the same fate as thousands of other individuals who have been sued by various recording company plaintiffs who follow the motto usually attributed to *Soldier of Fortune* magazine: 'Kill them all; let God sort them out.'"

The recording industry, appalled by the rhetoric, asked the judge to put a damper on such talk; Toder promised to restrain himself unless the record companies made the case about the broader issues of "the danger of piracy running through America." In that case, he would have no choice to but to highlight the industry's "kill them all" missteps.

It didn't take long. After lunch on the trial's first day, while grilling his very first witness, Toder asked, "How many dead people have you sued?" The combative questioning was Toder's attempt to show the jury that such lawsuits had missed the mark on many occasions, a by-product of the fairly basic techniques used to identify file-sharers. Even assuming that nothing went wrong in the process of turning an IP address into a name—and file-sharing networks sometimes seeded themselves with bogus IP addresses just to cause such problems—the best that an investigator could do was link an IP address to a particular machine. In most cases, that machine wouldn't be a person's computer, either, but the DSL or cable modem with which they connected to the Internet.

Perhaps a boyfriend had shared the songs? Perhaps Thomas's children had installed a file-sharing program without their mother's knowledge?

Perhaps an overnight guest had used a computer of her own, connecting through Thomas's Internet connection? Toder even posited an unlikely hypothetical—that five people might have held a "computer party" in Thomas's home, each logging into the file-sharing network Kazaa with Thomas's e-mail address. Who knew?

The question arises in many Internet investigations, and the answer usually is no, an IP isn't *personal proof*. No investigator worth her salt would rely on an IP address alone to make a case. While an IP address cannot identify a person or even an address with total reliability—police on multiple occasions have raided homes looking for child porn before confused residents finally figured out that their IP address was being used by a neighbor accessing their wireless connection—it provides a reasonable place to start. Other facts, obtained by search warrants or through the civil discovery process, are always needed. This case had several.

For one thing, the person using Thomas's IP address to share songs in 2005 had logged in using the screen name "tereastarr." Thomas had used that name extensively online for not one but three e-mail addresses, an instant messaging account, her MySpace page, online dating site Match. com, and even online accounts she had created at stores like Best Buy. "Tereastarr" was also the main account name on the Compaq Presario computer Thomas kept in her bedroom. After moving to Brainerd in 2004, Thomas had password-protected this account and admitted during trial that she had given the password to no one, not even to her new boyfriend.

"And so the only person with access to the 'tereastarr' portion of your computer was you?" asked recording industry lawyer Rich Gabriel.

"Correct," Thomas replied.

It certainly looked as though Thomas's machine and Thomas's Kazaa account had shared the files; still, it might not have been Thomas herself behind the keyboard. To look for clues, the recording industry asked for the computer's hard drive. Thomas provided it. A copy was made for the labels's hired expert, computer science professor Doug Jacobson of Iowa State University, while the original drive went to Thomas's own expert, Eric Stanley, who oversaw electric power control systems—and who knew Toder's brother.

The investigation went about as badly as it could have for Thomas. For one thing, Jacobson noted that the hard drive contained plenty of music, but the songs didn't appear to have been ripped from her own CDs, as Thomas had claimed. Instead, the song files carried extra information (known as "metadata") such as "uploaded by Off$3+"— suggesting that the files had been obtained from the Internet, where they had first been acquired and uploaded by a person or group using a creatively spelled variant of "Offset" as its name. Still, Jacobson could find no evidence that the hard drive had ever held the Kazaa file-sharing software at issue in the case. In fact, he saw no file-sharing software of any kind. So how had the songs been downloaded?

Thomas's own expert supplied a possible answer. In examining the hard drive, Eric Stanley noticed a sticker showing the drive's date of manufacture: January 22, 2005. Thomas had told everyone that the computer's hard drive had been replaced in 2004—obviously not true—and that the one she turned over had been the one whirring away in her computer on the date of her alleged infringement. Stanley suspected a more likely scenario: Thomas had replaced her hard drive some time *after* the recording industry saw "tereastarr" sharing those 1,700 songs online. Records from Best Buy later confirmed his hypothesis; Thomas had taken the computer in for service in March 2005 and had the hard drive replaced—one month after the alleged infringement.

Toder put a brave face on the news. "Our expert, who is not here today because we can't afford to pay him, he's not here today because he found something," he told the jury during his opening remarks. "Our expert found nothing on there and their expert found nothing on there."

(Stanley did ultimately appear as a witness in the trial—but one called by the music labels.)

While true, the statement was also irrelevant. And though Thomas insisted she had simply been off by a year with all of her dates, she wasn't helped by testimony from her own ex-boyfriend. When Thomas had been notified by letter of her suspected infringement in mid-2005, her boyfriend said he had reminded her that the labels would find nothing on the new drive, because it had recently been replaced.

Rich Gabriel stressed the restraint showed by the music labels, which could have sued Thomas for "hundreds upon hundreds of sound recordings. They sued on just 24 because the point here is not to get the biggest number we could get, this big verdict. The number is to hold her responsible."

The recording industry refused to offer any guidance about what number might, in its view, be a fair one. Saying that actual damages were too difficult to calculate, the labels instead elected to sue for statutory damages. This entitled them to anywhere between $750 and $150,000 per infringement—a tremendous range. How was a Duluth jury that included a funeral director, a bartender, and a steelworker supposed to know that this range had been passed into law years ago to deter for-profit corporate infringement? How could they know the history of infringement awards, a history that might help them slot Thomas's alleged bad behavior into its proper place on the ladder of damages? How might they come up with a fair procedure for picking a number?

The law offered a few general factors, but Gabriel had a suggestion of his own, one that went beyond his initial talk about the need to hold Thomas personally responsible for her own actions. The jury must pick a number that would catch the attention of the millions of other Americans engaged in file swapping. "I only ask that you consider that the need for deterrence here is great," he said.

At the conclusion of the trial, Judge Michael Davis gave the jury until

4:15 p.m. to reach a verdict. If the twelve members could not agree by then, they would have to return the next day. They just made the cutoff; at exactly 4:15 p.m., the jury shuffled back into their seats. Thomas sat with Toder at a table on the left side of the courtroom; the recording industry lawyers clustered at a table on the right. A handful of tech reporters, banned from using their beloved electronic devices, waited with paper copies of the special verdict form, pens hovering over the pages.

"Members of the jury, have you reached a verdict in this matter?" Judge Davis asked.

Jury leader Jill Forseen, who had already warned the judge that she had a "mousy voice," stood up. "Yes, we have, Your Honor," she said.

"Would you turn it over?"

A court official passed the special verdict form to Davis, who looked it over without comment. He passed the paper down to his law clerk, who began to read out Jammie Thomas's fate.

/////

Copyright poses a unique scale problem. Make child pornography licit and few would take you up on the opportunity. Legalize fraudulent spam and most people would instead continue to work legitimate jobs as pediatric nurses, chemical engineers, and trainers of miniature quarter horses. But copyright? Millions wanted to share and experience new music. Once it became possible to do so online, and at no cost, millions did.

Defenders of the current copyright regime have faced unusual public resistance, not seen in the case of any other ill on the Internet—and they have taken unusual steps to counter it. One of those steps was the music labels's 2003 decision to start suing fans of their own product on a scale never seen before in copyright cases. But even with all the resources at their command, this was still about deterrence more than it was about catching every guilty party. In 2007, in Brainerd, you could have thrown a rock in the air and had a solid chance of hitting someone who had infringed copyright; despite Toder's claim, the industry simply couldn't afford to "sue 'em all and let God sort it out."

Consider the jury pool for the Thomas trial. While Thomas faced potential multi-million-dollar fines for sharing music online, even this random group of nonfelonious Minnesota residents contained people who openly admitted to doing the same thing. These weren't the proverbial "young people" always said to know so much about technology, either. Most of the jurors clustered around middle age and worked middle-class jobs, yet they said surprising things.

"The songs that I did download were of such poor quality and other people kind of mess with them along the way and they add different sounds and slow them down and stuff so by the time you get it, it's really not the same as if you go out and buy a CD," said one prospective juror from Crow Wing County during the jury-selection process. "I guess I could look at it like when I was a teenager and we would tape stuff, you know, when tape recorders first came out and somebody would make a tape and they would share it with you and stuff."

A hospital accountant with an associate's degree, a nineteen-year-old daughter, and an admitted lack of computer savvy, she hardly seemed a typical downloader. But so long as she didn't sell music to other people, and so long as the quality of the downloads wasn't too great, the woman didn't believe sharing music online was wrong. "So, yeah, I guess I was surprised when people were getting in trouble for it, for downloading it free," she concluded. She was eventually dismissed from the jury.

Another prospective juror, who remained on the jury, "did it once too, downloaded on my MP3 player. I have no idea how it got there, not a clue. I did it once. That's it. I was just pushing buttons."

Even those who hadn't downloaded music often had trouble seeing the issue in the same stark terms as the recording industry. A high school English teacher noted that his students loved to write on the issue: "It was a pretty popular topic because kids were into downloading and there were lots of issues, so it made for a good controversial, debatable topic for students to write about." Those papers—and his own subscription to *Rolling Stone*—had educated him on the questions involved. "Most of my students aren't necessarily on the side of, when it comes to a lawsuit, on the side of the labels or the corporations," he said. "They're probably more on the side of the downloaders themselves because that's who they relate to. But having read a lot about it, I know that it's a very debatable topic and there's lots of issues surrounding it. So I don't know that I've come to my own conclusions on it. I feel like I sometimes go back and forth on the issue."

Sometimes go back and forth on the issue? While the law clearly proscribes much of this activity, the mere proscription failed to convince both students and teacher of its innate justice. Though the recording industry had embarked on its campaign of lawsuits to help "educate" the public about copyright law, they actually faced a more difficult problem: convincing those who already knew the law that unauthorized file-swapping wasn't just illegal but wrong.

Many file-sharers lack this view, seeing themselves as fans who also buy music and attend concerts. As Toder pointed out repeatedly during trial, Thomas had spent plenty of money on music. At one point, she owned more than four hundred CDs and she had legally purchased music online from places like Walmart. "Jammie Thomas is one of the best customers that record companies ever had around here," Toder said in his closing remarks. "I mean, she bought hundreds of these things and she paid dearly for them. She bought all kinds of CDs before February 21, 2005. She bought all kinds of CDs after February 21, 2005."

Academic studies on the effects of unauthorized online sharing have been mixed, though most recent ones find some measure of harm to recorded music sales. Teasing out that harm has proved notoriously tricky, since the rise of file swapping coincided with a shift to online distribution—where songs are generally sold as singles rather than requiring a full album purchase—and the price of songs and albums dropped. In addition, the Internet, television, and video game consoles have soaked up huge amounts of time and money that might have otherwise been spent on music, making it difficult to devise a precise study of just how much the recording industry's financial decline has been caused by file swapping in particular.

Even those with little digital savvy recognize that copyright is a murkier legal concept than most. In the Thomas trial, prospective jurors understood that they could rip music to their computers and move it to their digital music players, and that they could make mixtapes or CD compilations for friends. They knew that people could tape songs off the radio (even as radio stations pay nothing to music labels for the music) or movies from television. And the "fair use" doctrine adds to the ambiguity, offering four broad principles under which unauthorized use of copyrighted works may be allowed. Federal judges have sometimes ruled that even sharing entire works is fair use, usually in cases where people have posted complete news stories to encourage commentary on them. Still, one thing remained clear in the midst of the ambiguity: sharing music merely for the purpose of enjoying it free of charge is not protected activity.

The wholesale sharing of music online with potentially millions of strangers poses few real questions of existing copyright law—except for the interesting question of when and how middlemen like Napster and Kazaa and LimeWire might be responsible for infringement conducted using their services. But copyright law has always felt more like a commercial bargain than a moral imperative, and even unauthorized commercial copying with the intent to profit hasn't always been outlawed. In the nineteenth century, America famously refused to recognize copyright on foreign works; printers ripped off popular authors like Dickens with abandon.

Even a top legal scholar, Stephen Breyer, recognized the unique complexities around copyright before he became a Supreme Court justice. In a well-known 1970 *Harvard Law Review* article titled "The Uneasy Case for Copyright," Breyer came down on the side of continued copyright protection—but only just. "Taken as a whole," he wrote, "the evidence now available suggests that, although we should hesitate to abolish copyright protection, we should equally hesitate to extend or strengthen it." (Congress utterly ignored this advice over the next four decades.)

So it wasn't surprising that when compression squeezed the size of music files down to something manageable, when dial-up Internet gave way to broadband, and when CD burners and later iPods became ubiquitous, that infringement flourished. And it wasn't surprising that opinions about how to deal with it would vary wildly, even within the Jammie Thomas jury pool.

"We, the jury, impaneled in this matter, hereby answer the special verdict questions put to us as follows," began Judge Davis' law clerk as she read it out. Did the labels own the copyrights to the twenty-four songs at issue in the case? Yes, said the jury. Did Thomas infringe those copyrights? Yes. Was that infringement willful? Yes.

Then came the key question: how much would Thomas owe? The jury settled on $9,250 per song, for a total of $222,000.

Toder and Thomas left the courthouse quickly after the verdict, offering only a terse "no comment" when asked about the possibility of an appeal. But Gabriel took questions from a small knot of reporters gathered on the courthouse steps. "This does send a message, we hope," he said, "that both downloading and distributing music is not okay."

Thirty-eight-year-old juror Michael Hegg, a steelworker who had never used the Internet, later told *Wired* that the jury made its decision about Thomas' infringement within five minutes. Settling on the damages took longer; at least two jurors thought $150,000 per song was completely fair, while one held out for the $750 minimum. Hours of haggling finally produced the $9,250 per song compromise. "She lied," Hegg said, pointing to the fact that Thomas turned over the wrong hard drive. "There was no defense. Her defense sucked. . . . I think she thought a jury from Duluth would be naïve. We're not that stupid up here. I don't know what the fuck she was thinking, to tell you the truth."

The week after the case concluded, Thomas appealed. Several months later, Judge Davis threw out the verdict. If the recording industry wanted to get its money—and to send its message—it would have to fly its pin-striped and power-skirted crew back to Minnesota for a do-over.

/////

No one wanted to be in that Duluth courtroom. Thomas certainly could have done without the years of legal hassles—to say nothing of the bill she ran up with Toder, her lawyer. The recording industry, burning wheelbar-rows of cash just to mount one legal attack on a single mom, expressed constant exasperation that she wouldn't settle for a few thousand dollars. Even Judge Davis, the long-serving chief justice of the Minnesota District Court, made clear how appalled he was by the entire proceeding. He granted Thomas a new trial after deciding, on fairly technical grounds, that one of his instructions to the jury had been fatally flawed. In an unexpectedly passionate aside to his order, Davis begged Congress to change the law he had been forced to act upon:

> While the Court does not discount Plaintiffs' claim that, cumulatively, illegal downloading has far-reaching effects on their businesses, the damages awarded in this case are wholly dispro-portionate to the damages suffered by Plaintiffs. Thomas allegedly infringed on the copyrights of 24 songs—the equivalent of approxi-mately three CDs, costing less than $54, and yet the total damages awarded is $222,000—more than 500 times the cost of buying 24 separate CDs and more than 4,000 times the cost of three CDs . . .

Surely damages that are more than 100 times the cost of the works would serve as a sufficient deterrent....

The Court would be remiss if it did not take this opportunity to implore Congress to amend the Copyright Act to address liability and damages in peer-to-peer network cases such as the one currently before this Court.... The Court does not condone Thomas' actions, but it would be a farce to say that a single mother's acts of using Kazaa are the equivalent, for example, to the acts of global financial firms illegally infringing on copyrights in order to profit.

So why did the trial take place at all? Chalk it up to the difficulties of private policing at Internet scale. The US music labels had for decades acted against for-profit pirates throughout the world, of course, but the high costs of reproduction and distribution of physical CDs had always allowed them to target major stamping operations, distribution facilities, or large markets for illicit goods. As computers and then Internet access made reproduction and distribution simple and nearly free, the challenges multiplied.

Cary Sherman, a vice president (and later president) of the Recording Industry Association of America (RIAA), talked about this shift when he testified before Congress back in 1997. "In 1991, 12 counterfeiting operations, employing hundreds of individuals, manufactured approximately 28 million counterfeit cassettes," he said. "Today, one individual, in less time than it takes me to read this testimony, can send a full-length album to more than 50 million Internet users. As I said, the rules of the game have radically changed."

Traditional enforcement techniques stood no chance of stopping so many people online. David Post, the cyberlibertarian law professor we met in the first chapter when he was arguing about the difficult of policing the "borderless" Internet, has recently turned his attention to the sheer size of the Internet.

"I am obsessed with trying to understand Internet scale," Post wrote on his blog in January 2012. "The TCP/IP network had to solve a number of very profound scaling problems before it could perform the tasks it now performs—700,000 Google searches, 11 million IM conversations, 1 million Facebook status updates, etc. etc., every minute of every day, more content posted to YouTube every month (probably, by now, every three weeks or so) than the combined output of all US television networks since their inception in the 1940s, etc.—and the idea that our legal system, and the 19th and 20th century tools it contains, can somehow magically 'scale up' to work well on the Net is, frankly, laughable."

The recording industry certainly agreed and so set out to craft new tools. In the late 1990s, the music labels recognized that the chaotic digital ecosystem still had choke points. Gadget manufacturers were an obvious one, and the labels had previously convinced Congress to hobble and then tax technologies like digital audio tape (DAT) in a bid to prevent rampant "serial copying" and to compensate the labels for whatever copying did take place. When the first MP3 players appeared in the late 1990s, the labels sued—using the DAT law to demand that digital music players follow a similar scheme. At the heart of the effort was a simple question: would the electronics industry need to build copyright enforcement technology into its products?

The plan did require expensive litigation, but that posed no problem so long as the number of cases remained limited. Given the expertise required and the difficulty of building a device and bringing it to market, lawsuits against hardware manufacturers could be handled so long as the gadget makers were forced to take responsibility for the copyright apocalypse by then underway. But the recording industry lost its lawsuit badly. It would have no design power over the way digital music devices were built, a decision that paved the way for products like Apple's iPod, which generated huge profits for the hardware makers but little enough for the music labels, thanks to widespread file-swapping and an initial lack of good online music stores.

Thwarted in their war against hardware, the labels turned to the next major choke point: the online file-swapping services that made infringement easy in the first place. Even if you owned an iPod that played pirated music with ease, you still had to get it from somewhere. Such music sites remained primitive for years; in 1997, Sherman was reduced to complaining to Congress about a website called "Jon's Take But Don't Tell Page," which had attracted a mere 36,000 visitors in three months. The website posed no actual threat to the labels, but the industry knew that a truly mainstream service offering similar functionality was inevitable. When such a mainstream service finally arrived, its name was Napster.

In the late 1990s, millions flocked to Napster for free music, especially on college campuses. The service let users search other users' computers for songs, albums, or bands, but it also offered rudimentary community features. Find an obscure band that you like and you could page through the libraries of the people offering that music, looking for other things worth hearing; you could even send them messages. When you found music you wanted, you downloaded it by connecting directly to the user who had a copy, not from Napster (hence the designation "peer-to-peer" to describe the system and its many future incarnations).

Napster's service blew open the doors of the digital revolution and millions of people poured through the breach. But how many Napsters could there be, especially if the labels could send a clear warning to clone sites by winning a major court case? Like the gadget makers, the software looked potentially controllable. Despite talks between Napster and the labels about turning its service-of-dubious-legality into a fully licensed operation, the two sides couldn't reach a deal, and the labels sued the company on December 9, 1999.

Unlike the case against the gadget makers, where the music labels had tried to stand firm on swampy legal ground, the Napster situation posed fewer legal problems. In 2001, the Ninth Circuit Court of Appeals in San Francisco concluded that a middleman like Napster was indeed responsible for the actions of its users, insofar as it knew about those actions. As evidence that Napster knew exactly what happened through its network of connected music fans, the court pointed to a "document authored by Napster cofounder Sean Parker [that] mentioned 'the need to remain ignorant of users' real names and IP addresses 'since they are exchanging pirated music'" and to the fact that the recording industry had notified Napster about thousands of specific works being exchanged through the service. In addition, the court noted that "Napster executives have downloaded copyrighted songs from the system."

Though the Supreme Court had famously exempted the makers of videocassette recorders manufacturers from this sort of liability for user conduct back in the 1980s, Napster knew what its users were doing in a way that no VCR maker ever could, since Napster's own servers centrally indexed all of the music people made available on the system to make searching for music easier. In response to the court decision, Napster shuttered its main file-swapping system and limped through multiple attempts at reinvention over the years, but it never regained its former popularity. Perhaps the labels had found a choke point amenable to pressure after all.

The music labels industry racked up numerous wins against companies like Napster. On March 29, 2005—just a month after its investigators had seen "tereastarr" sharing those 1,700 files online—the labels argued a case against file-swapping company Grokster before the Supreme Court. Grokster had specifically engineered its operation to avoid the liability that tripped up Napster—it made sure its central servers never saw and indexed the songs its users were searching for and sharing. Despite these efforts, the Supreme Court came up with a new theory of liability that swept up Grokster anyway.

This "inducement doctrine" was summed up by Justice David Souter. "We hold that one who distributes a device with the object of promoting its use to infringe copyright, as shown by clear expression or other affirmative steps taken to foster infringement, is liable for the resulting acts of infringement by third parties," he wrote. Grokster hadn't helped itself by promoting its services as a "Napster alternative" after Napster lost its court cases, nor by sending out an electronic newsletter "containing links to articles promoting its software's ability to access popular copyrighted music." Soon Grokster too was out of action.

The labels sued Aimster, Morpheus, Audiogalaxy, iMesh, LimeWire, and Kazaa—the service Thomas was accused of using—while other outfits like DearShare tried to go legit in order to head off such lawsuits of their own; most went extinct instead. The labels won case after case. But for some reason, the hydra couldn't be killed; no matter how many file-swapping services got lopped off, more appeared almost instantly.

One reason for this was the engineering involved in building these systems. When Napster launched in 1999, its founder had to write most of the code for the system from scratch, which took time and effort and deterred entrants. Within a few years, however, core file-swapping components (such as the underlying code for the decentralized Gnutella file-sharing network) appeared as open-source software that anyone could freely use or improve upon.

As the effort needed to build a file-sharing client dropped, the number of clients exploded. Columbia University law professor Tim Wu compiled a 2003 list of the file-swapping programs that existed just between 1999 and 2002. It included: Abe's MP3 finder, Aimster, Ares, Audiogalaxy, AudioGnome, BadBlue, Bearshare, Blubster, CuteMX. Com, DirectConnect, eDonkey, FileAngel, Filetopia, File Navigator, File Rogue, FileSpree, Free Haven, Freenet, Frost, Gnotella, Gnucleus, Gnutella, Gnutmeg, Grokster, Groove Network, Hotline Communications, iMesh, iSwipe, Jungle Monkey, Kazaa, KonSpire, LimeWire,

Mactella, Mojo Nation, Morpheus, MyNapster, Myster, NapMX, Napster, Nutella, Ohaha, OnSystem, OpenNap, Phex, Phosphor, Pointera, Publius, Qtella, Qube, Scour.com, Shareaza, Spinfrenzy, SongSpy, Taxee, Voodoo Vision, WinMX, and Xolox.

As the companies behind these programs were sued, file sharing moved away from specific clients. Sites like The Pirate Bay, a Swedish site built around the efficient BitTorrent file-sharing protocol and accessed through the Web, dominated the middle part of the 2000s. The site, counting on jurisdiction to keep US firms at bay, brazenly mocked takedown notices it received. One 2005 law firm demanded in a letter that The Pirate Bay remove links to unreleased music from Smashing Pumpkins front man Billy Corgan. Pirate Bay admins posted and then made fun of this: "'First Notice of Infringement'? Is that kind of like when I don't pay my bills on time? 'First notice,' 'Second notice,' 'Third notice,' 'WE KILL YOU!', then a package with the sawed-off head of a pig? . . . We are well aware of the fact that The Pirate Bay falls outside the scope of the DMCA [Digital Millennium Copyright Act]—after all, the DMCA is a US-specific legislation, and TPB is hosted in the land of vikings, reindeers, Aurora Borealis and cute blonde girls."

BitTorrent, like most peer-to-peer systems, had a weakness, however—it exposed the IP addresses of those sharing and downloading files. (Indeed, it had to do so in order to allow users to share files as "peers" directly with one another; without knowing the other person's IP address, the two machines couldn't connect.) Copyright holders continued to file suit against individual users, and they kept up the pressure against the websites hosting huge directories of the files available through BitTorrent. They finally managed to bring a suit in Sweden against The Pirate Bay's four key creators—and they won, securing short jail sentences and a huge collective fine against the men. (The trial was tied up in appeals for several years, when the Swedish Supreme Court upheld modified verdicts against the men. Still, showing just how difficult the traditional court process was at reining in Internet abuses, the three principals behind the site left Sweden and neither served the jail sentences nor paid the fine. One was eventually arrested in Cambodia in 2012 and deported to Sweden, where he remains in custody. The Pirate Bay website remains operational.)

So file-sharing innovated again, trying to protect both the users and the websites. "Cyberlockers" like Megaupload and RapidShare moved away from the peer-to-peer model and back to centralized servers, offering direct downloads that could not be publicly tracked by industry investigators and that did not reveal user IP addresses to outsiders. Material stored on the sites was generally not searchable or publicly listed, as the files on The Pirate Bay were, to provide deniability about any illicit file-sharing that might take place through the cyberlockers. Problem solved—except now it was hard to locate the content. Separate "linking sites" soon sprang up consisting of nothing but aggregated collections of copyrighted content uploaded to the cyberlockers by users.

As with spam, the tick/tock of innovation has frustrated the initial hopes of the antipiracy warriors who hoped that squeezing a few choke points could control the problem without too much trouble. How was this possible when attacking the choke points had worked relatively well in the old world of physical media?

Australian professor Rebecca Giblin wrote an entire book to answer the question. She concluded that the music label strategy ran into problems because of "mismatches between physical world assumptions and software world realities." Thanks to the Internet, new methods of sharing content had become easy to build; the plummeting cost of bandwidth made them cheap to operate, too. And because people badly wanted to share music, someone somewhere in the world always proved willing to meet the need. Attacking choke points and gatekeepers worked best when those services were difficult to replicate and costly to run.

"Although they prevailed in every major court action instituted against P2P [peer-to-peer] providers, software developers remained unfazed," Giblin wrote in a 2011 paper distilling her book's research. "By 2007, more software programs facilitating P2P file sharing were available than ever before. The average number of users sharing files on P2P file sharing networks at any one time was nudging 10 million, and it was estimated that P2P traffic had grown to comprise up to 90 percent of all global Internet traffic. At that point, rights holders tacitly admitted defeat."

If targeting gadgets that played music hadn't worked and targeting the services and software that made file sharing possible hadn't worked, what was left? Suing the individuals actually sharing the songs. (More positively, the labels also made belated strides to license their music to services like iTunes and Amazon's MP3 music store, and finally even removed the digital locks known as "DRM" they had long insisted upon—and had even sued to enforce.)

The problem with suing individual file swappers was that there were just so damn many of them. No one could afford lawyers to actually take all these people to trial, so the legal campaign that launched in 2003 focused on partial automation: outside firms developed software to troll services like Kazaa for infringers. Federal lawsuits were filed en masse; letters demanding payments to make the case go away were mailed in bulk. Payment could be made over a telephone hotline—and later simply by visiting a website with a credit card.

The process required oversight, but at least it could scale significantly. The recording industry filed 35,000 lawsuits against 18,000 individuals over the next several years (many lawsuits were filed first as "Doe" cases, and then later became named lawsuits after an individual was identified), and it collected millions in settlement money. But the plan had a flaw: even if the industry could avoid targeting children, cheerleaders, grandparents, stroke victims, and dead people, just a few people who refused to settle could derail the litigation pain train from its automated track.

And people did fight back. The moment they started to fight, the cases became grinding exercises in legal brief drafting and argument; each could drag on for years and require hundreds of court filings. The labels were even countersued by those who felt they were being extorted under the threat of those $150,000-per-song damages. Their initial, easy methods for matching names to IP addresses were challenged successfully by Internet providers like Verizon. And their investigators were repeatedly sued for operating without state-issued private-investigation licenses (claims that were repeatedly dismissed).

In Thomas, the labels saw the fullness of their litigation nightmares come to life. They couldn't just let her win—what kind of "educational" message would that send?—but each over-the-top victory only made them look worse. (When a chief federal judge implores Congress to change its laws because of a case you just won, you know you're not running a popular operation.) And that's to say nothing of the sheer money pit the case was becoming, with no serious hope of recovering any real cash from Thomas.

What the labels needed, as in their battle against the middlemen, was something more suited to the Internet age than to the courtroom. The trial process wasn't built for suing 35,000 people; the labels needed a way to blast out millions of warnings with minimal fuss and they wanted a system where not every user with an implausible claim about innocence could ring up millions of dollars in billable hours for a label-backed law firm.

This required the voluntary cooperation of Internet providers, who alone could match IP addresses to subscribers without a court order. It was the Internet providers who could see what traffic passed through their wires and fiber-optic cables. And it was the Internet providers who could block that traffic, or censor foreign websites that might be hard to sue, or cut subscribers off from the Internet completely.

But the providers had little incentive to crack down hard on their own customers. Around the world, they refused to comply with copyright-holder demands for help unless judicial authorities vetted the accusations first. In Australia, Internet provider iiNet famously stood up to a movie-industry lawsuit demanding that it take action against accused file swappers. iiNet's CEO Michael Malone complained about the copyright holders' stance, saying that an Internet provider cannot act simply on the basis of private allegations.

"They send us a list of IP addresses and say 'this IP address was involved in a breach on this date,'" he told *ComputerWorld Australia*. "We look at that say, 'Well, what do you want us to do with this? We can't release the person's details to you on the basis of an allegation and we can't go and kick the customer off on the basis of an allegation from someone else.' So we say, 'You are alleging the person has broken the law; we're passing it to the police. Let them deal with it.'"

During the trial, movie industry lawyers asked Malone whether he had ever cut off one of his his subscribers for repeatedly infringing copyright. Malone said he had not, since none of his customers had ever been "found to infringe copyright." The studios's lawyer asked him if he was making a "joke" response, but he wasn't. Malone was making the point that "infringement" was something established by a judge and, while he was happy to act in any case on which a judge had ruled, he wasn't going to take serious steps like customer disconnection based wholly on allegations from "Jo Blow." The studios later complained to the judge that "they, being the major film studios, could not possibly be considered 'Jo Blow' when copyright infringement of their films is under consideration." In other words, the studios wanted their allegations treated as true by default, even in the absence of a court order.

In 2010, iiNet won its case in the Federal Court of Australia. In 2012, it won again on appeal to the Australian High Court, which confirmed that an Internet provider did not have to take any action in response to purely private allegations that provided no "reasonable basis for sending warning notices to individual customers containing threats to suspend or terminate those customers' accounts."

Only one entity had the brawn to force Internet providers to take action against their users: the government. So it's no surprise where the labels turned next.

/////

"I never downloaded Morbid Angel's 'World of Shit,'" said Jammie Thomas from her spot in the witness box in Judge Davis's wood-paneled fifteenth-floor courtroom. She looked over the list of songs the labels accused her of sharing, which included Swedish death metal. "I didn't even know there *was* a Swedish death metal genre," she said.

Thomas's June 2009 retrial had a touch of the surreal about it. The mass "John Doe" lawsuits, meant to liberate the labels, had instead become a millstone weighing them down; by December 2008, the recording industry had abandoned the tactic. The Internet rejoiced at the news; Jammie Thomas did not. Despite the change of strategy, the labels offered no amnesty. All past cases would continue.

The predictable result was a retrial that felt like a zombified retread of the first. Identical witnesses, identical testimony, identical facts. Zombies feast on brains, of course; as the only journalist apparently willing to sit through the four days of retrial testimony, I often felt that the case was feasting on my own. The feeling also appeared to have reached Judge Davis, who spent much of the retrial looking displeased that he had to see any of these people again.

A few small changes enlivened the proceedings. Recording industry lawyer Rich Gabriel had secured an appointment to the judiciary back in Colorado and had been replaced. Brian Toder, who wanted out of the case even before the first trial, finally got his wish and was replaced by the team of "Kiwi" Camara and Joe Sibley, lawyers from Texas who were angry at the label lawsuit campaign and represented their client pro bono. Thomas had married and now went by the name Thomas-Rasset. And the setting had shifted from Duluth to Minneapolis.

But it was Thomas-Rasset's own testimony, more extensive this time around, that proved most riveting. The labels had grilled her already about all the old issues, especially her replacement of the hard drive— standard fare after the first trial. When it came time to present a defense, however, Thomas-Rasset took the stand again. (In her first trial, the defense had called no witnesses at all.) Even more intriguingly, she suddenly had some new suggestions about who might have been sitting at the computer, sharing the files in question.

Her lawyer Joe Sibley walked through some of the 1,700 tracks belonging to the "tereastarr" account, tracks by metal bands like Wumpscut, VNV Nation, and Morbid Angel. Thomas-Rasset insisted that she disliked many of the groups—but that her ex, Justin, had been a big fan. Even after their 2004 split, he still watched the two children on occasion for a week at a time in her Brainerd apartment. Perhaps he had done it?

She followed that speculation with a totally different scenario. She had caught her ten-year-old son looking at some online pornography with a friend about that time, she said. The son knew how to use computers, and it's possible that *he* had installed the Kazaa file-swapping software without her knowledge.

This move infuriated the label attorneys. They noted that Thomas-Rasset had never aired either scenario in the four years since the infringement had been detected, had never mentioned them through multiple interrogatories and depositions, and had not even conjured them during her first trial. And now—now, when it was too late to investigate the theories—she was willing to blame an ex-boyfriend or a child?

Thomas-Rasset then raised the emotional temperature in the

courtroom even further by claiming that Doug Jacobsen, the Iowa State computer science professor, had been brought in to give "false testimony" against her and that the labels had tried to "extort $5,000 from me." The bluntness of the charges caused gasps in the courtroom and brought an immediate objection from the labels. Judge Davis halted Thomas-Rasset's weepy monologue about how the case had affected her life. She stepped down from the stand.

"This could happen to any of us," said Sibley in combative closing remarks to the jury. As for the music labels, they were run by out-of-towners who "hop on a jet back to New York or LA or wherever they're from" and they had no trouble suing harmless local residents like Thomas-Rasset. Cross them and they would "come after you like the Terminator."

The new jurors were wild cards. They had no knowledge of what had happened in the first trial and didn't know about the $222,000 judgment or Judge Davis's remarks about its injustice. They began with a blank slate, knowing only that if Thomas-Rasset was found liable, they must choose a figure between $750 and $150,000 per song. They had heard from a Sony Entertainment executive during the retrial who, when pushed, agreed that even the full $150,000 per song would be an appropriate remedy.

Sibley worked on them, noting just how easily the jurors, their friends, or their children might be on trial facing similar charges. Even if he couldn't get Thomas-Rasset off completely, perhaps he could secure a minimal judgment. "There but for the grace of God go I," he added, imploring the jurors not to sentence Thomas-Rasset to "a life of financial misery."

The jury retired. I spoke to the defense team while we waited; it was their hope, they said, that they had secured a complete victory. Several more reporters had arrived by the time the jury reached a verdict and had filed back into the courtroom. Judge Davis repeated his routine, looking at the verdict and handing it off to his clerk.

The jury found Thomas-Rasset liable again. What about damages? As the clerk reached the first song on the list, tension crackled through the courtroom.

"$80,000," she announced.

Thomas-Rasset gasped, her eyes wide. A quick scribble in the corner of my notepad totted up the total damage award—$1.92 million. Given their decision to pull the plug on the mass-lawsuit campaign, the only real way the labels could continue generating horrific press on this issue was to secure an exorbitant judgment against Thomas-Rasset for offering what amounted to two CDs worth of music online. They had just managed to do so.

The labels knew it, too. Rather than touting their victory, the only statement an RIAA spokeswoman would offer in the moments after the verdict was about how the industry remained willing to settle with Thomas-Rasset for a much, much lower amount.

Not that Thomas-Rasset had any intention of settling. The jury's decision was not "the end of the war," she told me as she left the courtroom. As for the damage award—"Good luck trying to get [the money] from me," she said. "It's like squeezing blood from a turnip."

Shortly after the verdict, *Chicago Sun-Times* music critic Jim DeRogatis called the decision "a ruling that already is infamous as one of the most wrong-headed in the history of the American judicial system—not to mention that it will forever stand as the best evidence of the contempt of the old-school music industry toward the music lovers who once were its customers." Even Richard Marx, one of the artists Thomas-Rasset was charged with ripping off, complained that "this show of force posing as judicial come-uppance is clearly abusive. Ms. Thomas-Rasset, I think you got a raw deal, and I'm ashamed to have my name associated with this issue."

Just as no one had wanted to take the case to trial in the first place, so no one wanted the verdict they got. Thomas hated it, the labels knew it was far too high, and Judge Davis was unlikely to be pleased, either, given his earlier remarks. In the end, he took seven months to make his feelings felt, but when he did in January 2010, his opinion took on the tone of an Old Testament prophet on a bad day.

He didn't *like* Thomas-Rasset, that much was clear; indeed, Davis singled out for particular condemnation her willingness to direct new suspicion on her own children. "Thomas-Rasset lied on the witness stand by denying responsibility for her infringing acts and, instead, blamed others, including her children, for her actions," he wrote.

But that was no excuse for a "monstrous" judgment. "The need for deterrence cannot justify a $2 million verdict for stealing and illegally distributing 24 songs for the sole purpose of obtaining free music," he added. "$2 million for stealing 24 songs for personal use is simply shocking. No matter how unremorseful Thomas-Rasset may be, assessing a $2 million award against an individual consumer for use of Kazaa is unjust."

Davis used "remittitur," his common-law power to cut the amount of an excessive jury verdict, to slash the award from $1.92 million to $54,000. He arrived at this number by tripling the statutory minimum of $750 (tripling is a common remedy for harms conducted "willfully"). Even this new amount was a "higher award than the Court might have chosen to impose in its sole discretion," Davis wrote, but the decision had been the jury's to make. His only role was to reduce the $1.92 million verdict to "the maximum amount that is no longer monstrous and shocking." If left to his own devices, the damages would clearly have been lower still.

Five years, two trials, and 366 court filings had elapsed since investigators saw "tereastarr" sharing 1,700 music files online. The music labels had abandoned the entire mass-litigation strategy that had started this fight. Thomas-Rasset had little money to pay a judgment, no matter how small. And yet—the case would set a key precedent.

The music labels faced a choice after Judge Davis's remittitur: they could accept the lower award, creating an understanding that online file-swapping was a relatively minor crime deserving of relatively modest fines, or they could accept a third trial against Thomas-Rasset.

They chose trial.

/////

The combined political and economic power of the movie and music industries looked like it had met its match on the Internet. Controlling gadgets had failed. Lawsuits against file-swapping services took forever and cost a fortune—and new services kept appearing anyway. Internet providers, who could have deployed automated surveillance tools, weren't willing to start scanning their user's traffic or to play private Internet cops. And trying to litigate millions of ordinary users into compliance with copyright law through federal courts had created the Thomas-Rasset fiasco and the sort of public relations debacle about which case studies get written.

But just because the labels couldn't get the job done didn't mean someone bigger couldn't. As the sheer scale of the problem they faced became apparent, the labels and their allies in Hollywood turned increasingly toward government, and government was sympathetic.

Copyright holders had (largely) given up on the plan to gimp devices by legislative fiat. And they were prepared to fund the time-intensive lawsuits against specific file-sharing services. But they simply couldn't keep pace with lawsuits against individuals, as the Thomas-Rasset case was making abundantly clear, so rights holders demanded that the government force a faster, automated process on Internet providers and on Internet users.

In the United States, rights holders turned to the Federal Communications Commission (FCC), where Hollywood had previously waged a battle to control all digital video-recording devices like the TiVo, demanding that they respect a "do not copy" signal called the "broadcast flag." (This, the Hollywood version of the music labels's lawsuit against music players, actually passed the FCC but was fortunately tossed by a federal court.)

In 2007, Rick Cotton, general counsel for NBC Universal, warned the FCC that "stolen intellectual property is not the occasional needle in the haystack of legitimate content . . . instead, it threatens to become the entire haystack." He had a bold request—order Internet providers "to use readily available means to prevent the use of their broadband capacity to transfer pirated content."

Resistance proved especially strong from companies like Verizon that had begun life offering telephone service. They had no responsibility to police crimes committed over the phone, and bringing any sort of liability to Internet middlemen struck them as a terrible idea. Where might it end? In 2008, Verizon's top lobbyist remarked, "Once you start going down the path of looking at the information going down the network, there are many that want you to play the role of policeman. Stop illegal gambling offshore. Stop pornography. Stop a whole array of other kinds of activities that some may think inappropriate."

AT&T filed a regulatory document raising questions about how becoming a private policeman might expose the company to increased liability. "Private entities are not created or meant to conduct the law enforcement and judicial balancing act that would be required," the company warned. "They are not charged with sitting in judgment of facts; and they are not empowered to punish alleged criminals without a court order or other government sanction . . . The government and the courts, not ISPs, are responsible for intellectual property enforcement, and only they can secure and balance the various property, privacy, and due process rights that are at play and often in conflict in this realm." This was the iiNet argument, and it won the day at the FCC.

Rights holders shifted pressure to Congress, which was unwilling to impose rules on intermediaries like Internet providers but might do something more modest. In 2008, copyright owners convinced Congress to target college campuses, and lawmakers agreed that US universities would lose federal student aid money unless they became copyright cops. Schools had to develop and implement "written plans to effectively combat the unauthorized distribution of copyrighted material by users of the institution's network," and even had to educate incoming students about "appropriate versus inappropriate use of copyrighted material." No matter that the key, Hollywood-backed study used to justify the measure turned out to be hugely flawed (by Hollywood's own admission, it misstated the rate of collegiate piracy by a factor *of three*)—the bill became law, and it remains so.

Though Congress would not go further at the moment, the music industry has a powerful lobbying operation in place around the world. Even though the major labels consist only of four companies (to be three after two merge), they were able to run a coordinated lobbying strategy to pass "graduated response" legislation, under which Internet providers would forward the labels' notices of infringement to their users and eventually turn over user information without a court order. After a certain number of such notices, disciplinary action could be taken, starting with a fine or with "educational" material.

The French government agreed to such a law in 2009. It created an administrative authority called HADOPI to accept complaints and mete out punishments to users, including the threat of total Internet disconnection. The law, which dished out penalties without trial and began with a presumption of guilt, was quickly ruled out by the "Sages" on the country's Constitutional Council. A revised version, which sent third-time infringers to the judiciary instead, passed successfully later in the year.

The system was a triumph of automation. A technology firm used software to scan file-swapping networks for music and movies, then generated long reports of what IP addresses were sharing which files. The reports went to the central clearinghouse at HADOPI, Internet providers turned over the relevant subscriber addresses, and threatening letters went out. Between October 2010 and December 2011, HADOPI contacted 755,015 French Internet subscribers with at least one warning. Given that France has 19.5 million homes with broadband Internet access, this means that nearly 4 percent of all French broadband subscribers received such a notice in just over a year's time. (HADOPI claims that 95 percent of those receiving a notice have yet to earn a second.)

Other countries, including South Korea and Japan, adopted similar plans, and all needed some form of government power to get the job done; graduated response remains unpopular with many Internet providers and users. In 2009, the New Zealand government had to pull a badly drafted graduated-response law after intense public opposition. InternetNZ, which runs the country's top-level .nz domain, said in a statement at the time, "Terminating an Internet account was always a disproportionate response to copyright infringement, and to force ISPs and other organisations to be copyright judges and policemen was never an acceptable situation."

Rights holders, seeing how unpopular their ideas were, headed down a darker path; rather than give up on government help for such schemes, they worked to get them through with limited public debate. New Zealand's revised law, which began with the presumption that the accused were in fact infringers, was pushed through in 2011 under "urgency" rules in the wake of the major Christchurch earthquake. In the United Kingdom, the Digital Economy Act laid the groundwork for a similar scheme and had to be passed during a hurried "wash-up" session with little discussion just before new elections in 2010.

In the United States, the graduated-response idea never even reached the legislature; after much music label urging, the White House brought Internet providers and content companies together in private to hash out a deal. Government pressure might push the agreement forward, but the result would not be "law"—and thus could face only limited legal challenges. In summer 2011, both sides agreed to a graduated-response scheme a bit less punitive than the French model. Despite their earlier objections about becoming the Internet's private police, most major Internet providers in the United States went along with the White House–brokered plan. Whether users will accept it remains unclear—implementation has been repeatedly delayed. As of early 2013, the system had still not started, though it was promised soon. In France, the 2012 election of president François Hollande led the government to talk about shutting down HADOPI altogether or at least scaling back its budget.

Even as these schemes passed, they became dated. Graduated response depends on a third party having the ability to see what IP addresses are downloading which files—possible in most file-swapping networks, but far more difficult on the cyberlockers that gained popularity in the last few years.

Still, graduated response was something, and it established new and often nonjudicial ways of dealing with online infringement in a quick and automated fashion. Graduated response has prompted plenty of criticism from those who note that speed and automation aren't always the hallmarks of justice and that privatizing so much of the enforcement system risks losing the protections offered to defendants at law. On the other hand, law has handed US rights holders an astonishing stick with which to beat people into settlements—the chance that they could win up to $150,000 per infringement. Whatever the weaknesses of graduated response—and they are numerous—such systems look positively sane compared with the succession of judgments against people like Thomas-Rasset.

Rights holders weren't content just with the creation of graduated-response systems targeting users, however. They wanted government help against the file-sharing sites, too. Civil lawsuits were tough, slow, and expensive—much better for them to get cases prosecuted as a criminal matter, throwing site operators into jail.

For years, rights holders had tried to "criminalize infringement down," setting the bar for criminal activity low enough that nearly anyone could trip over it (willfully distributing copyrighted works with a total retail value of $1,000 is the current threshold). Still, the Department of Justice showed little interest in prosecuting such cases. Thus, even major cases like those against Napster, Grokster, and LimeWire involved civil lawsuits, not criminal charges.

But the 2008 PRO-IP Act put an Intellectual Property Enforcement Coordinator in the White House and gave the feds new authority to seize the Internet domain names of allegedly infringing sites. Parts of the government took on their expanded roles with gusto. Immigration and Customs Enforcement (ICE) launched Operation In Our Sites and has seized hundreds of domain names since 2010, with raids often linked to themed events. (Sports-video site names were seized right before the Super Bowl, for instance.) Handed long lists of names by rights holders, ICE then investigated and took a subset of them before a federal judge for a one-sided (ex parte) hearing at which no defense could even be offered. The judge signed off on the seizures, and the domains were transferred without warning to ICE control and their content replaced with a scary-looking banner. Surprise! Those who wanted their website names back had to sue.

The seizures did take out a host of small foreign counterfeiting operations and few midlevel file-sharing sites, but their effect was limited. ICE didn't grab the actual servers powering the sites, many of which hummed away in data centers overseas, and it had no control over domain names not registered with US companies. Numerous site operators simply purchased new names not registered in the United States (www.ihatecopyright.eu, for instance) and continued with business as usual.

It didn't help the campaign that ICE made high-profile mistakes, in one case seizing a United States–based blog's domain name and handing it back a year later without explanation and without pressing charges. In another case, it seized the domain name for a company that appeared to be legal in its native Spain; in 2012, it also handed that name back without apology after tying the issue up in court for a year.

The secrecy of the process angered people like Rep. Zoe Lofgren, a former prosecutor, who told me when we spoke about the issue in 2011 that ICE's "effort to essentially seize—I think illegally—these domain names lacks due process, in some cases has violated the First Amendment rights of individuals. . . . You've got the prosecutors coming in, they have a judge sign something, and the people whose property is being seized are never heard from. It doesn't appear, honestly—though it would not solve the due process problems—that there's much inquiry on the part of the prosecution, either. Is there a fair use right? Is there an authorized use? Is there legitimate business going on? There's no opportunity for that to be raised, and once the damage is done, it's done."

Government officials involved with the process defended it as a simple application of existing seizure law—often used in narcotics cases—to the Internet. This brought a strong retort from Lofgren, who told me, "You're never going to have a free speech issue when it comes to a pile of cocaine. . . . This is prior restraint of speech, and you can't do that in America."

But domain-name seizures were small ball compared to the big-league battles about to get underway in Congress. Rights holders wanted to go much further than the PRO-IP Act, and they didn't waste much time doing it. Beginning in 2009, a new rights-holder approach emerged, one predicated on creating a blacklist of specific pirate and counterfeiting sites. Under this idea, those on the blacklist would be subject to four massive penalties.

First, search engines would have to "de-list" the offending sites. Rights holders targeted search engines like Google for displaying results that linked to file-sharing sites, in many cases ahead of legitimate sites.

(Search for a film name and you were likely to get a BitTorrent tracking site in response, for instance.) Google responded repeatedly that its links were a reflection of the Web as it was, not as it was wished to be; besides, rights holders could already file takedown notices against specific links and Google would remove them. But rights holders considered that older approach a sucker's game—the only way to win was not to play at all. They wanted entire sites removed, or at least demoted, from search results.

The campaign behind the idea was explicit and worldwide; in its January 2012 annual report, the international music industry trade group IFPI laid out its global lobbying plan. "Search engines need to rank search results factoring in clear indication of legality or illegality," the report said. "A basic measure such as this would help consumers not only avoid viruses and malware, but also being directed unwittingly towards content piracy."

Chris Dodd, head of the Motion Picture Association of America, said in a 2011 speech, "How do you justify a search engine providing for someone to go and steal something? A guy that drives the getaway car didn't rob the bank necessarily, but they got you to the bank and they got you out of it, so they are accessories in my view." This was an astonishing point of view—a search engine that indexes the Web was somehow liable for all of the content on the billions of Web pages in the world? Like Internet providers, the search engines wanted a model in which they were only conduits to content.

Second, rights holders wanted payment processors like MasterCard, Visa, and PayPal to cut off suspected pirates voluntarily, without any sort of court order or judgment. Government has already helped with such schemes; the City of London Police now works with content owners and credit card companies. The coppers "review the evidence, verify its integrity, and notify payment providers that their services should not be provided to such sites," said IFPI. For the accused, there is no recourse to the courts. Under the new plan, the payment processors would *have* to cut off sites on the blacklist. Without the ability to accept donations or fees from users, revenue to the pirates would shrink.

Third, rights holders also went after ad revenue, demanding the power to force advertising networks to cut cooperation with blacklisted sites. Ad networks didn't like the plan, but some had been compromised already by their own shady dealings; even Google had been caught with its hand in the cookie jar on this issue, taking money from advertisers who were engaged in fraud. In 2011, Google reached a $500-million settlement with the Department of Justice over ads for illicit online pharmacies that it apparently took with the knowledge of what was happening. Such examples made it harder for the ad networks to claim they were innocent bystanders.

Finally, the labels wanted Internet providers to engage in site blocking—a measure said to be necessary to stop offshore pirate operators. Such blocks wouldn't remove the site from the Internet, but they could prevent most users of an Internet provider from accessing it easily. In defending the idea, content owners like Chris Dodd didn't help their argument by pointing out that China had forced even a company like Google to censor material—surely companies could censor sites if the US government demanded it.

All four proposals showed up in the Stop Online Piracy Act (SOPA) of 2011, introduced by Rep. Lamar Smith (R-TX). SOPA was odiously one-sided—even the witness hearings on the topic were tilted so heavily towards rights holders that a cynic might still have felt some shock. Its draconian remedies spawned worldwide outrage and a day of protest by sites like *Wikipedia* and Google on January 18, 2012. (*Wikipedia* took its entire English-language encyclopedia offline; Google put a link to a petition on its home page. Both acts of protest were nearly unprecedented for Internet companies of this scale.) Millions of people signed anti-SOPA petitions. Members of Congress were flooded with calls; many backpedaled that very day. The Internet had spoken—shouted, even—and SOPA was quietly and immediately shelved.

It will no doubt return, in pieces and under other names, both in the United States and elsewhere; IFPI still lists all of SOPA's core provisions as key legislative priorities.

People want to copy, and the Internet is built to make it simple. No surprise, then, that any comprehensive attempt to minimize legal process and maximize penalties eventually reaches a point at which many people believe the cure is worse than the disease.

Even with SOPA's remedies thwarted, though, copyright holders have been able to get the government to take over the prosecution of entire sites and site operators. One key player in this effort has been US attorney Neil MacBride, who holds sway in the Eastern District of Virginia, near Washington, DC. MacBride was formerly an antipiracy official with the Business Software Alliance, a software trade group, and he has brought a string of criminal cases against file-sharing operations since moving into government. He targeted a video-sharing site called NinjaVideo, for instance, securing a twenty-two-month jail sentence and $200,000 in restitution for one of the site's operators, a twenty-nine-year-old woman named Hana ("phara") Beshara.

According to her lawyer, Beshara was an "emotional and high strung woman" who "used up many Kleenexes crying in counsel's office, at the arraignment and afterwards." After her sentencing in early 2012, Beshara remained free while awaiting instructions to report to jail. She returned home and almost immediately posted bluster-filled messages to Facebook, such as "I hold my head high. Always. Ride or die, no? THIS SHIT IS NINJA." MacBride's office, which apparently spent its time monitoring Behsara's Facebook account, immediately went back to the judge and argued that she showed a lack of remorse—and that she posed a safety risk based on claims that she could "shank it up with the best of them."

Not even a contrite letter to the judge could save her; Beshara was sent immediately to prison.

In addition to smaller criminal cases like these, MacBride helped the industry take on Public Internet Enemy No. 1, a Hong Kong–based cyberlocker called Megaupload. In January 2012, just after the public protests against SOPA, the FBI announced the end of a two-year investigation against the site. It conducted coordinated raids around the world to search servers and arrest site operators. New Zealand police descended on the home of Megaupload's principal, a hefty German man-child and convicted fraudster who had legally changed his name to Kim Dotcom, lived in the largest private home in the country, and owned a stable of luxury cars with vanity license plates like "GUILTY." Police swept in with overwhelming force, including helicopters, to arrest him, eventually cutting their way into a safe room where he had holed up, allegedly in fear that he was being abducted or robbed by armed men. A New Zealand judge later found the entire raid illegal and the search warrant invalid; the prime minster was forced to apologize when it came out that the country's Government Communications Security Bureau had spied on Dotcom illegally. To date, the attempt to extradite Dotcom has largely confirmed an impression of investigative overreach and made him an almost sympathetic figure—no easy feat, given his background. Still, the whole operation was a reminder that, when the United States gets involved, it can in fact reach Internet users in many parts of the globe.

It also showed just how far copyright cases have progressed (or regressed, depending on your point of view). Sean Parker and Sean Fanning built Napster and went on to become Internet legends—yet Kim Dotcom was arrested, his assets seized, and his company shut down even before trial (and even though his company claimed it complied with US takedown notices for infringing content). His extradition to the United States is pending; if upheld, he would be tried in Virginia by MacBride's office.

Such tough international measures appear to be the future. The United States spent two years seeking to extradite a University of Sheffield student named Richard O'Dwyer, who ran a "linking site" (that is, it hosted no content directly, pointing instead to files stored on sites like Megaupload) called TV Shack. The UK government declined to prosecute O'Dwyer for anything; indeed, his site might be legal under British law. His servers were not in the United States, but he did have a US-based domain name, which ICE seized in 2010; O'Dwyer simply re-registered it with a non-US company instead. ICE wanted to haul him to the United States to face criminal charges under US law, and the UK's Home Secretary eventually agreed.

His mother, Julia, a pediatric nurse, was nearly frantic over the case. "Forcing Richard to stand trial in the United States would be a severe hardship for his family," she told my colleague Timothy B. Lee in 2011. "It will cost £1,500 at least to have a trip to America. And then you go all that way for an hour's visiting time in jail. It seems ridiculous. The threat of being extradited is like an extra punishment that you're given before you even get to any charges."

Only after widespread publicity in the United States and United Kingdom, including a campaign launched by *Wikipedia* founder Jimmy Wales, did the US government back down on its extradition demand. In November 2012, it agreed to lift the extradition threat that had hung over O'Dwyer's head and accepted something far more proportional to the harm—a "deferred prosecution" agreement. If O'Dwyer stayed out of trouble in the future, he would not face criminal charges.

O'Dwyer was making money from his site through advertising, and Kim Dotcom likewise raked in mountains of cash. Neither is an especially sympathetic figure, but neither case is as clear-cut as the harsh pretrial responses might suggest. The United States has sought almost no previous extraditions on online copyright issues—indeed, on computer crimes in general—yet it now pursues them with vigor. Cases that would have been matters of civil contention a few years before have turned into serious federal criminal charges.

If another industry wants to do Internet-wide policing, it could do worse than follow the music and movies playbook: find ways to automate or offload complaints against users, intermediaries, and sites by getting the government to do much of the work. This only works if you can convince the government that your industry needs its attention—but the movie and music businesses didn't spend decades building some of the most impressive lobby shops in Washington for nothing.

This shifting of the copyright enforcement burden to government has been good for some rights holders. Deposit a list of names and turn over some evidence, and the governmental machine hums away. It may run for years at a time, burning tax dollars for fuel, but it can handle an enormous volume of work—and it has the power to snatch and jail those accused of copyright violations; not even SOPA promised to grant such powers to private agents. Whether the shift has been as good for the public remains an open question.

Copyright enforcement will always be with us, but rights holders have found many ways to automate enforcement and to offload costs. That's fortunate for them; they'll need the money to pay for things like the Jammie Thomas-Rasset trial, which has dragged on so long it appears headed for Dickensian territory.

/////

Judge Davis, resigned to running through the Thomas-Rasset trial for a third time, entered his courtroom on November 2, 2010 and looked about with a slow smile. "It is Groundhog Day," he announced, a reference to the Bill Murray film in which a man repeatedly lives a single day. Before him sat the same defendant, the same lawyers, the same small knot of observers and witnesses.

The only major change: Thomas-Rasset was already liable for

infringement this time around. Her third trial would not be on the facts of the case, which had been settled by the previous jury, but only on the proper amount of damages. With his remittitur order, Davis had already drawn a bright red line through the range of statutory damages, saying that anything over $54,000 ($2,250 per song) would be "monstrous and shocking."

Since Thomas-Rasset's previous trial, the recording industry had taken a second case, against a Massachusetts college student named Joel Tenenbaum, all the way to trial. There, it had won $22,500 per song, which the judge promptly chopped down to $2,250 a song, just as Judge Davis had done. In the only two such cases to proceed all the way to verdicts, the judges agreed that anything above this amount was so shockingly disproportionate to the harm involved that it could not stand.

The Thomas-Rasset jury knew nothing of this, however, setting the stage for an obvious problem. What happened if they, like the two juries before them, arrived at a damage award higher than $54,000? Davis had already made clear he would throw the decision out once more.

Potential jurors again offered themselves up as unwitting object lessons to the commonplace nature of Thomas-Rasset's activities. A local car-wash magnate, who owned and ran five locations around Minneapolis, admitted to using LimeWire to download unauthorized music. Follow-up questions revealed that he continued to do so. Another, younger man admitted to using both Napster and then Kazaa since his college days at the University of Minnesota. His own creative work had been appropriated without permission, which made him "angry," he said, but not until recently had he abandoned piracy. Neither man made the final cut for the jury; each walked out the door of the courtroom owing nothing.

The re-retrial ran in fast-forward. Judge Davis gave the lawyers only two days to make their case since this trial was to focus only on damages, but the music labels rushed through all of their underlying evidence anyway. I bumped into Thomas-Rasset outside the courtroom during a break in proceedings. How did it feel to be back downstate for go-round number three in federal court? "Like Groundhog Day," she said.

The case wrapped up as scheduled on its second day. The jury retired and returned after only two hours. In their view, Thomas-Rasset should now pay $62,500 per song, for a total of $1.5 million. Thus, to recap the three Thomas-Rasset trials and the Tenenbaum suit, juries had heard similar accounts about file-swapping and had reached the following conclusions on the damages owed for this conduct:

Thomas 2007: $9,250 per song
Thomas-Rasset 2009: $80,000 per song
Tenenbaum 2009: $22,500 per song
Thomas-Rasset 2010: $62,500 per song

Stacked beside each other in list form, the verdicts make an unspoken argument: juries largely pluck these numbers from thin air. And why wouldn't they? They have no context for making their decisions.

I asked Thomas-Rasset's lawyer Kiwi Camara after the trial if he had a reaction to the verdict. "Groundhog Day," he said. But the chance this all might happen a fourth time was one the labels hoped to nip. "Now with three jury decisions behind us along with a clear affirmation of Ms. Thomas-Rasset's willful liability," a recording industry spokesperson told me immediately after the trial, "it is our hope that she finally accepts responsibility for her actions." Fat chance. Because the award was above the threshold Judge Davis had already announced, Thomas-Rasset and her lawyers asked him to move beyond remittitur and to find the $1.5 million award unconstitutional. In the summer of 2011, Davis did as they asked. Because the new finding involved a constitutional claim rather than the common-law process of remittitur, the trial court case was finally over. The matter could now be taken to the Eighth Circuit Court of Appeals—and it was.

In late 2012, the music labels won at the Eighth Circuit, which simply reinstated the first (and smallest) of her damage awards from the trial in Duluth. After that ruling, Kiwi Camara told me that Thomas-Rasset plans to take the only step still left to her, asking the Supreme Court to hear her case. Seven years, three trials, and one appeal after the labels first accused her of file-sharing, the Thomas-Rasset case does the one thing most detrimental to any attempt to sue the Internet masses into compliance: it continues.

9
PRODUCTIVE CHAOS

My Internet hunt for heroin took five minutes—less time than lacing up my shoes and backing out of the driveway. I was spoiled for choice: 121 options for opioids, 243 for ecstasy, 339 varieties of weed, 45 dissociatives. Stimulants, downers, psychedelics—a global network of sellers stood ready to ship them all to my door in "discreet packaging" that might arrive from Switzerland, Germany, the United Kingdom, the United States, or even India. Tabs of LSD might be slipped into greeting cards, marijuana vacuum-packed to contain its scent, MDMA crystals crushed into powder for flatter packaging, yet all would travel through the ordinary mail system. Welcome to Silk Road, an online almost-anything-goes bazaar launched in early 2011. Like the ancient trade route for which it is named, the modern website can provide just about anything for the right price.

At Silk Road, buyers leave feedback on the sellers and their product, just as they do at more conventional Internet retailers after buying a pair of sneakers or a book. "Just pulled the needle out of my arm and all I can say is 'ahhhhhhhhhh,'" wrote one heroin buyer after receiving an order.

"This dope is among the best and cleanest I've had. The shipping was fast as all hell too. . . . Thanks a ton, bro!"

A pleased purchaser of ecstasy wrote, ".200 mg floored everyone that tried it. Out of my mind! Lots of lovin' but not very stimulating (since it is pure MDMA after all). And best of all, I slept in an instant. Great clean product."

One would be hard pressed to design a site more likely to anger the drug warriors, and Silk Road quickly did so. In June 2011, soon after Silk Road picked up some unwanted media attention, West Virginia senator Joe Manchin wrote a letter to the Department of Justice and to the Drug Enforcement Administration asking for help. (West Virginia has one of the highest rates of drug overdose fatalities in the United States.) Manchin urged both agencies "to take immediate action and shut down the Silk Road network." He noted that they had the authority to seize the site's domain name, too.

Nothing happened. Indeed, in 2012, Silk Road expanded, branching out into "small-arms weaponry for the purpose of self defense" by launching a spinoff site called The Armory, which traffics in powerful weaponry. As of mid-2012, $1.2 million each month was passing through the site, as estimated by Carnegie Mellon's Nicolas Christin in a provocative paper that attempted to gauge Silk Road's size.

Not surprisingly, Silk Road's proprietor has powerful libertarian leanings. In a "State of the Road Address" posted to the site's discussion forum in January 2012, the owner explained the site goal: "To grow into a force to be reckoned with that can challenge the powers that be and at last give people the option to choose freedom over tyranny."

This borders on the grandiose, but Silk Road's users really seem to think the site offers something more potent than Super Lemon Haze 28% THC primo weed. After buying heroin through Silk Road, one anonymous writer penned a lengthy piece about the site for alternative publication *The Austin Cut*:

Hackers, anarchists, and criminals have been dreaming about these days since forever. Where you can turn on your computer, browse the Web anonymously, make an untraceable cash-like transaction, and have a product in your hands, regardless of what any government or authority decides. We're at a new point in history, where complicated, highly-technical systems have become freely available and pretty easy to use....

This goes beyond people trying to get around laws and use the Internet to commit crime. This goes beyond that nasty scar on the face of human history, the "war on drugs." This is about real freedom. Freedom from violence, from arbitrary morals and law, from corrupt centralized authorities, and from centralization altogether. While Silk Road and Bitcoin may fade or be crushed by their enemies, we've seen what free, leaderless systems can do. You can only chop off so many heads.

The site offers the freedom from government interference that HavenCo hoped to find, but without the bother of shuffling servers into rusting North Sea forts. "Weird offshore jurisdictions" were "just a hack, and if they worked, wouldn't scale," admitted Ryan Lackey a decade after returning from Roughs Tower.

As law professor James Grimmelmann puts it, "HavenCo was always an awkward way station on the road to the real cypherpunk vision: perfect, anonymous cryptography in the hands of the masses. It doesn't matter where the bits are stored if no one can tell what they are. HavenCo's founders understood this. Sealand was just a temporary stopgap until the good crypto was up and running."

Silk Road can operate brazenly because it takes full advantage of a decade's worth of advances in cryptography. It accepts no cash or credit, relying instead on an anonymous, encrypted digital currency called Bitcoin. Buyers are told to encrypt their mailing addresses before sending them to sellers and pointed toward tools to help them do so. Most importantly, the site isn't accessible by simply opening a Web browser and typing in "silkroad.com"; instead it can only be reached through the encrypted online "onion routing" service Tor. Tor hides Silk Road in the shadows, just as it shadows all sorts of other hard-to-trace behavior. As a *VICE* magazine writer put it, anonymizing services like Tor are used largely by "hackers, libertarians, and child pornographers." This oversells the seediness of the situation—Tor has been a powerful tool in the hands of political dissidents, among others—but it has indeed provided cover for some technically savvy child pornographers and drug pushers.

What crafty libertarian hacker built a tool so destabilizing to the order that authorities have tried to impose on the 'Net for the last decade? The US Navy.

Computer scientists developed "onion routing" in the 1990s as a way to disguise communications over the public Internet, and they presented their work at conferences with names like Information Hiding Workshop. Onion routing works by bouncing a user's Internet traffic through an encrypted network of computers around the globe. After passing through these internal layers, each using a new encryption key, the traffic emerges from an "exit node" that dumps it onto the public Internet with its layers of encryption finally peeled away. The traffic thus appears to originate from the exit node rather than from the original computer, disguising its source. Most of the computers in the encrypted network also remain unaware of the originating computer's actual IP address.

In the early 2000s, the US Naval Research Laboratory built on this research to create Tor (originally an acronym for The Onion Router, now simply the name of the project), a next-generation implementation of onion routing. The Navy wanted ways to disguise military communications on the public Internet. While the armed forces routinely use nonpublic military networks, these become liabilities in certain situations. For instance, a military intelligence agent might want to keep up on what happens with jihadi websites—but connecting directly from a US military network would blow whatever cover the agent used on the site. Or reverse the scenario and imagine military, intelligence, or diplomatic officials on sensitive or undercover missions to foreign countries; connecting from within the country to a far-off US military network could give the game away.

The Naval Research Laboratory paid for Tor research and development between 2001 and 2006, but it quickly became clear that making Tor public and easy to use would empower all sorts of other uses by political dissidents, reporters, broadcasters, and even persecuted religious minorities—the grant-giving National Christian Foundation has sponsored Tor the last three years for this very reason. More users would also make military and police users of the network more secure by hiding their work within a blizzard of other traffic. If government agents were the main users of Tor, simply accessing the network would raise suspicions that the user was some kind of spy or cop; adding the dissidents, the drug dealers, the reporters, the feds, the child pornographers, the spooks, the privacy-conscious, and the hackers all provided greater anonymity for everyone.

The Electronic Frontier Foundation provided funding in 2004 and 2005, and the private Tor Project took over leadership of the project in 2006 and maintains the code today. The network itself is largely made up of volunteers around the world who opt their machines into serving as relay and exit nodes for the network, and funding comes from a wide variety of sources. The US government still provides major funding through the Broadcasting Board of Governors (which oversees US government media operations like Radio Free Europe), National Science Foundation grants, and the Naval Research Laboratory. The Swedish International Development Agency, Google, Human Rights Watch, and even privacy-conscious individuals have all ponied up to keep the project running.

I have repeatedly invoked "government," though of course there is no such abstraction. Hardly a monolith, government is instead a mass of agencies and departments and commissions and offices and fiefdoms and—ultimately—individuals, with all the cross-purposes this suggests. Key elements of government impose order on the Internet, but they compete with other powerful interests who actually sow disorder and anonymity. Tor resists the ordered world of the Internet police, but in that very lack of accountability lies its value; the US government built a tool of use to criminals because that was the only way to make it useful to everyone else.

/////

On January 21, 2010, US Secretary of State Hillary Clinton took the stage at Washington, DC's Newseum to deliver a pivotal speech on Internet freedom. She peppered her speech with bland bromides about the power of Twitter to change the world. But when Clinton got specific, one could sense government censors around the planet sitting up a bit straighter in their chairs: "We are also supporting the development of new tools that enable citizens to exercise their rights of free expression by circumventing politically motivated censorship," Clinton said beneath the glare of the Newseum's lights. "We are providing funds to groups around the world to make sure that those tools get to the people who need them in local languages, and with the training they need to access the Internet safely."

These tools, which included technologies like Tor, became part of the State Department's "21st Century Statecraft." Practical deployments include a Mexican project "to help combat drug-related violence by allowing people to make untracked reports to reliable sources to avoid having retribution visited against them," said Clinton, though she was careful only to mention projects that had the support of their local governments.

In the wake of the speech, more disruptive ideas emerged. The *New York Times*, for instance, reported on an "Internet in a suitcase" project funded by the State Department. The goal: private wireless networks, built on an ad-hoc basis, which would let activists communicate apart from the public (and government-monitored) Internet. "We're going to build a separate infrastructure where the technology is nearly impossible to shut down, to control, to surveil," said Sascha Meinrath of the New America Foundation—a remark likely to displease police all over the world, not just the censors in Iran and Syria for which the system is built. "The implication is that this disempowers central authorities from infringing on people's fundamental human right to communicate."

In 2011, State launched a series of tech camps that brought together activists from Europe, Eurasia, and Asia to learn about social media, mobile apps, and Internet safety. At a tech camp in Vilnius, Clinton told the assembled activists that "we have to be willing to keep coming up with new ways of getting over, under, around, and through the walls and other techniques that are used to prevent people from freely communicating."

This alarmed national leaders like authoritarian Belarussian President Alexander Lukashenko. Days before Tech Camp Vilnius, Lukashenko blasted his opposition in Minsk for using social networks to call for a strike. "I will watch and observe, and then whack them in such a way that they won't even have time to run across the border," he said on state television.

Shortly after a Belarussian contingent returned from Tech Camp Vilnius, Lukashenko complained about "information intervention" from other countries. "We understand that the goal of these attacks is to sow uncertainty and alarm, to destroy social harmony, and in the end to bring us to our knees and bring to naught our hard won independence," he said. Other countries with an interest in censoring and surveilling the Internet have also expressed displeasure at the US government's $50 million effort.

Still, this is relatively tame stuff. Governments, which routinely proclaim their horror at "cyberwar," hackers, botnets, and viruses, also create thriving markets for these tools. And unlike Carnivore, such tools can be deployed internationally with near-legal impunity. The market is hardly secret; companies like Xetron, a unit of giant defense contractor Northrup Grumman, announces publicly on its website that it will help government agencies perform "computer assault." But to understand what's actually on offer, you need nonpublic sources. Thankfully, we have some.

In early 2011 a small security company called HBGary had its network invaded by the hacking collective known as Anonymous. Anonymous then released tens of thousands of private e-mails from the company, though with little idea of what they contained. After a week immersed in the message cache, I found the outlines of a little-told story: how thousands of security contractors function as high-level hackers for government agencies. HBGary is only a minnow swimming in a sea of sharks, but its e-mails provide hints of how deep and murky the waters are.

The company's top coder, Greg Hoglund, had published books with titles like *Exploiting Software* and *Rootkits: Subverting the Windows Kernel*, but the e-mails explained how he put this knowledge to more private uses. As part of a government contract, Hoglund built a next-generation rootkit system called "12 Monkeys," which would be almost impossible to detect and remove once installed on a target computer. It could gather usernames, passwords, website addresses—then "exfiltrate" them to a remote server for later pickup, disguising the data as ad-clicks and sending it only when the computer had other outbound traffic. A document found among the e-mails showed that the company routinely built its systems to bypass common security and firewall software, then provided a checklist to customers showing just which tools it could avoid. An earlier version of the company's rootkit went for about $60,000; 12 Monkeys might earn as much as $240,000.

How to get a rootkit like this onto a computer in the first place?

HBGary, which announced in private presentations that it had expertise in "computer network attack," kept a stockpile of unpatched "zero-day" flaws for common operating systems and software packages. Rather than notify the vendor about security flaws that affected millions of users around the world, companies like HBGary investigate and hoard zero-day flaws in order to resell them. The company even kept a list of which ones had been sold on a "nonexclusive basis" and thus could be sold again. The more widely a zero-day attack vector was distributed, the more likely it would be found and patched, so deep-pocketed government agencies could also pay a premium for exclusive information on a particular software flaw.

Companies like HBGary provide only specific attack tools; they generally know little about their intended purpose—but we do have hints about how such tools get deployed. Hoglund at one point forwarded to several colleagues a Microsoft Word document he had obtained from a "dangler site for Al Qaeda peeps." The document, written in English, begins, "LESSON SIXTEEN: ASSASSINATIONS USING POISONS AND COLD STEEL" and goes on to describe a host of techniques for killing enemies with knives (try "the area directly above the genitals") and crafting ricin at home. But the document appears to have been only a hook to attract jihadist sympathizers.

"I think it has a US govvy payload buried inside," Hoglund wrote. "Would be neat to [analyze] it and see what it's about. DONT open it unless in a [virtual machine] obviously . . . DONT let it FONE HOME unless you want black suits landing on your front acre. :-)"

HBGary itself had worked on projects with bland names like "Task B" in which it investigated spy-movie scenarios for infiltrating computers. For example, "Man leaves laptop locked while quickly going to the bathroom. A device can then be inserted and then removed without touching the laptop itself except at the target port. (i.e. one can't touch the mouse, keyboard, insert a CD, etc.)"

The famous Stuxnet virus, apparently designed by US or Israeli intelligence to infiltrate and disrupt computerized control systems at Iranian nuclear research facilities, was reportedly delivered this way—through a memory stick taken into the target facilities. When inserted in computers there, the virus installed itself by exploiting a zero-day flaw and propagated among connected computers, looking for machines attached to specific industrial control hardware, which it then disrupted.

Through their funding and their actions, government agencies ratify their belief that too much Internet order is counterproductive. Chaos—even the kind that clears the way for sites like Silk Road—has important uses, but it's not hard for some to see in the Internet's disruptive anarchy a challenge to the basic ordered structure of civilization itself.

/////

French president Nicolas Sarkozy spent the last few years of his presidency calling for a "civilized" Internet, one from which chaos would be banished by law, treaty, force, and social norm. The Internet was whole new frontier, just as the Internet exceptionalists had argued—but Sarkozy had no time for hippies spouting nonsense about governing themselves online by the "Golden Rule." When he looked at Internet companies, Sarkozy saw their fundamental philosophical alignment with a philosophy of creative destruction, bottom-up innovation, and outright disorder. What he saw was companies who built chat applications and video conferencing tools but wouldn't voluntarily build in backdoors for government wiretaps. What he saw was Amazon threatening traditional French booksellers with low prices (France imposes "no discount" controls on books, to keep prices uniform and high). What he saw was Google threatening French newspapers by indexing and aggregating their headlines (the French government in late 2012 announced it was "studying" a law that would force Internet sites to pay for citing and linking to news content in French). What he saw was the Internet auction sites that had no problem selling Nazi memorabilia in France, where such sales are illegal (Yahoo famously had to be dissuaded from the practice by lawsuit back in the early 2000s). In all, it looked like a cross-border assault on a carefully crafted French social system by players from outside that system. It looked like chaos.

So in 2011, he asked a friend to organize the first-of-its-kind "e-G8" conference in Paris ahead of a major G8 meeting on the French coast a few days later. Suspicions among the Internet classes ran high, and many saw the entire event as a government-and-big-business stitch-up that would only result in calls for more Internet rules, more tracking, more asking for permission to innovate. (One invitee who declined to attend called it "a whitewash, an attempt to get people who care about the Internet to lend credibility to regimes that are in all-out war with the free, open 'Net." He then added, "On the other hand, I now have a dandy handwriting sample from Sarkozy should I ever need to establish a graphological baseline for narcissistic sociopathy.")

Perception of the event became so negative that organizers turned at the last minute, in a bid for inclusiveness, to a man with a hugely different view of what "civilization" meant on the Internet and how it developed: John Perry Barlow.

Urged not to go by those wanting to deny legitimacy to the event, Barlow nonetheless packed his bags for the flight to France. When he got there, he found an elite group of business and government leaders gathered in a tent in the Tuileries Gardens on the bank of the Seine. In his keynote address, Sarkozy rose to address the gathered worthies and did nothing to dispel Barlow's fears. "The universe that you represent is not a parallel universe which is free of rules of law or ethics or of any of the fundamental principles that must govern and do govern the social lives of our democratic states," thundered Sarkozy at the Internet execs in their folding chairs below his platform. "Don't forget that behind the anonymous Internet user there is a real citizen living in a real society and a real culture and a nation to which he or she belongs, with its laws and its rules."

And yet he recognized the practical weakness of his position. Unable to bend a global ecosystem easily to his will, Sarkozy instead went to Internet companies with a plea. Governments "wish to enter into dialogue with you so that we can defend one another's interests," he said. "What I am calling for is for everyone to be reasonable."

Yet reason and culture are both contested. Those gathered beneath the tent in the Tuileries had, for instance, already seen Sarkozy's party pass the first version of the HADOPI antipiracy agency, the one which treated the accused as guilty until proven innocent and which denied them due process, until it was overturned by the country's Constitutional Council. They had seen the proposals for cutting off Internet access—almost a necessity, in their view—after sharing a few songs online. The system had seemed utterly reasonable to those who passed it, and the longer they had listened to those affected by file-sharing, the more reasonable it had presumably appeared—but it had few admirers among companies born online. (Even the French government has announced plans to curtail or scrap HADOPI, with a new culture minister saying that Internet disconnection was a disproportionate penalty and that HADOPI cost too much to run.)

When Sarkozy had finished, Barlow prepared to mount the futuristic stage to face off with a panel of luminaries from music and movie companies. "I am about to enter the Lion's Den at #eG8," he tweeted.

The discussion began; each man got a turn to make opening remarks. Barlow talked about his surprise at simply being invited, "because I don't think I'm from the same planet, actually." Fifteen years after writing his declaration, the suit-and-cowboy-boots-clad pioneer was still fighting gamely for a chaotic Internet in the name of both productivity and freedom. The e-G8 meeting, he said, had thus far been about "imposing the standards of some business practices and institutional power centers that come from another era on the future, whether they are actually productive of new ideas or not."

When some in the audience broke into applause at his remarks, Barlow looked out over the crowd with obvious surprise. "This is a different audience than I thought it was," he said. Indeed, it may have been a different audience than Sarkozy thought it was, too. The French leader had more trouble getting an agreement out of the e-G8 than he had anticipated; the group came to no conclusions of substance, and at least a minority of attendees remained wary of the entire Internet "civilization" project.

The old view, that government has nothing to do with the Internet and indeed couldn't police it even if it tried, has been overtaken by events. But deciding when and how the government can act online remains a key problem of the next decade. The first e-G8 conference, as a gathering of the world's most powerful leaders, showed just how important the Internet "chaos vs. order" debate has become at the highest levels of business and government—and how contested the terms of that debate remain.

/////

Life is a messy business on the Internet as it is everywhere else, and we're never going to engineer the mess out of it. That doesn't mean we ever *accept* crime, piracy, or boorish behavior, but we *tolerate* them online just as we tolerate a certain amount of drunk driving, tax fraud, or jaywalking. Many such problems could be nearly eliminated if we just tried hard enough—required breath tests before every car start, conducted audits on every tax return, posted cops at every corner. But the cost of total order is totalitarianism; the real challenge is making prudential judgments about how we weigh risks and rewards, costs and benefits, order and chaos.

To do that, we need public and private actors who can police the Internet's chaos—and who also recognize that such chaos comes in two forms. The first is productive, allowing new and disruptive innovations to launch without permission and letting free speech thrive; productive chaos is the fertile soil in which the future grows. The second is unproductive, mere crime and anarchy, spam and spyware and child pornography and credit card theft.

The two often look hopelessly tangled. Porous online borders, relative anonymity, and innovation at the edges have led to international spam networks, The Cache, and The Pirate Bay—but also to Skype, blogs, instant messaging, Google, e-mail, Netflix, video chatting, and *Wikipedia*. The difficulty of disentangling them was one of Barlow's key points in his long-ago declaration. Remember what he said in 1996? "All the sentiments and expressions of humanity, from the debasing to the angelic, are parts of a seamless whole, the global conversation of bits," he wrote, arguing that we can't "separate the air that chokes from the air upon which wings beat."

That doesn't make the Internet an "anything goes" forum in which bad actors destroy the platform's value for the rest of us, and the stories in this book show just how far creative policing can go when dealing with online ills. In the case of Silk Road, for instance, the police don't need a backdoor that bypasses Tor's encryption in order to catch drug dealers; Australian police secured the first guilty plea from a Silk Road buyer in January 2013 after simply intercepting and opening all of his international mail. We should generally prefer such conventional investigative approaches over technical attempts to remove any hint of chaos from the Internet.

Requiring strong encryption to be crackable by governments would make it easier to prosecute just about every online crime today, but at the cost of destabilizing nearly all commerce and communication on the Internet. Eliminating the Internet's default (and modest) veil of anonymity could do wonders for copyright lawsuits, online libel cases, and child pornography investigations, but at the cost of widespread user tracking, less anonymous communication, and less whistleblowing. Making it *too* simple to snatch or extradite an Internet criminal from another country would also endanger everyone from American pornographers to critics of the Thai king to Chinese dissidents writing from Australia—anybody writing online may be breaking some country's law.

Investigative tools simply can't get too easy to use without creating significant problems for the vast majority of Internet users doing nothing wrong; the very fact that online investigations require real resources helps keep the Internet police focused on true priorities and makes it more difficult for them to create the kinds of massive automated systems that risk turning the Internet into a surveillance paradise.

Such a "paradise," besides sounding more than a bit dystopian, would also have unequal effects on the Internet-using public. As James Grimmelmann, the professor who wrote extensively about Sealand, told me as he looked to the future, "I'm worried about having a worst-of-both-worlds situation in which motivated people who are hiding their tracks are hard to track down—but ordinary individuals have lost a lot of their privacy."

Pragmatism is required—even the most creative and effective policing cannot always operate at Internet scale, and certain specific problems call out for more international cooperation, legislative tinkering, or regulatory changes. Some online ills might be better served with less judicial oversight but with correspondingly small penalties; others might benefit from more automated enforcement. But we should also be skeptical—such requests should only be granted after a rigorous vetting process, and they must be as narrowly tailored as possible.

The Internet is not the world's loosest slot machine, spitting out jackpots no matter what comes up on the screen. It can become an agent of surveillance and repression, it can become a playground on which corporations play, and it can become so infested with crime that commerce falters and communication is overwhelmed by noise. To avoid the first two outcomes, we need to preserve the productive chaos that arises from anonymous speech, from creativity at the network edge, and from strong encryption; we just need to understand that this also makes all sorts of unproductive chaos not just possible but unavoidable. To deal with the unproductive chaos and to avoid the third outcome, we need the Internet police, but we need to keep a close eye on them—and on their tools.

AFTERWORD: THE SPY AND THE POLICEMAN

Descriptions of the Internet as history's greatest surveillance network might sound hyperbolic. Hackers aren't well resourced enough to surveil entire populations, and they would have few reasons to do so, while police pursue more targeted investigations under at least some judicial oversight. But fund a hacker ethos with a nation-state's budget, then remove the shackles that govern law enforcement, and the 'Net's real surveillance potential becomes clearer. While we might, through policy, limit the extent of such surveillance, the Internet's technical design imposes no such limits. Indeed, what it allows is little short of astonishing.

Thanks in particular to the 2013 revelations of Edward Snowden, a former contractor for the US National Security Agency (NSA) who leaked masses of documents to the press, we now have a much better window into the ways that spies seek mastery over computer and mobile-phone networks. From the comfort of their offices—that is, without deploying a man in a trench coat to intercept someone's mail or a surveillance team to track his movements—the NSA can:

Read your text messages. An NSA program code-named DISHFIRE collects and stores nearly 200 million text messages per day from cell-phone users around the globe (only known US numbers are not collected). Apart from their contents, the messages also reveal the sender's social network and sometimes the sender's location (texts are commonly sent to phones as they cross national borders and automatically join new cell networks).

Watch your webcam. Because they have access to parts of the Internet's backbone and have tapped private corporate networks like Yahoo and Google, digital spies can collect much of what people do online without having to target them individually. And if there's one thing people around the world love to do online, it's wave their genitalia in front of a webcam.

Working in concert with the NSA, the United Kingdom's Government Communications Headquarters (GCHQ) developed a program called OPTIC NERVE to spy on webcam transmission and to store some of the images for long-term use. This particular program—there may be others—focused on Yahoo, which runs a popular instant messaging service with support for video chatting. Because the service does not appear to use encryption, it's a relatively simple task for the spooks to decode and store the video data; all they have to do is figure out the format in which it is transmitted over the Internet.

OPTIC NERVE was "untargeted" collection that scooped up everything it could find; in one six-month period during 2008, it logged webcam images from 1.8 million Yahoo accounts. (GCHQ saved one still image from each five minutes of video.) According to OPTIC NERVE documents seen by *The Guardian*, somewhere between 3 percent and 11 percent of this imagery involved "undesirable nudity." One GCHQ analyst noted that a "surprising number of people use webcam conversations to show intimate parts of their body to the other person."

See your Facebook posts in real time. Much of the NSA's surveillance takes place on the Internet backbone, which provides a powerful perch but comes with the burden of complexity. The packets of millions of users are jumbled together, and the NSA must isolate them and reconstruct the data flows into buckets—e-mail, instant message, web browsing, Skype call, webcam, etc. Each bucket requires a different protocol to understand, and some buckets are covered with locked lids (encryption) preventing the spooks from peering inside.

It's easier (but more limited) just to go directly to the most popular online services—most of which conveniently happen to be based in the United States—and pull user information right from their servers. The NSA does this through its PRISM program, which in 2013 provided "collection directly from the servers" of Microsoft, Skype, Yahoo, Google, Facebook, AOL, Skype, YouTube, Apple, and PalTalk. According to NSA slides, agency analysts can access both "stored communications" and also "real-time collection," apparently after obtaining a secret court order.

What comes back depends on the provider, of course, but PRISM can provide stored and real-time access to just about anything, including e-mail, chat (video, voice), videos, photos, file transfers, notifications of target activity (such as an account login or logout), and "online social networking details." No wonder that the PRISM slide deck boasts that the tool is one of those used most by signals intelligence; even the most America-hating target probably has a Facebook account.

Know when your computer crashes. Computers running Windows have long offered to send reports back to Microsoft when the machine crashes. Because the NSA sits on major Internet backbone points around the globe, it can see these crash reports, which are transmitted without encryption over the Internet.

The German magazine *Der Spiegel* revealed in late 2013 that the NSA captured these crash reports when they came from machines previously targeted by the agency. While the technique appears to be only modestly useful—it reveals a bit about the configuration of the target computer— it shows the creativity of a well-resourced spy agency for whom no "that's crazy!" idea has ever been too crazy to try.

Leaf through your Rolodex. While spies are widely assumed to be vacuuming up the content of phone calls, e-mails, and instant messages, then perusing them for secrets, the reality is that metadata (data about data) can often be just as useful. Knowing where someone is and who his or her friends are can expose the social networks of any organized activity, from money laundering to terrorism.

Thus, once the NSA and its allies got access to Internet backbone links, they began siphoning off and storing the full contact lists of Internet users around the world, including Americans. These lists—also known as "buddy lists" in instant messaging programs—are routinely transmitted across the Internet by some e-mail and instant messaging programs. The NSA uses the data to build a massive database of social connections.

According to the *Washington Post*, which revealed this particular insight from the Snowden documents, such collection is widespread. "During a single day last year, the NSA's Special Source Operations branch collected 444,743 e-mail address books from Yahoo, 105,068 from Hotmail, 82,857 from Facebook, 33,697 from Gmail and 22,881 from unspecified other providers, according to an internal NSA Power-Point presentation," it noted. "Those figures, described as a typical daily intake in the document, correspond to a rate of more than 250 million a year."

Track your location . . . with WiFi. Cell-phone tracking technology is already so good that the NSA uses it to target drone strikes. But many devices don't have mobile radios, and the spooks would like to track them, too. One Snowden document revealed a Canadian pilot program that captured information from devices connected to one Canadian airport's free WiFi network. The information was then used to "track the travellers for a week or more as they—and their wireless devices—showed up in other Wi-Fi 'hot spots' in cities across Canada and even at US airports," according to the CBC.

This capability, which Canadian spies called "game changing," was naturally built in partnership with the NSA.

Infect your computer. The NSA runs a series of QUANTUM computer servers that sit on or near Internet backbone links. These servers watch traffic passing across the Internet and, when they see any originating from a targeted machine, they react like a traffic cop. Because of their location, QUANTUM servers can respond milliseconds faster than the legitimate server that a target is trying to access. Rather than receiving a copy of the LinkedIn website, for instance, an NSA target browsing the Internet might be silently redirected by a QUANTUM server to a different FOXACID server. FOXACID machines essentially contain a malware menu; they can run down a long list of options depending on the configuration of the target machine and serve up the most appropriate exploit. In most cases, the target computer can be automatically infected with government-controlled code. At this point, the machine is open to whatever the NSA might want to do with it.

These examples are a small fraction of the Snowden revelations. The NSA also has no trouble collecting and reading e-mail (which is rarely even encrypted), instant messages, and Web-browsing histories. It monitors financial networks. It has developed custom malware that can turn cell phones into bugging devices by activating their microphones. It has built custom hardware and software that can slip malware across the air gaps that physically isolate sensitive computers from the Internet and can then "exfiltrate" the stolen payloads back out. It can spy on documents as they are sent over printer cables. It has designed USB cables with built-in radios that can broadcast every key being typed. It watches the pornographic habits of its targets with the goal of discrediting them. Its hackers have infiltrated more than 50,000 computer networks.

In short, the agency and its partners have helped make the Internet the primary playground of modern spies.

/////

When listed together, NSA capabilities can feel like Big Brother's gaze—and many of those caught in its gaze want to blind the agency, even if they've done nothing wrong. Given the networked nature of modern telecommunications, that's difficult to do by using private networks or relying on geographical isolation. The only viable approach is robust encryption of data traveling on the Internet—and the NSA is therefore determined to thwart that.

It is a tricky job, because the agency has two duties, one offensive and one defensive—spying on others while defending the US government and US business from such spying by others. But as we've seen repeatedly, the strong cryptography that protects bank records and defense schematics is the same crypto that also cloaks terrorists and criminal hackers. So what is the NSA to do?

What it *has* done remains controversial. It treats all encrypted information on the Internet as a threat and stores as much of it as possible, hoping that future breakthroughs will enable decryption. It also works to break cryptography algorithms, finding secret weaknesses that would let the NSA's powerful computer networks crack encrypted communications without manual intervention. In September 2013, the *New York Times* said that the NSA "has circumvented or cracked much of the encryption, or digital scrambling, that guards global commerce and banking systems, protects sensitive data like trade secrets and medical records, and automatically secures the e-mails, Web searches, Internet chats and phone calls of Americans and others around the world."

Even if this all took place by finding existing vulnerabilities in crypto algorithms, the extent of the crypto cracking would be controversial. The crypto routines in question aren't algorithms used only by a foreign military or government, as they might have been in Cold War days; they are the building blocks of privacy and trust on the Internet, which makes them the building blocks of all commercial activity on the Internet. By not revealing the fact that the algorithms have weaknesses and by not helping to improve them, the NSA has made everyone from ordinary Internet users to dissidents less safe online.

But the NSA isn't just passively weakening the Internet's security; it is actively seeking to destroy it. One of the Snowden documents revealed a $250 million "SIGINT [signals intelligence] Enabling Project" that tries to "influence and/or overtly leverage" the design of commercial cryptography products. The money is used to "insert vulnerabilities into commercial encryption systems, networks, and endpoint communications devices used by targets" and to "influence policies, standards, and specification for commercial technologies." In other words, the NSA is building backdoors into every cryptographic product it can. Examples of NSA targets under this program include commercial satellite services, peer-to-peer communications tools (such as Skype), and cell phones.

More general targets may include wide-ranging cryptography algorithms with many different uses. In the best-known example, the NSA apparently played a role in weakening an algorithm known as

"Dual_EC_DRBG." Soon after it became a US government standard, researchers questioned the strength of the algorithm, noting that it could be easily broken if an attacker knew the relationship between the numbers used to seed the algorithm. Did the NSA know this relationship? We don't know for certain—but reporting from Reuters revealed that the NSA paid well-known security vendor RSA $10 million to push the Dual_EC_DRBG algorithm as a default choice in its software.

/////

This is spycraft, not police work, but it gives us the best single look at the Internet's surveillance potential. Not even the most outrageous of the examples discussed here are theoretical. They are real—and the NSA is only one spy agency in a world filled with countries making similar attempts to "own" the Internet.

But the examples also aren't all that far from current police work, except in scope. Cops today routinely subpoena Twitter and Facebook accounts, cell-phone-location data, e-mail, and text messages, and they check the phones of suspected drug dealers for contacts. Less routinely, they install data-gathering malware on target computers and they activate webcams. Forensic labs break or bypass encryption on seized laptops and cell phones.

And police are piloting broad new experiments, such as automated license-plate readers (ALPRs) that log the time and then the plate number of all passing cars. (The Department of Homeland Security recently announced—and then canceled—a trial attempt to build a national tracking database from all these local data sources.) Live in a city that doesn't yet use ALPR? Electronic toll transponders offer cruder location data, but their records are easily obtained during an investigation.

In addition, we know that the spies are passing information to the cops—and often disguising its provenance. In August 2013, Reuters revealed the existence of a secret Special Operations Division (SOD) within the US Drug Enforcement Administration. To belong to the unit, you need to work for a TLA—a Three Letter Acronym—such as the FBI, CIA, NSA, IRS, and DHS (all of which have agents in the unit). SOD exists to funnel information "from intelligence intercepts, wiretaps, informants and a massive database of telephone records to authorities across the nation to help them launch criminal investigations of Americans," according to Reuters.

The cases aren't often about national security, and agents are reminded that "the utilization of SOD cannot be revealed or discussed in any investigative function," according to an SOD training document. Instead, agents pretend the investigation began some other way—a technique called "parallel construction." Told by SOD to stop a certain car at a certain time, local police might find some excuse to halt the vehicle for a traffic violation and then just happen to find drugs inside. Should the case proceed to court, the beginning of the investigation would appear to be the "random" traffic stop, not a tip gleaned from Internet surveillance. Even without involving SOD, the NSA has broad latitude to pass along evidence of American criminality to the FBI, and it's not clear how often it does so.

While intelligence and law enforcement continue to have different goals, they share investigative techniques far more similar today than they were a generation ago. Digital evidence gathering is policing's new paradigm now, and it has plenty of upside. But ease is always seductive, and the danger is just how simple the 'Net and digital devices have made mass dragnet-style surveillance, sweeping up the data of those not (currently) under suspicion. Without legal or technical innovation, anyone who uses a car, cell phone, or the Internet will soon be tracked and trackable at all times, establishing guilt a mere matter of querying databases.

A new series of Katz-style judicial decisions will probably be required to bring privacy protections up to date with modern technology, setting limits on tools like ALPR and facial recognition databases. But the protection of privacy also depends on agencies like the NSA accepting the chaos (most of it productive!) brought about by strong encryption and by tools like Tor. As security guru Bruce Schneier put it in a February 2014 speech, "We have built an insecure Internet for everyone. When you think of the NSA surveillance, it breaks political systems, legal systems, commercial systems—and the technology protocols we rely on are now not trusted."

Tempting as it might be to keep the entire Internet in a weakened state in order to have the run of it, this is a terrible long-term approach. The very basis of trust online is now effective encryption, which encourages everything from economic development to unpopular political speech. Encryption also discourages dragnet surveillance by imposing such a high price on each decryption attempt that mass decryption is untenable (though targeted techniques and traditional policing will continue to be effective).

The Snowden revelations have shown us what sort of surveillance is truly possible in the digital world; it's time to decide if we want to limit those possibilities.

CODA

Final resolution of several stories covered in *The Internet Police* came too late for inclusion in the main text, but for those who like tidy endings, here are a few more.

ROGER LOUGHRY

The accused Cache coadministrator got his second federal trial in January 2013, when the same witnesses and the same evidence were trotted out before a new jury in an Indianapolis courtroom. The jury's conclusion stayed the same, too: guilty. On February 12, 2013, Loughry was sentenced to 360 months in jail, with a recommendation to the Bureau of Prisons that he "be evaluated to determine if mental health counseling would be beneficial."

Loughry has appealed again.

AN FBI RAT

The FBI has moved far beyond the CIPAV software it rolled out in 2007 to solve the Timberline bombing. Evidence of just how far the Bureau has come was revealed on April 22, 2013, when a pro-privacy judge from Texas issued a public order denying a novel FBI search request.

"The Government does not seek a garden-variety search warrant. Its application requests authorization to surreptitiously install data extraction software on the Target Computer," wrote Magistrate Judge Stephen Smith. "Once installed, the software has the capacity to search the computer's hard drive, random access memory, and other storage media; to activate the computer's built-in camera; to generate latitude and longitude coordinates for the computer's location; and to transmit the extracted data to FBI agents within this district."

But the judge noted that the FBI had no idea where its surveillance software might end up. "What if the Target Computer is located in a public library, an Internet café, or a workplace accessible to others?" he asked. "What if the computer is used by family or friends uninvolved in the illegal scheme? What if the counterfeit e-mail address is used for legitimate reasons by others unconnected to the criminal conspiracy? What if the e-mail address is accessed by more than one computer, or by a cell phone and other digital devices?"

The request was denied, but it did reveal an important fact: FBI agents do have full remote administration tool (RAT) capability today, should a judge let them use it.

OLEG NIKOLAENKO

Nikolaenko finally pled guilty to controlling the Mega-D spam botnet. His plea agreement revealed that the FBI had seized his laptop when Nikolaenko was arrested in Las Vegas; on that laptop agents had found spreadsheets detailing Nikolaenko's spam earnings, along with a control script for Mega-D. Nikolaenko also admitted to making "in excess of $400,000" from his botnet.

His parents, Egor and Luidmila, sent a touching letter from Russia, begging the judge to go easy on their son. "It was very difficult and shocking to realize that our son had unexpectedly stumbled," they wrote. "Honourable Court! Definitely, Oleg has made an inconsiderate act, mainly due to this mindlessness and youth. And life has given him a hard lesson to learn. He has paid his freedom for that. But Oleg is our son, our flesh and blood. . . . [W]e hear that Oleg is honest in his repentance for what he had done, and he will never do anything like that in the future."

A friend also weighed in with the court, explaining what it was like to work daily with Nikolaenko in the car-tuning business they shared. "Day after day, month after month we were busy with cars, often hanging in the workshop till morning," he wrote. "It was very difficult to earn money. Often we slept three–four hours a day after tuning cars at night. I was seating [*sic*] behind the wheel, while Oleg was adjusting parameters of the engine. To do that we have to trust each other to the maximum." Nikolaenko, said the friend, was "the Real Man."

On February 27, 2013, a judge sentenced Nikolaenko to the time he had already served in prison, along with three years of probation. No victims came forward to assert damages, so restitution was not required.

JAMMIE THOMAS-RASSET

Without comment, the US Supreme Court declined Thomas-Rasset's final appeal on March 18, 2013. She owes the record labels $222,000 and continues to say that she cannot pay it.

SILK ROAD

The notorious online drug bazaar called the Silk Road was shut down in late 2013. The site's alleged founder, twenty-nine-year-old libertarian

Ross Ulbricht, was tackled by FBI agents at the Glen Park branch of the San Francisco Public Library after he opened his laptop and entered his various passwords. Ulbricht was accused of running a business so vast that he had made $80 million in commissions—despite a lifestyle in which he paid just $1,000 a month to live in one bedroom of a shared San Francisco home. More luridly, the feds accused Ulbricht of attempting to hire hit men on multiple occasions to take out those he felt had crossed him. Ulbricht has pleaded not guilty to all charges. His case, which is being heard in New York, remains ongoing.

In the weeks that followed the arrest, a new version of Silk Road opened under the operation of a new "Dread Pirate Roberts" (the same name Ulbricht had allegedly used to run the site). In February 2014, after several successful months of operation, the site claimed it had been hit in a sophisticated bitcoin heist and said that it was now bust.

ACKNOWLEDGMENTS

This book might have attained perfection had it been written by someone with Shakespeare's grasp of language, Methuselah's free time, and God's knowledge. Instead, it was written by me. The long list of those who pushed it closer to the Platonic ideal begins with my agent, Piers Blofeld, and his colleagues at Sheil Land in London. While it's fashionable in today's e-book age to suggest that major publishers are unnecessary, my prose was greatly improved by the care of my editor, Brendan Curry, and his colleagues at Norton. (Even I shudder to imagine the crayon drawing that would have served as the cover illustration had I been left in charge of such matters.) Many of the threads spun out in this book began as woolgathering during my editorial work at *Ars Technica*, where editor-in-chief Ken Fisher has been an unfailingly supportive boss and a model to media magnates everywhere in how they should treat employees. Thanks too to everyone interviewed for this book, each of whom gave generously of their time and proved eminently quotable. Finally, my wife and three children supported a project that took me away from them on more evenings and weekends than I like to count.

NOTES

1 CHAOS, STRENGTH OF THE INTERNET

Page

1 *"squatting in an abandoned warehouse"*: From Lackey's description of life on Sealand in response to a question on Quora, a question-and-answer website. Ryan Lackey, "What was living in Sealand like?" Quora.com, July 1, 2010, http://www.quora.com/Ryan-Lackey-what-was-living-in-Sealand-like.

1 *100 enlisted men bunked*: More detail on the "Maunsell Forts," as they were known, available from Project Redsand in the UK. Together, the forts in southern England did have some impact. "The Thames forts shot down 22 planes, 30 flying bombs, and were instrumental in the loss of one U-boat, which was scuttled after coming under fire from Tongue sands tower," notes the site. See Frank Turner, "The Maunsell Forts of the Thames Estuary," Project Redsand, 2006, http://www.project-redsand.com/history.htm.

2 *"it was intolerable for the crews"*: "'Fort Madness:' Britain's Bizarre Sea Defense Against the Germans," *Der Spiegel*, December 11, 2010, http://www.spiegel.de/international/zeitgeist/0,1518,728754,00.html.

2 *"artistic exploration of isolation"*: Read Turner's blog about the experience at Stephen Turner, "Seafort – Blog," 2005, http://www.seafort.org/blog/index.html.

2 *Sharman had ordered his men*: Ibid.

2 *"Rusty precipitation falls"*: Ibid.

3 *"our shower wasn't properly grounded"*: Ryan Lackey, "What was living in Sealand like?"

3 *"worse than I expected"*: Ryan Lackey, "HavenCo: One Year Later" presentation, DEF CON 9, 2001, https://media.Defcon.org/dc-9/audio/dc-09-ryan-lackey-audio.m4b.

3 *"They didn't like living"* and *"She went off to the north"*: Ibid.

3 *No rules governed*: The HavenCo site is no longer available. See an archived version of the site's "acceptable use policy" using the Internet Archive's "Wayback Machine" at http://web.archive.org/web/20040710104113/http://www.havenco.com/legal/aup.html.

3 *And the extraordinarily powerful*: Pirates have long seen the value of having their own beyond-the-law hosting site; the internationally famous Swedish site The Pirate Bay announced plans in 2007 to buy Roughs Tower after legal troubles began brewing; nothing ever came of the scheme.

4 *"If somebody comes to us"*: Lackey, DEF CON 2001.

4 *"There's really no middle ground"*: Ibid.

5 *"captured stealing a fishing boat"*: James Bates, "Prince Roy of Sealand aka Roy Bates (passed away 9th October 2012) Obituary," Official Sealand website, October 10, 2012, http://www.sealandgov.org/_blog/Sealand_News/post/Prince_Roy_of_Sealand_aka_Roy_Bates_(passed_away_9th_October_2012_Obituary)/.

5 *"I will never die of boredom"*: Ibid.

6 *"Radio Caroline didn't go down"*: James Grimmelmann, "Sealand, HavenCo, and the Rule of Law," *Illinois Law Review*, 2012, http://illinoislawreview.org/wp-content/ilr-content/articles/2012/2/Grimmelmann.pdf. Grimmelmann's eighty-page law review paper is a tour-de-force, heavily researched account of the entire Sealand/HavenCo business, and contains far more detail than most will ever want or need. Its footnotes reference everyone from Ursula LeGuin to Scrooge McDuck. (In March 2012, Grimmelmann produced a 5,000-word adaptation for *Ars Technica* that may be of interest to those desiring more overview than dissertation. See http://arstechnica.com/tech-policy/news/2012/03/sealand-and-havenco.ars).

6 *Sealand's history over the next decades only got more bizarre*: Ibid.

6 *invested over one million pounds*: Ibid.

7 *"the latest in a string of bizarre stories"*: See "Sealand Launches Casino," *Ipswich Star*, August 1, 2007, http://www.ipswichstar.co.uk/news/sealand_launches_casino_1_115333.

8 *"the British will deal with it"*: Lackey, DEF CON 2001.

8   *"very dangerous to be in a country"*: Ibid.

9   *"Governments of the Industrial World"*: John Perry Barlow, "A Declaration of the Independence of Cyberspace," February 8, 1996, https://projects.eff .org/~barlow/Declaration-Final.html.

10   *"You claim there are problems"*: Ibid.

10   *"All the sentiments"*: Ibid.

13   *"Pornography from, say, Amsterdam"*: Stewart Dalzell, Opinion, *ACLU v. Reno*, June 11, 1996, case no. 96-963, available at http://law.duke.edu/boylesite/ aclureno.htm.

13   *"Congress may not regulate indecency"*: Ibid.

13   *"True it is that many find"*: Ibid.

14   *"I just couldn't believe it"*: Stewart Dalzell, Penn Law School Legal Oral History Project Files, Box 4, Folder 8, October 29, 1999, https://www.law.upenn .edu/library/archives/other/oralhistory/interviews/transcripts/dalzell.php.

14   *"Really? What about fraud"*: Cathleen Cleaver, "Cyberchaos: Not First Amendment's Promise," September 9, 1996, archived at http://groups.csail .mit.edu/mac/classes/6.805/articles/cda/cleaver-cyberchaos.html.

15   *"the enemy of chaos and anarchy"*: Ibid.

15   *"We all share the goal of a robust Internet"*: Quoted in Nate Anderson, "RIAA: Google/Verizon deal needs yet another gaping loophole," *Ars Technica*, August 19, 2010, http://arstechnica.com/tech-policy/2010/08/ riaa-googleverizon-deal-needs-yet-another-gaping-loophole/.

15   *"US Customs officials have generally given up"*: David Post and David Johnson, "Law And Borders: The Rise of Law in Cyberspace," *Stanford Law Review* 48, no. 5 (1996): 1372–73. http://www.temple.edu/lawschool/dpost/Borders .html.

15   *"Individual electrons"*: Ibid.

17   *"Viewed through this lens"*: James Boyle, "Foucault in Cyberspace: Surveillance, Sovereignty, and Hardwired Censors," *University of Cincinnati Law Review* 66 (1997): 177–205, http://law.duke.edu/boylesite/foucault.htm.

17   *"We were worried"*: Lackey, DEF CON 2001.

18   *"It's not a big deal"*: Ibid.

18   *"The huge support cylinders"*: Simpson Garfinkel, "Welcome to Sealand, Now Bugger Off," *Wired*, June 2000, http://www.wired.com/wired/archive/8.07/ haven_pr.html.

19   *"Five years from now"*: Ibid.

19   *"A good deal of this is actually my fault"*: Ryan Lackey, "HavenCo: what really happened," DEF CON 11, August 3, 2003. Video and audio of the

presentation available at https://www.Defcon.org/html/links/dc-archives/ dc-11-archive.html#Lackey.

20 *"so much press inquiry"*: Ibid.

20 *Roy finally died*: Bates, "Prince Roy of Sealand."

21 *"Informal and inconsistent restrictions"*: Lackey, "HavenCo: what really happened."

21 *Zediva was sued out of business*: The key injunction came in 2011. See Timothy B. Lee, "Judge orders shutdown of DVD-streaming service Zediva," *Ars Technica,* August 2, 2011, http://arstechnica.com/tech-policy/2011/08/ judge-orders-shutdown-of-dvd-streaming-service-zediva/.

22 *"Ryan got the hump"*: Author e-mail interview with Michael Bates, October 13, 2011.

22 *"So the answer is"*: Ibid.

22 *"[W]e wouldn't do anything which was anti-British"*: Quoted in Grimmelmann, "Sealand, HavenCo, and the Rule of Law."

22 *"HavenCo was not an exercise in pure lawlessness"*: Ibid.

23 *"Political and contract stability is critical"*: Ryan Lackey, DEF CON 2003.

23 *"This cost me $220,000"*: Ibid.

23 *"Our [cybercrime] case load is increasing"*: Louis Freeh, Testimony to the Senate Committee on Judiciary, Subcommittee for the Technology, Terrorism, and Government Information, March 28, 2000.

23 *"enhanced vigilance at the local level"*: Hamid Ghodse, Foreword, *Report of the International Narcotics Control Board for 2001.*

24 *"the Internet's good old days"*: Adam D. Thierer and Clyde Wayne Crews Jr., "Everybody Wants to Rule the Web," Cato.org, December 17, 2003, http:// www.cato.org/pub_display.php?pub_id=3343.

24 *"Let this dream now come"*: Milton Mueller, "Securing Internet Freedom," Address to Technology University of Delft, October 17, 2008, http://faculty .ischool.syr.edu/mueller/opzet1.pdf.

24 *"governments have a role to play"*: G8 Summit, "Deauville G8 Declaration," May 26–27, 2011, http://ec.europa.eu/commission_2010-2014/president/ news/speeches-statements/pdf/deauville-g8-declaration_en.pdf.

24 *"building consensus on responsible behavior"*: White House Office of the Press Secretary, "Joint Fact Sheet: U.S. and U.K. Cooperation on Cyberspace," May 25, 2011, http://iipdigital.usembassy.gov/st/english/texttrans/2011/ 05/20110525121339su0.4443432.html#ixzz29IKlTqoz.

26 *"Cyberspace transactions are no different"*: Jack Goldsmith, "Against Cyberanarchy," *University of Chicago Law Review* 65 (1998), http://cyber.law.harvard .edu/property00/jurisdiction/cyberanarchy.html.

26 *"What we have seen, time and time again"*: Tim Wu and Jack Goldmsith, *Who Controls the Internet? Illusions of a Borderless World* (New York: Oxford University Press, 2006), Kindle edition.

28 *"What does ICE have to do with the Internet?"*: John Morton, Remarks, State of the Net Conference, January 18, 2011, http://www.ice.gov/doclib/news/library/speeches/011811morton.pdf.

28 *"We will follow criminal activity"*: Ibid.

28 *"ICE is not the police of the Internet"*: Ibid.

2 OPERATION NEST EGG

31 *On the morning of September 10, 2008*: The term "child pornography" is contested. Some groups contend that such sexual images and video of children cannot by definition be "pornography" but are better described simply as "child sex abuse." For instance, the UK's Internet Watch Foundation says that it "uses the term child sexual abuse content to accurately reflect the gravity of the images we deal with. Please note that child pornography, child porn and kiddie porn are not acceptable terms. The use of such language acts to legitimise images which are not pornography, rather, they are permanent records of children being sexually exploited and as such should be referred to as child sexual abuse images." But US prosecutors and the press still routinely refer to such images as "child pornography," as they did in The Cache case. This book uses both terms to refer to the same imagery.

31 *Without it, the raid was on hold*: Unless otherwise noted, details in this chapter are drawn from *USA v. Savigar et al.*, the criminal case that eventually put away the leaders of The Cache. The massive docket, now over 1,000 entries, contains a detailed archive of material related to The Cache. The key documents are docket numbers 910–913, the transcripts of Loughry's four-day first trial, along with docket number 915, the transcript of his sentencing. The case is 1:08-cr-00132 in the Southern District of Indiana. Quotations are not reconstructions, but the actual words either used at trial or recorded in court filings.

32 *Heath arrived shortly*: This sentence reconstructs events based on photos of Loughry's home and the timeline of the raid.

32 *The team had broad license*: See the copy of the search warrant in *USA v. Savigar*, Southern District of Indiana, docket no. 593, January 4, 2010.

33 *Savigar would later plead guilty*: See "'Dangerous sexual predator' facing lengthy jail sentence for three separate schoolgirl assaults," *Daily Mail*, January 13, 2010, http://www.dailymail.co.uk/news/article-1242969/Dangerous-sexual-predator-facing-lengthy-jail-sentence-separate-schoolgirl-assaults.html.

33 *"The only functions I performed"*: Testimony of Lori Heath in *USA v. Savigar*, Southern District of Indiana, docket no. 911, October 5, 2010, p. 191.

33 *"We expect his essential defense"*: Steve DeBrota in *USA v. Savigar*, Southern District of Indiana, docket no. 911, October 5, 2010, p. 213.

34 *The long road to Loughry's run-down Baltimore home*: For details on how the Australia investigation led to Europe and then to the US, see Department of Justice, "Department of Justice Announces Ongoing Global Enforcement Effort Targeting Child Pornographers," December 12, 2008, http://www.justice.gov/opa/pr/2008/December/08-crm-1095.html.

34 *who spoke with a Flemish accent*: Detail recorded in FBI Press Release, "Rescuing Our Children," FBI.gov, February 9, 2009, http://www.fbi.gov/news/stories/2009/february/jointhammer_020909.

35 *US Attorney General Michael Mukasey*: Ibid.

35 *In 2007, a US postal inspector*: Arney was the first witness at Loughry's trial once opening statements had been made.

36 *"not request, offer, and/or post child pornography"*: Trial transcript 2, docket no. 911, p. 15.

37 *With 1,000 members at its height*: Michael Baratta, another Cache coadmin, testified at Loughry's trial that The Cache had hit 1,000 users at its peak, but that admins eventually pruned it down to 530 or so by removing users who didn't participate or who were suspected of having been arrested by the police. See Trial transcript 3, docket no. 912, p. 115.

38 *"I didn't see any problem"*: Quoted in Ivan Penn, "Unlikely candidate runs for mayor," *Baltimore Sun*, July 10, 1999, http://articles.baltimoresun.com/1999-07-10/news/9907100223_1_drug-charges-mayoral-race-mayor-s-job.

39 *His bid didn't go far*: Election results available from Maryland State Board of Elections, 1999—Baltimore City, http://www.elections.state.md.us/elections/baltimore/1999.html.

39 *Loughry's mother Margarete*: See property lookup at the Maryland Departments of Assessment & Taxation, http://dat.state.md.us/.

39 *He grew estranged from his family*: Much of this detail comes from Transcript of August 18, 2010 Sentencing Hearing, *USA v. Savigar*, docket no. 915, October 10, 2010.

39 *Pictures posted to the account*: Seventy-seven pictures of Loughry and his life are still publicly accessible on his MySpace account.

40 *"You could say I was sexually molested"*: Trial transcript 2, docket no. 911, p. 76.

40 *"I used to look at LGs"*: Ibid.

41 *"If he were in custody"*: Trial transcript 3, docket no. 912, p. 115.

41 *"Paranoia about what?"*: Ibid, p. 119.

41 *"Yes, it was paranoia"*: Ibid, p. 122.

42 *"Yes, sir. There—I, I don't know"*: Ibid, p. 212.

43 *"If you let it get warm"*: Author interview with Steve DeBrota, September 12, 2011.

44 *"Very dangerous offenders"*: Ibid.

44 *In Loughry's case, that job fell*: Kiley's report is attached to "Notice Of Computer Forensics Experts," *USA v. Savigar*, docket no. 596, January 11, 2010.

44 *"the content of the chat"*: USA v. SAVIGAR, docket no. 596.

45 *"approximately 200 pictures and 40 videos"*: Ibid.

45 *"It was immensely satisfying to catch people"*: DeBrota interview.

45 *"We had what they said"*: Ibid.

47 *"Loughry's fixation extends"*: Joseph Cleary, "MOTION for Order of Competency to Stand Trial by ROGER LOUGHRY," *USA v. SAVIGAR*, docket no. 255, January 22, 2009.

47 *"I did not re-raise the issue in this case"*: E-mail interview with Joseph Cleary, September 1, 2011

47 *"It was a place where we traded"*: Trial transcript 3, docket no. 912, p. 189.

48 *"had child pornography in his house"*: Trial transcript closing arguments, docket no. 936, p. 36.

48 *"My job is to zealously advocate for my client"*: Cleary interview.

48 *"I realize now that my actions"*: Letter from Thomas "Arthurgrey" Lenti to the court, *USA v. Savigar*, docket no. 617, February 5, 2010.

49 *"I've had my face rearranged in Kentucky"*: Transcript of August 18, 2010 Sentencing Hearing, docket no. 915, p. 34.

49 *"The deputy here or guard"*: Ibid., p. 34.

50 *"Everything pertaining to this case"*: Ibid., p. 19.

50 *"At my wife's prodding"*: Ibid., pp. 29–32.

51 *"It was a Sunday"*: Ibid., pp. 21, 32.

51 *"may not be a fully one-dimensional character"*: Ibid., pp. 43–44.

52 *"Clearly the offenses"*: Ibid., p. 49.

52 *"I would suspect that it's a difficult road"*: Ibid., p. 38.

53 *"Operation Delego represents the largest prosecution"*: "Attorney General and DHS Secretary Announce Largest US Prosecution of International Criminal Network Organized to Sexually Exploit Children," Department of Justice, August 3, 2011, http://www.justice.gov/opa/pr/2011/August/11-ag-1001 .html.

53 *"other Internet forums dedicated"*: Harkless quotes from the "Motion For Downward Departure For Substantial Assistance To Authorities," *USA v. SAVIGAR*, docket no. 568, October 26, 2008.

54 *"The Internet has connected all of us"*: Quoted in Joint Hammer press release.

54 *"24/7 Network"*: See the "Convention on Cybercrime," Council of Europe, http://conventions.coe.int/Treaty/en/Treaties/Html/185.htm.

55 *"actually two operations after Nest Egg"*: DeBrota interview.

55 *"It simply cannot be tolerated"*: Quoted in 2010 Annual Report, Internet Watch Foundation, p. 2, http://www.iwf.org.uk/accountability/annual-reports/2010-annual-report.

56 *"Child pornography is great"*: Quoted in Rick Falkvinge, "Cynicism Redefined: Why the Copyright Lobby Loves Child Porn," Falkvinge.net, May 23, 2012, http://falkvinge.net/2012/05/23/cynicism-redefined-why-the-copyright-lobby-loves-child-porn/.

56 *Though Falkvinge has extreme views on plenty of issues*: See Rick Falkvinge, "Three Reasons Child Porn Must be Re-legalized in the Coming Decade," Falkvinge.net, September 7, 2012, http://falkvinge.net/2012/09/07/three-reasons-child-porn-must-be-re-legalized-in-the-coming-decade/.

56 *European digital rights group EDRI*: "Toward a Single Secure European Cyberspace," February 17, 2011, http://www.edri.org/files/virtual_schengen.pdf.

57 *"be possible to broaden the cooperation"*: Ibid.

57 *"effectively beyond the reach of this court"*: See Hon. Mr. Justice Arnold, "Approved Judgment," *20th Century Fox v. BT*, July 28, 2011, http://www.judiciary.gov.uk/Resources/JCO/Documents/Judgments/twentieth-century-fox-film-corp-others-v-bt.pdf.

57 *"In essence, what the Studios seek"*: Ibid.

58 *"pointed out to him"*: Ben Sisario, "To Slow Piracy, Internet Providers Ready Penalties," *The New York Times*, July 7, 2011, http://www.nytimes.com/2011/07/08/technology/to-slow-piracy-internet-providers-ready-penalties.html.

58 *"making things easier for predators"* and *"either stand with us"*: See this and other comments in Staff, "Online surveillance critics accused of supporting child porn," CBC News, February 13, 2012, http://www.cbc.ca/news/technology/story/2012/02/13/technology-lawful-access-toews-pornographers.html.

58 *"the first time that a Western democracy"*: Derek Bambauer, "Filtering in Oz: Australia's Foray Into Internet Censorship," Brooklyn Law School, *Legal Studies Paper No. 125*, December 22, 2008, http://papers.ssrn.com/sol3/papers.cfm?abstract_id=1319466.

58 *"If people equate freedom of speech"*: See "Conroy announces mandatory internet filters to protect children," ABC News (Australia), December 31, 2007, http://www.abc.net.au/news/2007-12-31/conroy-announces-mandatory-internet-filters-to/999946.

59 *"paints a harrowing picture"*: Asher Moses, "Leaked Australian blacklist reveals banned sites," *Sydney Morning Herald*, March 19, 2009, http://www.smh.com.au/articles/2009/03/19/1237054961100.html.

59 *That same year, WikiLeaks also obtained*: "797 domains on Finnish Internet censorship list, including censorship critic, 2008," WikiLeaks, January 5, 2009, http://wikileaks.org/wiki/797_domains_on_Finnish_Internet_censorship_list,_including_censorship_critic,_2008.

59 *In addition, the list contained a block*: Wikipedia actually has a quite a solid overview of the particular issue around lapsiporno; see http://en.wikipedia.org/wiki/Lapsiporno.info.

59 *"Of the 1,203 Thai sites censored"*: "1,203 new websites censored by Thailand," WikiLeaks, December 21, 2008, http://wikileaks.org/wiki/1,203_new_websites_censored_by_Thailand.

59 *While legal scholars like Bambauer*: See, for instance, the law article by Derek Bambauer, "Cybersieves," *Duke Law Journal* 59, 3 (2009): 377–446, http://papers.ssrn.com/sol3/papers.cfm?abstract_id=1143582.

59 *Milton Mueller, a Syracuse professor*: Milton Mueller, *Nations and States: The Global Politics of Internet Governance* (Cambridge, MA: MIT Press, 2010), 197–98.

60 *"The saving grace of this option"*: Ibid.

60 *"Remove, don't block!"*: See the main English-language MOGiS page at MOGiS e.V.—Eine Stimme für Betroffene, MOGiS, http://mogis-verein.de/eu/en/.

61 *"images of young kids, male and female"*: Trial transcript 2, docket no. 911, p. 182.

61 *"are bad, Your Honor"*: Ibid., p. 219.

62 *"The particular videos you are referring to"*: Cleary interview, September 1, 2011.

62 *"highly inflammatory"*: Order, *USA v. Roger Loughry*, October 11, 2011, http://www.ca7.uscourts.gov/tmp/MT1DVNQS.pdf.

62 *"I am sure 'The Cache' is back up"*: Trial transcript 2, docket no. 911, p. 118.

62 *"Before the Internet was easily searchable"*: DeBrota interview.

63 *"Their arrogant assumption"*: Ibid.

3 "I FEEL THAT HE IS WATCHING ME"

65 *Amy contacted her boyfriend Dave*: Actual victim names have been obscured by the FBI; the victim names given in this section are my own creations. The case at issue here is *USA v. Mijangos*, case number 10-743 in the Central

District of California. See in particular Complaint, *USA v. Mijangos*, docket no. 1, June 17, 2010, which provides an overview of the charges. I first reported parts of this section in Nate Anderson, "How an omniscient Internet 'sextortionist' ruined the lives of teen girls," *Ars Technica*, September 7, 2011, http://arstechnica.com/tech-policy/2011/09/how-an-omniscient-internet-sextortionist-ruined-lives/.

65 *"visibly upset and shaking"*: Quoted in Anderson, "How an omniscient Internet 'sextortionist' ruined the lives of teen girls."

66 *"had a hard time trusting anyone"*: Ibid.

66 *"For the longest time I didn't know"*: Ibid.

67 *"You pissed me off"*: Ibid.

67 *Mijangos was an undocumented alien*: Details from Mijangos' lawyer, speaking during his client's sentencing, transcript of September 1, 2011 sentencing hearing, *USA v. Mijangos*, docket no. 96, December 13, 2011, p. 21.

68 *"Mijangos acknowledged he threatened"*: Quoted in Anderson, "How an omniscient Internet 'sextortionist' ruined the lives of teen girls."

69 *"dedicated considerable time to toying"*: Ibid.

70 *"The minute that he attacked me"*: Transcript of sentencing hearing, pp. 32–35.

70 *"The malware that was used in this case"*: Ibid, pp. 11–12.

71 *"Some of these girls are disgusting"*: While the actual posts at Hackfoums.net require registration to view, the "Remote Administration Tools" subforum resides at http://hackforums.net/forumdisplay.php?fid=114. Unregistered users can browse the subject lines of posts in the subforum, such as "Could have potentially ruined a marriage" and "ShowCase: Girl Slaves on Your RAT."

71 *"Will add more photos"*: Ibid.

72 *"While I was at work"*: Ibid.

72 *"What a great way to spend a Sunday"* and *"kept a couple of guys"*: Ibid.

72 *Federal judge George King sentenced*: King's quotes from transcript of sentencing hearing, p. 70.

72 *"These people were having fun"*: David Kushner, "The Hacker is Watching," *GQ*, January 2012, http://www.gq.com/news-politics/newsmakers/201201/luis-mijangos-hacker-webcam-virus-internet.

72 *"The FBI has seen a rise in similar cases"*: Quoted in "Orange County Man Who Admitted Hacking Into Personal Computers Sentenced to Six Years in Federal Prison for 'Sextortion' of Women and Teenage Girls," US Attorney's Office, September 1, 2011, http://www.fbi.gov/losangeles/press-releases/2011/orange-county-man-who-admitted-hacking-into-personal-computers-sentenced-to-six-years-in-federal-prison-for-sextortion-of-women-and-teenage-girls.

73 *Susan Clements-Jeffrey didn't wake up*: The details in this section come from the lawsuit *Clements-Jeffrey et al. v. Springfield City et al.*, case no. 3:09-cv-00084-WHR, filed in the Southern District of Ohio. Of most interest are the complaint (docket no. 1) and the lengthy depositions of Clements-Jeffrey (docket no. 65), police officer Ashworth (docket no. 67), Carlton "Butch" Smith (docket no. 66), and Absolute Software's investigator Kyle Magnus (docket no. 77). All quoted material is taken verbatim from depositions and the complaint.

78 *Keifer Alternative had spent around $30,000*: Details of the program can be found in the deposition of Jason Graver, Director of IT for the school, *Clements-Jeffrey et al v. Springfield City of et al*, case number 3:09-cv-00084-WHR, docket no. 76.

79 *For instance, 1,617 rent-to-own stores*: Dan Goodin, "Rent-to-own PCs surreptitiously captured users' most intimate moments," *Ars Technica*, September 25, 2012, http://arstechnica.com/security/2012/09/rent-to-own-pcs-surreptitiously-captured-users-most-intimate-moments/.

80 *The school did use screenshots*: See the final report on the school's program—"Regarding Remote Monitoring of Student Laptop Computers by the Lower Merion School District," Ballard Spar, May 3, 2010, http://lmsd.org/documents/news/100503_ballard_spahr_report.pdf.

80 *The scandal caused a national uproar*: John Martin, "Lower Merion district's laptop saga ends with $610,000 settlement," *Philadelphia Inquirer*, October 12, 2010, http://articles.philly.com/2010-10-12/news/24981536_1_laptop-students-district-several-million-dollars.

81 *"What was it about the sensitive nature"*: Quotes from Geoffrey Ashworth deposition, p. 23.

83 *"But you tell us you have no interest"*: Ibid., p. 30.

83 *"He showed you the computer?"*: Ibid., p. 39.

84 *"How does the fact that you"*: Deposition of Carlton Smith, p. 25.

86 *The threats began on May 30, 2007*: See Nate Anderson, "FBI uses spyware to bust bomb threat hoaxster," *Ars Technica*, July 18, 2007, http://arstechnica.com/security/news/2007/07/fbi-uses-virus-to-bust-bomb-threat-hoaxster.ars. Also see Kevin Poulsen, "FBI's Secret Spyware Tracks Down Teen Who Made Bomb Threats," Wired.com, July 18, 2007, http://www.wired.com/politics/law/news/2007/07/fbi_spyware?currentPage=all.

86 *"I will be blowing up your school"*: The most detailed public account of the case comes from FBI Special Agent Norman Sanders, Application and Affidavit for Search Warrant, Western District of Washington, case no.

3:07-mj-05114-JPD, docket no. 1, filed June 12, 2007. All bomb-threat quotes that follow come from the affidavit.

87 *"The CIPAV will be deployed"*: Ibid., p. 14.

88 *"the FBI cannot predict"*: Ibid., p. 16.

89 *"We all know that there are IPAVs"*: See the documents released to the Electronic Frontier Foundation, Jennifer Lynch, "New FBI Documents Provide Details on Government's Surveillance Spyware," eff.org, April 29, 2011, https://www .eff.org/deeplinks/2011/04/new-fbi-documents-show-depth-government.

89 *"We want to ensure"*: Ibid.

89 *"I am embarrassed to be approaching you"*: Ibid. The specific document is included in https://www.eff.org/sites/default/files/filenode/cipav/FBL_ CIPAV-08.pdf.

89 *In late 2011, the Chaos Computer Club (CCC)*: See the group's report on the Trojan at "Chaos Computer Club analyzes government malware," ccc.de, August 10, 2011, http://www.ccc.de/en/updates/2011/staatstrojaner.

90 *"Not only can unauthorized third parties assume control"*: Ibid.

91 *"the security level this trojan leaves"*: Ibid.

91 *A leaked presentation from DigiTask*: See Dr. Michael Thomas, "Remote Forensic Software," DigiTask presentation, http://cryptome.org/0005/ michaelthomas.pdf.

91 *"shows how sensitive we are"*: Quoted in "German spyware scandal expands to political, legal circles," *Deutsche Welle*, October 20, 2011, http://www.dw.de/ german-spyware-scandal-expands-to-political-legal-circles/a-15475258-1.

91 *"FBI employees fully understand that the unlawful interception"*: Drawn from FBI Assistant Director Donald Kerr, "Carnivore Diagnostic Tool" US Senate testimony, September 6, 2000, http://www.au.af.mil/au/awc/awcgate/fbi/ carnivore_tool.htm.

4 A CARNIVORE GOES DARK

93 *"commentators and the press have portrayed Carnivore"*: Orin S. Kerr, "Internet Surveillance Law After the USA Patriot Act: The Big Brother That Isn't," *Northwestern University Law Review* 97 (2003), http://ssrn.com/ abstract=317501.

95 *"Carnivore's first action is to filter"*: Donald Kerr, US Senate testimony.

96 *"I just received a call from [REDACTED]"*: From information released to consumer privacy group EPIC under a Freedom of Information Act Request and available at "FBI Memo on 'FISA Mistakes,'" epic.org, originally sent April 5, 2000, http://epic.org/privacy/carnivore/fisa.html.

97 *"The software was turned on"*: Ibid.

97 *"There are few, if any, investigative techniques"*: See "FBI Memo Responding to Carnivore Legal Questions," epic.org, originally sent April 12, 2000, http://epic.org/privacy/carnivore/response.html.

98 *In December 2000, the IIT Research Institute*: Steven Smith et al., "Independent Technical Review of the Carnivore System," IIT Research Institute, December 8, 2000.

98 *"By 2003, an FBI report to Congress"*: See FBI, "Carnivore/DCS-1000 Report to Congress," December 18, 2003, http://epic.org/privacy/carnivore/2003_report.pdf.

99 *Put your taps at the right place*: *Wikipedia* has a long and helpful overview of the whole NSA wiretap controversy, along with 175 links to other sources. See "NSA warrantless surveillance controversy," http://en.wikipedia.org/wiki/NSA_warrantless_surveillance_controversy.

100 *"There are few barriers that prevent"*: Evgeny Morozov, "Bugger Off: Spying Online Is Perilous and Unnecessary," *Boston Review*, October 4, 2011, http://www.bostonreview.net/BR36.5/evgeny_morozov_internet_spying_privacy.php.

101 *"Cisco went on to sell about $100,000"*: Sarah Lai Stirland, "Cisco Leak: 'Great Firewall' of China Was a Chance to Sell More Routers," Wired.com, May 20, 2008, http://www.wired.com/threatlevel/2008/05/leaked-cisco-do/.

102 *"At first we were just poking around"*: Quoted in Andy Greenberg, "Meet Telecomix, The Hackers Bent On Exposing Those Who Censor And Surveil The Internet," *Forbes*, December 26, 2011, http://www.forbes.com/sites/andygreenberg/2011/12/26/meet-telecomix-the-hackers-bent-on-exposing-those-who-censor-and-surveil-the-internet/.

102 *Blue Coat responded*: "Update on Blue Coat Devices in Syria," Bluecoat.com, December 15, 2011, http://www.bluecoat.com/company/news/statement-syria.

102 *a group of them purchased Blue Coat*: Sayantani Ghosh and Jim Finkle, "Blue Coat to go private for $1.1 billion," Reuters, December 9, 2011, http://uk.reuters.com/article/2011/12/09/us-bluecoat-thomabravo-idUKTRE7B80QE20111209.

102 *"create their own policies"*: Blue Coat public statement.

103 *the government transparently injected*: Steve Ragan, "Tunisian government harvesting usernames and passwords," The Tech Herald, January 4, 2011, http://www.thetechherald.com/articles/Tunisian-government-harvesting-usernames-and-passwords/12429/.

103 *"We've had to deal with ISPs"*: Quoted in Alexis Madrigal, "The Inside Story

of How Facebook Responded to Tunisian Hacks," *The Atlantic*, January 24, 2011, http://www.theatlantic.com/technology/archive/2011/01/the-inside-story-of-how-facebook-responded-to-tunisian-hacks/70044/.

103 *The* Wall Street Journal *and the secrets-sharing website WikiLeaks*: The Wikileaks project is called "The Spy Files" and is available at http://wikileaks .org/The-Spyfiles-The-Map.html. The *Wall Street Journal* document collection is dubbed "The Surveillance Catalog" and is online at http://projects .wsj.com/surveillance-catalog/.

104 *"Your investigative staff will likely collect"*: See Packet Forensics, "Developments" newsletter, vol. 1, no. 1, 2009, http://projects.wsj.com/surveillance-catalog/ documents/267777-documents-266261-packet-forensics-youve-got-a/.

104 *"This industry is, in practice, unregulated"*: See WikiLeaks, "The Spy Files."

105 *"In traditional spy stories"*: Ibid.

106 *This happened in 2009*: From the testimony of FBI General Counsel Valerie Caproni, "Going Dark: Lawful Electronic Surveillance in the Face of New Technologies," House Judiciary Committee, February 17, 2011, http://www .fbi.gov/news/testimony/going-dark-lawful-electronic-surveillance-in-the-face-of-new-technologies.

106 *"In this case, the FBI was able to build a case"*: Ibid.

108 *"Why should we hassle the social networks"*: Quoted in Andrei Soldatov and Irina Borogan, "The Russian state and surveillance technology," Opendemocracy .net, October 25, 2011, http://www.opendemocracy.net/od-russia/andrei-soldatov-irina-borogan/russian-state-and-surveillance-technology.

108 *"Essentially, officials want Congress to require all services"*: Charlie Savage, "US Tries to Make It Easier to Wiretap the Internet," *New York Times*, September 27, 2010, http://www.nytimes.com/2010/09/27/us/27wiretap.html.

108 *"What is it exactly that you would want"*: From "Going Dark," complete hearing transcript, available at "Going Dark: Lawful Electronic Surveillance In The Face Of New Technologies," House Judiciary Committee, February 17, 2011, http://judiciary.house.gov/hearings/printers/112th/112-59_64581 .PDF.

110 *"serving wiretap orders on providers"*: Ibid.

110 *"The lawful interception of voice and data communications"*: Ibid.

111 *"made it possible for investigators to get access to text-based chats"*: Craig Timberg and Ellen Nakashima, "Skype makes chats and user data more available to police," *Washington Post*, July 25, 2012, http://www.washingtonpost .com/business/economy/skype-makes-chats-and-user-data-more-available -to-police/2012/07/25/gJQAobI39W_story.html.

111 *"Because of this gap between technology and the law"*: Testimony of FBI

Associate Deputy Director Kevin L. Perkins, Senate Committee on Homeland Security and Governmental Affairs, September 19, 2012, http://www.fbi.gov/news/testimony/homeland-threats-and-agency-responses.

111 *In 2010, the US government's own public report on wiretaps showed*: Table 6, *Wiretap Report 2010*, Administrative Office of the United States Courts, http://www.uscourts.gov/uscourts/Statistics/WiretapReports/2010/Table6.pdf.

112 *"America requires telecommunications companies to build wiretapping capabilities"*: Bambauer discussed censorship with law professor Richard Epstein for a US State Department publication in 2010. See Derek Bambauer and Richard Epstein, "Who's Right: Debating Internet Censorship," America.gov, July 29, 2010, http://www.america.gov/st/democracyhr-english/2010/July/20100727140740enelrahc0.3175884.html.

112 *"This was seen most famously in Greece"*: One of the most thorough English-language write-ups of the bizarre case is Vassilis Prevelakis and Diomidis Spinellis, "The Athens Affair," *IEEE Spectrum*, July 2007, http://spectrum.ieee.org/telecom/security/the-athens-affair/0.

113 *"the most bizarre and embarrassing scandal"*: Ibid.

113 *"Wiretaps are a risky business"*: Susan Landau, *Surveillance or Security?: The Risks Posed by New Wiretapping Technologies* (Cambridge, MA: MIT Press, 2011), Kindle edition.

113 *"When you build wiretapping capability"*: Susan Landau testimony from the 2011 "Going Dark" hearing cited above.

113 *The paper he presented explained*: See Tom Cross, "Exploiting Lawful Intercept to Wiretap the Internet," Blackhat 2010 security conference, http://www.blackhat.com/presentations/bh-dc-10/Cross_Tom/BlackHat-DC-2010-Cross-Attacking-LawfulI-Intercept-wp.pdf.

114 *"conflict with the goal of freedom"*: See RFC 2084, "IETF Policy on Wiretapping," IETF, May 2000, http://www.ietf.org/rfc/rfc2804.txt.

114 *An example Landau often makes*: Included, among other places, in *Surveillance or Security?*

115 *Data from 2011 revealed by the US Marshals*: See Declan McCullagh, "Feds snoop on social-network accounts without warrants," CNET, September 27, 2012, http://news.cnet.com/8301-13578_3-57521680-38/feds-snoop-on-social-network-accounts-without-warrants/.

115 *"Privacy in an open society"*: Eric Hughes, "A Cypherpunk's Manifesto," 1993, http://www.activism.net/cypherpunk/manifesto.html.

115 *In 2000, the IETF stated its belief*: See "IETF Policy on Wiretapping."

116 *In 2001, FBI agents executing a search warrant surreptitiously installed*: See the court's decision in *USA v. Scarfo*, New Jersey District Court, December 26,

2001, http://scholar.google.com/scholar_case?case=121513540940436577
12&q=United+States+v.+Scarfo&hl=en&as_sdt=2002 or http://files.grim
melmann.net/cases/Scarfo.pdf.

117 *"Periodically, government eavesdroppers"*: Matt Blaze, "Wiretapping and Cryptography Today," July 12, 2011, http://www.crypto.com/blog/wiretap2010.

117 *"While traffic encryption is highly effective"*: Ibid.

117 *"In 2010, encryption was reported"*: See *Wiretap Report 2010*, cited above.

5 NATURAL MALE ENHANCEMENT

119 *Something extraordinary was also taking place*: Most of the information about
Berkeley's business comes from the criminal case against Steven Warshak,
his mother Harriet, and others, *USA v. Warshak et al.*, US District Court for
the Southern District of Ohio, case no. 1:06-cr-00111-SAS. The main outline
of the government's case can be found in the Indictment, docket no. 1. The
voluminous transcripts of the jury trial were also important, most notably the
testimony of James Teegarden, which offered a glimpse inside the company.
See transcript of Proceedings for January 15, 2008, afternoon session, docket
no. 495, filed May 9, 2008. Unless otherwise noted, the reconstruction of
events here comes from the trial transcripts and the indictment.

120 *In 2001 and 2002, Berkeley customers were "were simply added"*: See Opinion,
USA v. Warshak, United States Court of Appeals for the Sixth Circuit, case
no. 08-3997, December 14, 2010, p. 7, http://www.ca6.uscourts.gov/opinions
.pdf/10a0377p-06.pdf.

122 *"At one point, Enzyte customers seeking a refund"*: Ibid., p. 11.

124 *"a byproduct of unsophisticated business practices"*: See "Brief of Appellants
Steven Warshak, Harriet Warshak, and TCI Media, Inc.," *USA v. Warshak*,
United States Court of Appeal for the Sixth Circuit, case no. 08-3997, May
29, 2009.

124 *"A reasonable juror could easily conclude"*: Ibid., p. 69.

125 *But when the government finally turned over*: The backstory on the government's
behavior can be found most easily in Warshak's appeal, ibid., and in Opinion,
USA v. Warshak, United States Court of Appeals for the Sixth Circuit.

126 *"prospective surveillance tends to raise difficult questions"*: Orin Kerr, "Internet
Surveillance Law After the USA Patriot Act: The Big Brother That Isn't,"
Northwestern University Law Review, 97 (2003): 616, http://papers.ssrn.com/
sol3/papers.cfm?abstract_id=317501.

126 *The Department of Justice's own surveillance manual*: Quoted in "Brief Of Amici

Curiae Electronic Frontier Foundation et al.," USA v. Warshak, United States Court of Appeals for the Sixth Circuit, case no. 08-3997, June 10, 2009, p. 7.

126 *Warshak appealed his 2008 conviction*: See "Brief of Appellants Steven Warshak, Harriet Warshak, and TCI Media, Inc.," p. 53.

127 *"Put simply," it wrote, "the government misused the SCA"*: from "Brief Of Amici Curiae Electronic Frontier Foundation et al.," p. 3.

127 *To address the Fourth Amendment issue*: See Opinion, *USA v. Warshak*, United States Court of Appeals for the Sixth Circuit, p. 17.

127 *"Given the often sensitive"*: Ibid.

128 *Olmstead operated quite openly in Seattle*: For a nice overview of the Olmstead and Katz cases, see Matthew Lasar, "The crooks who created modern wiretapping law," *Ars Technica*, June 2, 2011, http://arstechnica.com/tech-policy/2011/06/the-crooks-who-created-modern-wiretapping-law/.

128 *"There was no searching"*: Ibid.

129 *"The Fourth Amendment protects people"*. See Opinion, Katz v. United States, Supreme Court of the United States, December 18, 1967, http://scholar.google.com/scholar_case?case=9210492700696416594.

130 *"[Agents] were not required, before commencing the search"*: Ibid.

131 *"Even just five years ago"*: Christopher Soghoian, "Caught in the Cloud: Privacy, Encryption, and Government Back Doors in the Web 2.0 Era," *Journal on Telecommunications and High Technology Law* 8, no. 2 (2010): 386, http://papers.ssrn.com/sol3/papers.cfm?abstract_id=1421553.

132 *"If we accept that an e-mail"*: Opinion, *USA v. Warshak*, United States Court of Appeals for the Sixth Circuit, p. 20.

132 *"To the extent that the SCA purports"*: Ibid., p. 23.

132 *"Today's decision is the only federal appellate decision"*: Kevin Bankston, "Breaking News on EFF Victory: Appeals Court Holds that Email Privacy Protected by Fourth Amendment," EFF.org, December 14, 2010, https://www.eff.org/deeplinks/2010/12/breaking-news-eff-victory-appeals-court-holds.

132 *Paul Ohm, a former Justice Department lawyer*: See Paul Ohm, "Court Rules Email Protected by Fourth Amendment," Freedom to Tinker blog, December 14, 2010, https://freedom-to-tinker.com/blog/paul/court-rules-email-protected-fourth-amendment/.

133 *Berkeley Nutraceuticals entered bankruptcy*: Dan Monk, "Kubicki company to buy Berkeley Premium Nutraceuticals," *Business Courier*, December 10, 2008, http://www.bizjournals.com/cincinnati/stories/2008/12/08/daily55.html.

133 *He forfeited homes, numerous bank accounts*: The complete forfeiture list is

available in the "Final Order of Forfeiture," *USA v. Warshak*, docket no. 760, March 4, 2009.

133 *Three years later, the Segway resurfaced*: This anecdote comes from "United States Marshals Service Notice of Modified Return Regarding Docket Entry 579," *USA v. Warshak*, docket no. 832, August 16, 2011.

134 *In May 2012, after the gear*: See "Justice Department to Return $24 Million to Victims of Berkeley Nutraceutical Fraud," FBI.gov, May 8, 2012, http://www.fbi.gov/cincinnati/press-releases/2012/justice-department-to-return-24-million-to-victims-of-berkeley-nutraceutical-fraud.

6 TICK/TOCK

135 *Twenty-four-year-old Oleg Nikolaenko*: The government account of Niko-laenko's doings is largely contained in Brett Banner, Affidavit in Support of Criminal Complaint, *USA v. Nikolaenko*, United States District Court—Eastern District of Wisconsin, case no. 2:10-mj-00093-AEG, docket no. 1, November 3, 2010.

135 *"you find in a basement munching nachos"*: Quoted in Associated Press, "Mus-covite Denies Spam in US," *St. Petersburg Times*, December 7, 2010, http://www.sptimes.ru/index.php?action_id=2&story_id=33214.

136 *Mega-D's owner had made $464,967.12 in just six months*: A popular write-up giving the figure, which ultimately comes from an Australian investigation, is Brian Krebs, "FBI Identifies Russian 'Mega-D' Spam Kingpin," *Krebs on Secu-rity*, December 1, 2010, http://krebsonsecurity.com/2010/12/fbi-identifies-russian-mega-d-spam-kingpin/#more-6899.

139 *"Green Card Lottery 1994 May Be The Last One!"*: The complete message is contained in the disciplinary action ultimately mounted against Canter by the Tennessee Bar. See In re Canter, Judgment of the Hearing Committee, Tennessee Board of Professional Responsibility, case no. 95-831-O-H, Febru-ary 25, 1997, http://www.tomwbell.com/NetLaw/Ch12/InReCanter.html.

140 *"the receptionist handed me a stack of angry faxes"*: Ray Everett-Church, "The Spam That Started It All," Wired.com, April 13, 1999, http://www.wired.com/politics/law/news/1999/04/19098.

141 *"The posting appeared on computer screens unsolicited"*: See In re Canter, Ten-nessee Board of Professional Responsibility.

141 *"The Usenet, to my way of thinking"*: Quoted in Sharael Feist, "The father of modern spam speaks," CNET, March 26, 2002, http://news.cnet.com/2008-1082-868483.html.

142 *"Also, if the term is to be used"*: See the corporate statement "SPAM® Brand and the Internet," Spam.com, undated, http://www.spam.com/about/internet .aspx.

145 *"the announcement of a seminar at Bell Labs"*: Official Transcript Proceeding, Day One, FTC Spam Forum, April 30, 2003, p. 286, http://www.ftc.gov/ bcp/workshops/spam/transcript_day1.pdf.

145 *"My son has grown up very, very good"*: Ibid., p. 299.

145 *"The situation is, folks"*: Ibid.

145 *"Although lately he's been asking"*: Ibid.

145 *"I was and remain powerless"*: Ibid., p. 167.

146 *A small Internet provider called Lava.net*: Ibid., p. 38.

147 *"Whenever Paul would make an update"*: Ibid., p. 243.

147 *So spammers took greater caution*: To understand in more detail how spammers worked their particular brand of black magic, see the report prepared for the FTC by Stanford computer science professor Dan Boneh, "The Difficulties of Tracing Spam Email," September 9, 2004, http://www.ftc.gov/ reports/rewardsys/expertrpt_boneh.pdf.

150 *One major Internet provider reported*: Anecdote contained in "National Do Not Email Registry: A Report to Congress," FTC, June 2004, p. 25.

150 *"lawsuits against spammers"*: Ibid., p. 25.

151 *"We have a delete button"*: See 2003 FTC Spam Forum transcript, Day One, p. 25.

151 *"really thought that this was a very serious problem"*: Ibid., p. 13.

151 *"toxic sea of spam"*: Ibid., p. 15.

151 *"Let me say that the spammers may not be quaking in their shoes"*: Ibid., p. 19.

152 *"Now, I'm busy, I will probably not participate"*: Ibid., p. 27.

153 *"Much of this sleuthing is based on intuition"*: "A CAN-SPAM Informant Reward System: A Report to Congress," FTC, September 2004, p. 3.

153 *"as a mechanism for verifying"*: See FTC's "National Do Not Email Registry," p. 16.

154 *"an abomination at the federal level"*: Quoted in Amit Asaravala, "With This Law, You Can Spam," Wired.com, January 23, 2004, http://www.wired.com/ techbiz/media/news/2004/01/62020.

154 *It worked with postal inspectors*: See "FTC Announces First Can-Spam Act Cases," FTC, April 29, 2004, http://www.ftc.gov/opa/2004/04/040429 canspam.shtm.

154 *"Once we pass a tough national law"*: 2003 FTC Spam Forum transcript, Day One, p. 21.

155 *Within a year of CAN-SPAM's passage*: See "FTC, International Agencies Adopt Action Plan on Spam Enforcement," FTC, October 12, 2004, http:// www.ftc.gov/opa/2004/10/spamconference.shtm.

155 *"the Act has provided law enforcement agencies"*: "Effectiveness and Enforcement of the CAN-SPAM Act: A Report to Congress," FTC, December 2005, http://www.ftc.gov/reports/canspam05/051220canspamrpt.pdf.

155 *"CAN-SPAM Act had no observable impact"*: Alex Kigerl, *International Journal of Cyber Criminology*, July-December 2009, Vol. 3 (2). Pp. 566–589, http:// www.cybercrimejournal.com/alexdec2009.htm.

155 *"Even if we apprehended all spammers"*: Author e-mail interview with Alex Kigerl, October 11, 2012.

155 *"I think a better solution"*: Ibid.

156 *Consider its global spam estimates*: See various reports from the company; for instance, January 2011 Intelligence Report, MessageLabs, http://www .symanteccloud.com/mlireport/MLI_2011_01_January_Final_en-us.pdf.

157 *"according to US laws"*: Quoted in "Chats With Accused 'Mega-D' Botnet Owner?" Krebs on Security, December 5, 2011, http://krebsonsecurity .com/2011/12/chats-with-accused-mega-d-botnet-owner/.

158 *Internet crime has flourished*: The current list of top global spammers is maintained by SpamHaus.org at http://www.spamhaus.org/statistics/spammers/.

158 *"The pursuit of Internet fraud is often a cat-and-mouse game"*: Mark Guarino, "E-mail spam: Will it abate with arrest of alleged master spammer?" *Christian Science Monitor*, December 3, 2010, http://www.csmonitor.com/ USA/2010/1203/E-mail-spam-Will-it-abate-with-arrest-of-alleged-master-spammer.

159 *"The officials' actions were a departure"*: Andrew Kramer, "E-Mail Spam Falls After Russian Crackdown," *New York Times*, October 26, 2010, http://www .nytimes.com/2010/10/27/business/27spam.html.

159 *FireEye decided to mount its own attack on Mega-D*: See the series of corporate blog posts from FireEye beginning with Atif Mushtaq, "Smashing The Mega-D/Ozdok Botnet In 24 Hours," FireEye blog, November 6, 2009, http://blog .fireeye.com/research/2009/11/smashing-the-ozdok.html.

160 *"Unless someone is committed enough to pre-register"*: Atif Mushtaq, "Killing the Beast, Part 4," FireEye blog, November 3, 2009, http://blog.fireeye.com/ research/2009/11/killing-the-beastpart-4.html.

161 *"After seeing all these fallback mechanisms"*: Ibid.

161 *"Based on the timing of the FireEye attack"*: See Affidavit in Support of Criminal Complaint, *USA v. Nikolaenko*, p. 11.

162 *"practically indestructible"*: Quoted in Peter Bright, "4 million strong Alureon

P2P botnet 'practically indestructible,'" *Ars Technica*, July 1, 2011, http://
arstechnica.com/security/2011/07/4-million-strong-alureon-botnet-
practically-indestructable/.

7 SLIPPERY FISH

164 *Fishel decided to proceed*: The reconstruction of the Jaynes case in this chapter
comes from my own on-background interview with the Virginia attorney
general's office and from Fishel's retelling of the case at an antispam summit. See transcript, "FTC Spam Summit: The Next Generation Of Threats
And Solutions," Day 2, July 12, 2007, pp. 8–20, http://www.ftc.gov/bcp/
workshops/spamsummit/draft_transcript_day2.pdf.

166 *"found cases and cases of hundred dollar bottles of wine"*: Ibid., p. 15.

167 *"Is forging headers on par with heinous crimes"*: Brian McWilliams, "Perspective. Free Jeremy Jaynes!" Betanews, April 11, 2005, http://betanews.
com/2005/04/11/perspective-free-jeremy-jaynes/.

167 *"major, major fraud case"*: Interview with Virginia attorney general's office,
January 24, 2012.

167 *"would prohibit all bulk e-mail"*: State Supreme Court of Virginia, Opinion,
Jaynes v. Commonwealth of Virginia, record no. 062388, September 12, 2008,
p. 26, http://www.courts.state.va.us/opinions/opnscvwp/1062388.pdf.

168 *"unconstitutionally overbroad on its face"*: Ibid., p. 28.

168 *"forged corporate documents"*: Bill of Information, *USA v. Jeremy Dagan Jaynes*,
case no. 5:06-cr-00054, US District Court for the Western District of North
Carolina, p. 7.

169 *the amended law*: See the text of the law, "An Act to amend and reenact §§
18.2-152.2, 18.2-152.3:1, and 18.2-152.12 of the Code of Virginia, relating
to unsolicited commercial electronic mail (spam); penalty," April 11, 2010,
http://leg1.state.va.us/cgi-bin/legp504.exe?101+ful+CHAP0489.

169 *"It has long been a commonplace"*: State Supreme Court of Virginia, Opinion,
p. 7.

170 *"We are not the biggest unit in the world"*: 2007 FTC Spam Summit, Day 2
transcript, pp. 12–13.

170 *"We just don't have enough people"*: Interview with Virginia attorney general's
office.

170 *"We figured, well, we'll just contact the debt-adjustment company"*: FTC Spam
Forum, Day 3 transcript, May 2, 2003, p. 177, http://www.ftc.gov/bcp/
workshops/spam/transcript_day3.pdf.

171 *"That's a lot steps"*: Ibid.

172 *"So, you know, a sort of happy ending"*: Ibid.

172 *Sanford "Spamford" Wallace showed up for his sworn deposition without a lawyer*: Wallace's deposition informs this section. See "Deposition of Contempt Defendant Sanford Wallace," FTC v. Odysseus Marketing and Walter Rines, United States District Court—District of New Hampshire, case no. 05-CV-330-SM, docket nos. 27–32, filed January 23, 2008.

173 *"Let me just state, for the record"*: Ibid., pp. 17–18.

173 *In 1997, Hormel sent him a letter*: Joanna Glasner, "A Brief History of SPAM, and Spam," Wired.com, May 26, 2001, http://www.wired.com/print/techbiz/media/news/2001/05/44111.

174 *Wallace was angry enough about the hacking*: Brian McWilliams, *Spam Kings* (Sebastopol, CA: O'Reilly Media, 2004), 22–25.

174 *Local residents were furious*: Deborah Scoblionkov, "Life In Spamalot," *Philadelphia Citypaper*, January 22–29, 1998, http://archives.citypaper.net/articles/012298/hr1.shtml

174 *"they put me into business—a business that worked"*: Quoted in Brian McWilliams, "Exiled Spam King's Go-Go Life," Wired.com, October 7, 2003, http://www.wired.com/techbiz/media/news/2003/10/60714.

175 *"I think the world of Sanford"*: Ibid.

175 *The Federal Trade Commission filed suit against Wallace*: "FTC Cracks down On Spyware Operation," FTC, October 12, 2004, http://www.ftc.gov/opa/2004/10/spyware.shtm.

175 *The two "wasted little time in violating the Court's Order"*: See "Memorandum In Support Of Plaintiff's Motion For An Order Holding Walter Rines, Online Turbo Merchant, Inc., And Sanford Wallace In Civil Contempt For Their Violations Of This Court's Permanent Injunction," *FTC v. Odysseus Marketing and Walter Rines*, United States District Court—District of New Hampshire, case no. 05-CV-330-SM, docket no. 27-2, p. 1, filed January 23, 2008.

176 *In one memorable exploit*: Ibid., pp. 7–8.

176 *50 million registered users*: Rowan Bridge, "MySpace looks to UK music scene," BBC News, January 24, 2006, http://news.bbc.co.uk/2/hi/technology/4642622.stm.

176 *"A message between two friends"*: Wallace deposition, p. 123.

177 *"It's not something coming from a stranger"*: Ibid., p. 132.

177 *"I basically could not pay"*: Ibid., p. 30.

177 *"Well, here's the kicker"*: Ibid., pp. 142–44.

178 *"I could not afford my rent"*: Ibid., p. 160.

179 *"Each time, MySpace waited"*: Greg Sandoval, "MySpace wins suit against

'spam king,'" CNET, April 28, 2008, http://news.cnet.com/8301-10784_3-9930977-7.html?part=rss&subj=news&tag=2547-1_3-0-20.

179 *In early 2009, Facebook filed suit against Wallace*: Sam O'Rourke, "The Fight Goes On," Facebook blog, October 30, 2009, https://blog.facebook.com/blog.php?post=58219622130.

180 *"The Court is not persuaded"*: Order Granting Plaintiff's Renewed Motion for Default Judgment, *Facebook v. Sanford Wallace*, US District Court for the Northern District of California, case no. 5:09-cr-00798, docket no. 91, p. 5.

180 *"While we don't expect to receive the vast majority of the award"*: "The Fight Goes On," Facebook blog.

180 *"I absolutely believed Sanford"*: Author e-mail interview with Pete Wellborn, October 11, 2012.

181 *"It's one thing to tell a fellow to go to hell"*: Author interview with Joshua Millard, February 9, 2012.

181 *The FBI investigated Wallace's Facebook activities*: See "Sanford Wallace Indicted for Spamming Facebook Users," US Attorney's Office, Northern District of California, August 4, 2001, http://www.fbi.gov/sanfrancisco/press-releases/2011/sanford-wallace-indicted-for-spamming-facebook-users.

182 *"I mean, if we got to it"*: Wallace deposition, p. 147.

183 *"the FTC needs to step up and quit being sissy's"*: Admin, "FTC Fail," Scam Times blog, November 1, 2009, http://www.scamtimes.com/ftc/ftc-fail/.

184 *"I have yet to have anyone be cheered"*: Interview with Joshua Millard.

8 GROUNDHOG DAY

185 *Here, the declining-but-still-mighty recording industry*: The long-running case against Thomas has been known by multiple names; it ended up as *Capitol Records v. Thomas-Rasset*, US District Court—District of Minnesota, case no. 06-cv-1497. The reconstruction of the first jury trial in 2007, and the quotations from it in this chapter, come largely from the three-volume trial transcript, docket nos. 220–22.

186 *"When you fish with a net"*: Quoted in Dennis Roddy, "The song remains the same," Pittsburgh Post-Gazette, September 14, 2003, http://old.post-gazette.com/columnists/20030914edroddy0914p1.asp.

187 *"brought the music industry some of the most favorable headlines"*: Ibid.

187 *"Kill them all; let God sort them out"*: From "Defendant's Statement of the Case," *Capitol Records v. Thomas-Rasset*, US District Court—District of Minnesota, case no. 06-cv-1497, docket no. 62, p. 1.

187 *The recording industry, appalled by the rhetoric*: See "Plaintiffs' Motion In

Limine To Preclude Defendant From Making Unfounded, Prejudicial Statements To The Jury," Capitol Records v. Thomas-Rasset, US District Court—District of Minnesota, case no. 06-cv-1497, docket no. 82.

190 *"hundreds upon hundreds of sound recordings"*: Thomas-Rasset trial transcript, vol. 3, p. 606.

190 *"I only ask that you consider"*: Ibid., p. 605.

192 *yet they said surprising things*: The juror material here comes almost exclusively from the voir dire jury selection process. For the first trial, this is contained in Transcript 1, docket no. 220.

193 *"Jammie Thomas is one of the best customers"*: Thomas-Rasset trial transcript, vol. 3, p. 572.

195 *"Taken as a whole,"* he wrote, *"the evidence now available"*: Stephen Breyer, "The Uneasy Case for Copyright." *Harvard Law Review* 84, no. 2 (December 1970): 281–351.

195 *"This does send a message, we hope"*: Quoted in Eric Bangeman, "RIAA trial verdict is in: jury finds Thomas liable for infringement," *Ars Technica*, October 4, 2007, http://arstechnica.com/tech-policy/2007/10/verdict-is-in/.

196 *"She lied"*: Quoted in David Kravets, "RIAA Juror: 'We Wanted to Send a Message'," Wired.com, October 9, 2007, http://www.wired.com/threatlevel/2007/10/riaa-juror-we-w/.

196 *"While the Court does not discount Plaintiffs' claim"*: From "ORDER GRANTING [109] Motion for New Trial and DENYING [116] Motion to Amend/Correct," Capitol Records v. Thomas-Rasset, US District Court—District of Minnesota, case no. 06-cv-1497, docket no. 197, September 24, 2008.

197 *"Today, one individual, in less time"*: Cary Sherman, Testimony on No Electronic Theft Act, Subcommittee on Courts and Intellectual Property, House Judiciary Committee, September 11, 1997, http://judiciary.house.gov/legacy/41104.htm.

198 *"I am obsessed with trying to understand Internet scale"*: David Post, "Talk about scale!" January 1, 2012, http://volokh.com/2012/01/01/talk-about-scale/.

200 *"document authored by Napster cofounder"*: Opinion, *A&M Records v. Napster, Inc.*, Court of Appeals, 9th Circuit 2001, April 3, 2001, http://scholar.google.com/scholar_case?case=14102696336550697309&hl=en&as_sdt=2,14&as_vis=1.

201 *"We hold that one who distributes a device"*: Opinion, *MGM v. Grokster*, US Supreme Court, case no. 04-480, June 27, 2005, http://www.copyright.gov/docs/mgm/opinion.pdf.

201 *"containing links to articles"*: Ibid.

201 *Tim Wu compiled a 2003 list*: Tim Wu, "When Code Isn't Law," *Virginia Law Review* 89 (2003), p. 151, http://ssrn.com/abstract=413201.

202 *Pirate Bay admins posted and then made fun*: See The Pirate Bay response from "anakata" at http://static.thepiratebay.se/warner_resp.txt.

203 *"mismatches between physical world assumptions"*: Rebecca Giblin, *Code Wars: 10 Years of P2P Software Litigation* (Cheltenham, UK: Edward Elgar Publishing, 2011), 141.

204 *"At that point, rights holders tacitly admitted defeat"*: Rebecca Giblin, "Physical World Assumptions and Software World Realities (and Why There are More P2P Software Providers than Ever Before)," *Columbia Journal of Law & the Arts* 35, no. 1 (2011), http://ssrn.com/abstract=1992711.

206 *"They send us a list of IP addresses"*: Quoted in Howard Dahdah, "Film industry sues iiNet over BitTorrent downloads," *Computerworld*, November 20, 2008, http://www.computerworld.com.au/article/268184/film_industry_sues_iinet_over_bittorrent_downloads/.

206 *In other words, the studios wanted*: See Nate Anderson, "Australia confirms ISPs are not copyright cops," *Ars Technica*, February 24, 2011, http://arstechnica.com/tech-policy/2011/02/australia-confirms-isps-are-not-copyright-cops/.

206 *iiNet won its case*: See Nate Anderson, "Studios crushed: ISP can't be forced to play copyright cop," Ars Technica, Feruary 4, 2010, http://arstechnica.com/tech-policy/news/2010/02/studios-crushed-isp-cant-be-forced-to-play-copyright-cop.ars.

206 *In 2012, it won again on appeal*: See Nate Anderson, "Australian High Court rules ISPs need not act on private infringement notices," *Ars Technica*, April 20, 2012, http://arstechnica.com/tech-policy/2012/04/australian-high-court-rules-isps-need-not-act-on-private-infringement-notices/.

207 *"I never downloaded Morbid Angel's 'World of Shit'"*: The account of Thomas' second trial come from my own notes on the case; I covered the entire trial for *Ars Technica* in 2009.

210 *"a ruling that already is infamous"*: Jim DeRogatis, "Richard Marx defends the RIAA's $1.92 million scapegoat," *Chicago Sun-Times*, June 23, 2009, http://blogs.suntimes.com/music/2009/06/richard_marx_defends_the_riaas.html.

210 *"this show of force"*: Quoted in Ibid.

211 *"Thomas-Rasset lied on the witness stand"*: See Nate Anderson, "Judge slashes 'monstrous' P2P award by 97% to $54,000," *Ars Technica*, January 22, 2010, http://arstechnica.com/tech-policy/2010/01/judge-slashes-monstrous-jammie-thomas-p2p-award-by-35x/.

211 *"The need for deterrence cannot justify"*: Ibid.

211 *"higher award than the Court might have chosen"*: Ibid.

213 *"stolen intellectual property is not the occasional needle"*: Richard Cotton and Margaret Tobey, "Comments of NBC Universal, Inc.," FCC WC docket 07-52, filed June 15, 2007.

213 *"Once you start going down the path"*: Quoted in Saul Hansell, "Verizon Rejects Hollywood's Call to Aid Piracy Fight," *New York Times*, February 5, 2008, http://bits.blogs.nytimes.com/2008/02/05/verizon-rejects-hollywoods-call-to-aid-piracy-fight/.

213 *"Private entities are not created"*: Quoted in Timothy B. Lee, "ISP flip-flops: why do they now support 'six strikes' plan?" *Ars Technica*, July 10, 2011, http://arstechnica.com/telecom/news/2011/07/why-did-telcos-flip-flop-and-support-six-strikes-plan.ars.

214 *No matter that the key, Hollywood-backed study*: See Nate Anderson, "Oops: MPAA admits college piracy numbers grossly inflated," *Ars Technica*, Jan 22, 2008, http://arstechnica.com/tech-policy/2008/01/oops-mpaa-admits-college-piracy-numbers-grossly-inflated/.

214 *The law, which dished out penalties without trial*: Nate Anderson, "French court savages 'three-strikes' law, tosses it out," *Ars Technica*, June 10, 2009, http://arstechnica.com/tech-policy/news/2009/06/french-court-savages-3-strikes-law-tosses-it-out.ars.

215 *Given that France has 19.5 million homes*: The OECD has long collected such data. See, for instance, the spreadsheet at http://www.oecd.org/dataoecd/19/46/34083096.xls. HADOPI's untitled report was written in March 2012 and is available in English at http://www.hadopi.fr/sites/default/files/page/pdf/note17_en.pdf.

215 *In 2009, the New Zealand government*: Nate Anderson, "'3 strikes' strikes out in NZ as government yanks law," *Ars Technica*, March 23, 2009, http://arstechnica.com/tech-policy/news/2009/03/3-strikes-strikes-out-in-nz-as-government-yanks-law.ars.

215 *"Terminating an Internet account"*: Ibid.

217 *It didn't help the campaign*: Timothy B. Lee, "ICE admits year-long seizure of music blog was a mistake," *Ars Technica*, December 8, 2011, http://arstechnica.com/tech-policy/2011/12/ice-admits-months-long-seizure-of-music-blog-was-a-mistake/.

218 *In another case, it seized the domain name*: See Nate Anderson, "Government admits defeat, gives back seized Rojadirecta domains," *Ars Technica*, August 29, 2012, http://arstechnica.com/tech policy/2012/08/government goes-0-2-admits-defeat-in-rojadirecta-domain-forfeit-case/.

218 *The secrecy of the process angered people*: Quoted in Nate Anderson, "Silicon

Valley Congresswoman: Web seizures trample due process (and break the law)," *Ars Technica*, March 14, 2011, http://arstechnica.com/tech-policy/2011/03/ars-interviews-rep-zoe-lofgren/.

219 *"Search engines need to rank search results"*: Quoted in Nate Anderson, "After terrific year, music biz demands that world adopt 'SOPA plus,'" *Ars Technica*, January 23, 2012, http://arstechnica.com/tech-policy/news/2012/01/after-terrific-year-music-biz-demands-that-world-adopt-sopa-plus.ars.

219 *"How do you justify a search engine providing for someone to go and steal something?"*: Quoted in Ted Johnson, "Dodd slams Google over legislation [sic]," *Variety*, Dec 8, 2011, http://www.variety.com/article/VR1118047080.

220 *China had forced even a company like Google*: Ibid.

221 *Beshara was an "emotional and high strung woman"*: Quoted in Nate Anderson, "NinjaVideo 'queen' gets 22 months in jail, owes $200,000 to Hollywood," *Ars Technica*, January 6, 2012, http://arstechnica.com/tech-policy/news/2012/01/ninjavideo-queen-gets-22-months-in-jail-owes-200000-to-hollywood.ars.

222 *Beshara was sent immediately to prison*: Nate Anderson, "Facebook posts show 'lack of remorse,' so NinjaVideo leader jailed early," *Ars Technica*, January 17, 2012, http://arstechnica.com/tech-policy/news/2012/01/facebook-posts-show-lack-of-remorse-so-ninjavideo-leader-is-in-jail.ars.

222 *A New Zealand judge later found*: Nate Anderson, "Mega-victory: Kim Dotcom search warrants "invalid," mansion raid 'illegal,'" *Ars Technica*, June 28, 2012, http://arstechnica.com/tech-policy/2012/06/mega-victory-kim-dotcom-search-warrants-invalid-mansion-raid-illegal/.

223 *ICE wanted to haul him to the United States*: Nate Anderson, "Copyright wars heat up: US wins extradition of college kid from England," *Ars Technica*, March 13, 2012, http://arstechnica.com/tech-policy/news/2012/03/copyright-wars-heat-up-us-wins-extradition-of-college-kid-from-england.ars.

223 *"Forcing Richard to stand trial"*: Timothy B. Lee, "Big Content's latest anti-piracy weapon: extradition," *Ars Technica*, July 21, 2011, http://arstechnica.com/tech-policy/news/2011/07/big-content-unveils-latest-antipiracy-weapon-extradition.ars.

224 *"It is Groundhog Day"*: The account of the third trial comes from my notes; I covered the trial for *Ars Technica* in 2010.

227 *In late 2012, the music labels won*: Greg Sandoval, "Appeals court sides with RIAA, Jammie Thomas owes $222,000," CNET, September 11, 2012, http://news.cnet.com/8301-1023_3-57510453-93/appeals-court-sides-with-riaa-jammie-thomas-owes-$222000/.

227 *After that ruling*: E-mail interview with Kiwi Camara, September 11, 2012.

9 PRODUCTIVE CHAOS

229 *"Just pulled the needle out of my arm"*: Quoted in Someone Who Wanted to be Anonymous, "Silk Road: A Vicious Blow to the War on Drugs," *The Austin Cut*, January 2, 2012, http://austincut.com/article/01012012/silk-road-a-vicious-blow-to-the-war-on-drugs.

230 *".200 mg floored everyone that tried it"*: Quote from Silk Road user. Silk Road, as will be explained, isn't reachable over the normal public Internet. Quotes from and descriptions of the site come from my own 2012 visits to Silk Road through the anonymizing Tor network.

230 *He noted that they had the authority*: Joe Manchin, "Manchin Urges Federal Law Enforcement to Shut Down Online Black Market for Illegal Drugs," manchin.senate.gov, June 6, 2011, http://manchin.senate.gov/public/index .cfm/2011/6/manchin-urges-federal-law-enforcement-to-shut-down-online-black-market-for-illegal-drugs.

230 *"As of mid-2012, $1.2 million each month"*: Nicolas Christin, "Traveling the Silk Road: A measurement analysis of a large anonymous online marketplace," unpublished working paper, November 28, 2012 revision, http://www.andrew .cmu.edu/user/nicolasc/publications/TR-CMU-CyLab-12-018.pdf.

230 *"To grow into a force to be reckoned with"*: Quote from Silk Road user.

231 *"Hackers, anarchists, and criminals have been dreaming"*: See "Silk Road: A Vicious Blow to the War on Drugs."

231 *"Weird offshore jurisdictions"*: See Lackey's comment on James Grimmelmann, "Death of a data haven: cypherpunks, WikiLeaks, and the world's smallest nation," *Ars Technica*, http://arstechnica.com/tech-policy/news/2012/03/ sealand-and-havenco.ars?comments=1#comment-22702770.

231 *"Sealand was just a temporary stopgap"*: James Grimmelmann, "Death of a data haven."

232 *"hackers, libertarians, and child pornographers"*: Ryan Broderick, "Traveling Down the Silkroad to Buy Drugs With Bitcoins," *VICE*, June 24, 2011, http:// motherboard.vice.com/2011/6/24/traveling-down-the-silkroad-to-buy-drugs-with-bitcoins.

232 *This oversells the seediness of the situation*: As for who uses Tor, the project itself provides a long and interesting list of use cases on its website, https://www .torproject.org/about/torusers.html.en. Tor is also understandably wary of being portrayed in sensationalist stories. "While it is thrilling to speculate about undesired effects of Tor, when it succeeds, nobody notices," says the project website. "This is great for users, but not so good for us, since publishing success stories about how people or organizations are staying anonymous

could be counterproductive. For example, we talked to an FBI officer who explained that he uses Tor every day for his work—but he quickly followed up with a request not to provide details or mention his name."

232 *In the early 2000s, the US Naval Research Laboratory*: See the US government's own overview of onion routing at "Onion Routing," US Naval Research Lab, http://www.onion-router.net.

233 *The Naval Research Laboratory paid for Tor*: See "Tor: Sponsors," Tor Project, https://www.torproject.org/about/sponsors.html.en.

233 *The Swedish International Development Agency*: Ibid.

234 *"We are also supporting the development of new tools"*: Hillary Clinton, "Remarks on Internet Freedom," January 21, 2010, http://www.state.gov/secretary/rm/2010/01/135519.htm.

234 *"to help combat drug-related violence"*: Ibid.

235 *"We're going to build a separate infrastructure"*: Quoted in James Glanz and John Markoff, "US Underwrites Internet Detour Around Censors," *New York Times*, June 12, 2011, http://www.nytimes.com/2011/06/12/world/12internet.html?pagewanted=all.

235 *"we have to be willing to keep coming up with new ways"*: Quoted in Nicole Gaouette, "Clinton's 'Tech Camp' Teaches Activists Web Savvy, Subversion," *Bloomberg*, July 1, 2011, http://www.bloomberg.com/news/2011-07-01/clinton-s-tech-camp-teaches-activists-web-savvy-subversion.html.

235 *"I will watch and observe"*: "Belarus leader threatens to 'whack' Internet protestors," Agence France Presse, June 14, 2011, http://www.google.com/hostednews/afp/article/ALeqM5jK8LN40ie4UScGD_4UHPv2jtuqtA?docId=CNG.b3569aafd06fe78f58be73c5faaa97a5.461.

235 *"We understand that the goal of these attacks"*: Quoted in Combined wire reports, "Belarus Fumes as US Teaches Activists," *Moscow Times*, July 4, 2011, http://www.themoscowtimes.com/news/article/belarus-fumes-as-us-teaches-activists/439940.html.

236 *The market is hardly secret*: See "About Xetron," Northrop Grumman, http://www.es.northropgrumman.com/by_division/landforces/xetron/#solutions.

236 *how thousands of security contractors function*: Nate Anderson, "Black ops: how HBGary wrote backdoors for the government," *Ars Technica*, February 21, 2011, http://arstechnica.com/tech-policy/news/2011/02/black-ops-how-hbgary-wrote-backdoors-and-rootkits-for-the-government.ars.

237 *"DONT let it FONE HOME"*: Ibid.

237 *"Man leaves laptop locked"*: Ibid.

238 *The famous Stuxnet virus*: For an easy-to-read primer on Stuxnet, see Michael

Joseph Gross, "A Declaration of Cyber-War," *Vanity Fair*, April 2011, http:// www.vanityfair.com/culture/features/2011/04/stuxnet-201104. For reporting on how the virus was introduced, see Richard Sale, "Stuxnet Loaded by Iran Double Agents," *ISS Source*, April 11, 2012, http://www.isssource .com/stuxnet-loaded-by-iran-double-agents/. For the best reporting to date confirming the link to US and Israel, see David Sanger, "Obama Order Sped Up Wave of Cyberattacks Against Iran," *New York Times*, June 1, 2012, http:// www.nytimes.com/2012/06/01/world/middleeast/obama-ordered-wave- of-cyberattacks-against-iran.html?pagewanted=all.

238 *What he saw was Google threatening French newspapers*: See, for instance, Sam Schechner, "Google Opposes Proposed French Search Law," *Wall Street Journal*, October 18, 2012, http://online.wsj.com/article/SB100008723963 904436841045780650315522211260.html?mod=googlenews_wsj.

239 *"a whitewash, an attempt to get people"*: Quoted in Nate Anderson, "France attempts to 'civilize' the Internet; Internet fights back," May 24, 2011, http:// arstechnica.com/tech-policy/2011/05/france-attempts-to-civilize-the- internet-internet-fights-back/.

239 *"The universe that you represent"*: Ibid.

240 *"wish to enter into dialogue with you"*: Ibid.

240 *"I am about to enter the Lion's Den at #eG8"*: Quoted in Nate Anderson, "Copy-fight: EFF co-founder enters e-G8 'lion's den,' rips into lions," *Ars Technica*, May 24, 2011, http://arstechnica.com/tech-policy/2011/05/eff-co-founder- enters-copyright-lions-den-rips-into-lions/.

240 *"because I don't think I'm from the same planet"*: Ibid.

242 *In the case of Silk Road*: Steve Butcher, "Secret website harboured drugs smorgasbord, court hears," *The Age*, January 31, 2013, http://www.theage .com.au/victoria/secret-website-harboured-drugs-smorgasbord-court- hears-20130131-2dlw3.html.

243 *"I'm worried about having"*: Author phone interview with James Grimmel-mann, April 13, 2012.

AFTERWORD: THE SPY AND THE POLICEMAN

246 *the messages also reveal*: James Ball, "NSA collects millions of text messages daily in 'untargeted' global sweep," *The Guardian*, January 16, 2014, http:// www.theguardian.com/world/2014/jan/16/nsa-collects-millions-text- messages-daily-untargeted-global-sweep.

246 *developed a program called OPTIC NERVE*: Spencer Ackerman and James

Ball, "Optic Nerve: millions of Yahoo webcam images intercepted by GCHQ," *The Guardian*, February 27, 2014, http://www.theguardian.com/world/2014/feb/27/gchq-nsa-webcam-images-internet-yahoo.

247 *The NSA does this through its PRISM program*: "NSA PRISM Program Slides," *The Guardian*, November 1, 2013, http://www.theguardian.com/world/interactive/2013/nov/01/prism-slides-nsa-document.

248 *The German magazine* Der Spiegel *revealed*: Spiegel staff, "Inside TAO: Documents Reveal Top NSA Hacking Unit," *Der Spiegel*, December 29, 2013, http://www.spiegel.de/international/world/the-nsa-uses-powerful-toolbox-in-effort-to-spy-on-global-networks-a-940969-2.html.

248 *According to the* Washington Post: Barton Gellman and Ashkan Soltani, "NSA collects millions of e-mail address books globally," *Washington Post*, October 14, 2013, http://www.washingtonpost.com/world/national-security/nsa-collects-millions-of-e-mail-address-books-globally/2013/10/14/8e58b5be-34f9-11e3-80c6-7e6dd8d22d8f_story.html.

249 *The information was then used*: Greg Weston, Glenn Greenwald, and Ryan Gallagher, "CSEC used airport Wi-Fi to track Canadian travellers: Edward Snowden documents," CBC, January 30, 2014, http://www.cbc.ca/news/politics/csec-used-airport-wi-fi-to-track-canadian-travellers-edward-snowden-documents-1.2517881.

249 *The NSA runs a series of QUANTUM computer servers*: Bruce Schneier, "Attacking Tor: how the NSA targets users' online anonymity," *The Guardian*, October 4, 2013, http://www.theguardian.com/world/2013/oct/04/tor-attacks-nsa-users-online-anonymity.

250 *It watches the pornographic habits*: Glenn Greenwald, Ryan Gallagher, and Ryan Grim, "Top-Secret Document Reveals NSA Spied On Porn Habits As Part Of Plan To Discredit 'Radicalizers,'" *Huffington Post*, November 26, 2013, http://www.huffingtonpost.com/2013/11/26/nsa-porn-muslims_n_4346128.html.

250 *It also works to break cryptography algorithms*: Nicole Perlroth, Jeff Larson, and Scott Shane, "NSA Able to Foil Basic Safeguards of Privacy on Web," *The*

New York Times, September 5, 2013, http://www.nytimes.com/2013/09/06/
us/ nsa-foils-much-internet-encryption.html.

252 *reporting from Reuters revealed*: Joseph Menn, "Exclusive: Secret contract tied NSA and security industry pioneer" Reuters, December 20,
2013, http://www.reuters.com/article/2013/12/20/us-usa-security-rsa-
idUSBR9BJ1C220131220.

253 *Reuters revealed the existence*: John Shiffman and Kristina Cooke, "Exclusive: U.S. directs agents to cover up program used to investigate Americans,"
Reuters, August 5, 2013, http://www.reuters.com/article/2013/08/05/us-
dea-sod-idUSBRE97409R20130805.

254 *As security guru Bruce Schneier put it*: Doug Drinkwater, "RSA 2014:
Bruce Schneier champions encryption in 'golden age' of government surveillance," *SC Magazine*, February 25, 2014, http://www.scmagazine.
com/rsa-2014-bruce-schneier-champions-encryption-in-golden-age-
of-government-surveillance/article/335678/.

CODA

255 *The jury's conclusion stayed the same, too*: See Judgment, *USA v. Savigar et
al.*, United States District Court—Southern District of Indiana, case no.
1:08-cr-00132, docket no. 1065, filed February 11, 2013.

255 *The FBI has moved far beyond the CIPAV software*: See Cyrus Farivar, "FBI
denied permission to spy on hacker through his webcam," *Ars Technica*,
April 24, 2013, http://arstechnica.com/tech-policy/2013/04/fbi-denied-
permission-to-spy-on-hacker-through-his-webcam/.

256 *Nikolaenko finally pled guilty*: See "Plea Agreement," *USA v. Nikolaenko*,
United States District Court—Eastern District of Wisconsin, case no.
2:10-cr-00246, docket no. 65, February 26, 2013.

257 *His parents, Egor and Luidmila*: All letters from family and friends of Nikolaenko are contained in "Letter of Support," *USA v. Nikolaenko*, United States
District Court—Eastern District of Wisconsin, case no. 2:10-cr-00246,
docket no. 68, February 27, 2013.

257 *Without comment, the US Supreme Court declined*: See David Kravets,
"Supreme Court OKs $222K Verdict for Sharing 24 Songs," Wired
.com, March 18, 2013, http://www.wired.com/threatlevel/2013/03/scotus-
jammie-thomas-rasset/.

INDEX

phone tapping *(continued)*
  "lawful intercept" backdoor capabilities in, 106, 107, 112
  laws and legal restrictions on, 129–30, 132
  warrantless, 128, 129–30
piracy, *see* copyright infringement; file-sharing services
Pirate Bay, 202–3, 242, 262*n*
Pirate Party, German, 91
Pirate Party (Piratpartiet), Swedish, 56
pirate radio, 4, 5–6, 26
Plum Crazy, 174–75
police raids, 131, 133, 222
  in child pornography investigations, 31–34, 38, 40–41, 42, 43, 53, 55, 116, 188
  in spam investigations, 165–66
police surveillance, 73–78, 81–85, 99–100, 107, 116, 117
  in Germany, 90–91
  phone taps in, 85–86, 111, 128–30
pornography, online, 3, 8, 59, 208, 213
  attempted regulation of, 11–13
  spam advertisements for, 144, 145
  see also child pornography
Post, David, 15–16, 197–98
postal inspectors, US, 25, 31, 35, 37, 38, 40, 41, 55, 61, 144, 154
Postal Service, US, 163
"preservation" requests, 125–27
Prevelakis, Vassilis, 275*n*
PRISM program, 247
Pristine Bay, 133
privacy issues, 65–134
  balancing effective investigative tools with concerns for, 242–44
  Berkeley Nutraceuticals case and, 119, 124–27, 130–33, 134
  corporate surveillance and, 73–85
  cyberstalking hackers and, 65–73
  government access to Internet servers and, 107–9, 111, 114, 124–27, 130–33
  government surveillance and, *see* government surveillance
  network surveillance and, 93–117
  pro-encryption arguments and, 115–16, 117, 242–43
  unsolicited spam and, 141
probable cause, 85, 126, 127, 130, 131, 132
productive chaos, unproductive chaos vs., 241–44
Prohibition, 128
PRO-IP Act (2008), 217, 218
Project Redsand, 261*n*

"prospective" surveillance, "retrospective" vs., 125–26
prostitution, 106, 110
Publius, 168
Punkbob (hacker), 101–2
Purdue University, 43

QUANTUM, 249
Queensland, 34, 52, 54, 55, 59

radio, pirate, 4, 5–6, 26
Radio Caroline, 5–6
Radio Essex, 5–6
Radio Free Europe, 233
RapidShare, 203
RAR'd files, 36
Rathbun, Michael, 146–47
Recording Industry Association of America (RIAA), 15, 197, 210
Reeder, Marc "Kingbee," 47
regulations, Internet, *see* Internet laws and regulations
remittitur, 211, 225, 226
remote access tool (RAT) software, 70–72, 78, 79, 92, 116, 256
  motion-detection features in, 71–72
  spammers use of, 149
"retrospective" surveillance, "prospective" vs., 125–26
Reuters, 252–53
Rhodes, 5
ricin, 237
Rines, Walter, 174, 175–76, 177, 179
Rolling Stone, 193
Rome, 87
Rootkits: Subverting the Windows Kernel (Hoglund), 236
rootkit systems, 236–37
Roughs Tower, 1–3, 4, 22, 231, 262*n*
  brutal conditions at, 2–3
  pirate-radio clashes on, 5–6, 22
  quasi-statehood of, 4, 6–7, 8, 20, 22
  see also Sealand, Principality of
routers, Internet, 100, 101
Rovicid, 119, 123
Russia, 137, 138, 157, 158, 159, 161
  System for Operative Investigative Activities in, 108
Russian Lolita BBS, 40, 44

Sanders, Norman, 87, 271*n*
Sara (cyberstalking victim), 66
Sarkozy, Nicolas, 238–40, 241
Saudi Arabia, 3, 100–101